Radical Economics

General Editor: SAM AARONOVITCH

Debates between economists are not just technical arguments amongst practitioners but often reflect philosophical and ideological positions which are not always made explicit.

Discontent grew with the prevailing economic orthodoxy as the long period of economic expansion in the advanced capitalist economies came to an end in the 1970s; disenchantment was expressed in open discussion about the 'crisis' in economics and in the rise of various kinds of radical economic theory, often using the general title of 'political economy'.

Many economists have looked for a more fruitful point of departure in the ideas of Marx and the classical economists and also in such contemporary economists as Kalecki and Sraffa. Although it is possible to identify a broad radical stream, it does not mean that there are no significant controversies within this radical approach and, indeed, it would be unhealthy if this were not the case.

Can radical economic theory interpret the world better than the current orthodoxy which it challenges? And can it show also how to change it? This is a challenge which this series proposes to take up, adding to work already being done.

Each book will be a useful contribution to its particular field and should become a text around which the study of economics takes place.

Radical Economics

Published

Amit Bhaduri, *Macroeconomics*
Michael Bleaney, *The Rise and Fall of Keynesian Economics*
Keith Cowling, *Monopoly Capitalism*
Paul Hare, *Planning the British Economy*
Michael Howard, *Profits in Economic Theory*
Antal Matyas, *History of Modern Non-Marxian Economics*
David Purdy, *Social Power and the Labour Market*
Malcolm C. Sawyer, *The Economics of Michał Kalecki*

Forthcoming

Terry Byres, *The Political Economy of Poor Nations*
Matthew Edel, *Urban Economics*
Michael Howard and John King, *A History of Marxian Economics*
  (2 volumes)
John E. Woods, *The Economics of Piero Sraffa: An Introduction*

Series Standing Order

If you would like to receive future titles in this series as they are
published, you can make use of our standing order facility. To place a
standing order please contact your bookseller or, in case of difficulty,
write to us at the address below with your name and address and the
name of the series. Please state with which title you wish to begin your
standing order. (If you live outside the United Kingdom we may not
have the rights for your area, in which case we will forward your order
to the publisher concerned.)

Customer Services Department, Macmillan Distribution Ltd
Houndmills, Basingstoke, Hampshire, RG21 2XS, England.

Social Power and the Labour Market

A Radical Approach to Labour Economics

DAVID PURDY

Lecturer in Economics
University of Manchester

M

MACMILLAN
EDUCATION

First published 1988

Published by
MACMILLAN EDUCATION LTD
Houndmills, Basingstoke, Hampshire RG21 2XS
and London
Companies and representatives
throughout the world

Typeset by Wessex Typesetters
(Division of The Eastern Press Ltd)
Frome, Somerset

Printed in Hong Kong

British Library Cataloguing in Publication Data
Purdy, David
Social power and the labour market: a
radical approach to labour economics.—
(Radical economics).
1. Labour market. Econometric models
I. Title   II. Series
331.12′0724
ISBN 0–333–29179–4 (hardcover)
ISBN 0–333–29180–8 (paperback)

In memory of Judith Gray

Contents

Acknowledgements

Among the people whose ideas and suggestions I have borrowed, adapted or resisted during the long gestation of this book I should particularly like to thank Beatrix Campbell, Pat Devine, Ann Long, Barbara MacLennan, Ian Steedman, Philippe Van Parijs, and the series editor Sam Aaronovitch. I am also grateful to the members of Manchester University's Economics Research Seminar for their helpful and sometimes provocative comments on draft versions of several chapters; to the members of the Basic Income Research Group; and to the participants at the first International Conference on Basic Income organised by the Collectif Charles Fourier at Louvain-la-Neuve, Belgium, in September 1986. I owe a special debt of gratitude to my friend and former colleague, Claudette Williams, who toiled with enthusiasm and patience to produce a first-class typescript. For the content of the book – errors, warts and all – I bear sole responsibility.

David Purdy

Part One
The Theory of the Labour Market

1
Two Paradigms: Exchange and Reproduction

1 Paradigms and Models

Since the time, some three centuries ago, when political economy began to take shape as a distinct intellectual endeavour, its practitioners have evolved two opposing theoretical approaches to the labour market. One, developed to a high degree of technical sophistication over the past hundred years by the neo-classical school, can conveniently be labelled the paradigm of exchange. The other, originating in the older classical and Marxist tradition, was long eclipsed by its rival, but underwent a certain rehabilitation following the publication of Sraffa's seminal *Production of Commodities by Means of Commodities* (Sraffa, 1960). It remains, however, a minority school of thought, and, as I argue later, has never performed at its full potential. Perhaps this is because, as an embattled minority, its followers have felt impelled to accept the terms of debate proposed by their adversaries. I have chosen to call this second approach the paradigm of reproduction.

Economists have, of course, devised a large variety of *models* of labour markets based on different institutional and behavioural assumptions. But this does not invalidate the claim that there are just two basic theoretical approaches to the labour market. I am using the words 'paradigm' and 'model' to refer to different orders of intellectual construct. Paradigms are arrangements of evaluative axioms, mental images and constitutive principles which support theoretical models. As the etymology of the word suggests, a paradigm provides a guiding framework. It shows

3

from the outside how specific models are to be interpreted. But it is not itself a model capable of being quantified, tested, refuted, and so on. Rather it is taken for granted as a condition of intelligibility. The investigations, experiments and judgements which it sustains can be compared with the movements of the waters on a river-bed.[1] There is a distinction, though not a sharp division, of the one from the other.

If this distinction is borne in mind, it will become apparent that the same paradigm may accommodate a number of theoretical currents, models and controversies. What divides the two paradigms of the labour market lies at a deeper level than disagreements over the weight to be accorded to this or that explanatory variable. Both begin from a working definition of the labour market as a set of institutional arrangements for enlisting labour performance, for allocating society's labour force to different productive uses, and for distributing income to those who participate in it. But the two offer very different accounts of the social meaning of these arrangements according to the activities and relationships which each selects as its central focus of attention.

2 The Exchange Paradigm

The exchange paradigm treats the mutual trading of money for services between employers and employees as a sub-class of the more general category of transactions between buyer and seller. That this sub-class may have certain peculiarities which mark it off from other kinds of trade is already indicated as soon as we try to define who the traders are. The nineteenth-century English tradition of common law insisted that contracts of employment were not essentially different from other commercial contracts. The contracting parties were both 'individual agents' with legal personality and equal status before the law. This doctrine conveniently ignored one very obvious source of inequality between employer and employee. 'The employer' is not a creature of flesh and blood, but a more or less complex organisation combining the skills and resources of many individuals. Workers, on the other hand, are genuine persons. Considered as individuals they typically have far fewer resources, options and powers of initiative than the organisation which employs them. This applies to individual salaried managers at the apex of the organisational pyramid as well as to their subordinates at the base. The former are usually less vulnerable, dependent and disadvantaged than the latter. But as individuals workers of all kinds normally stand in an unequal relationship to their employer.

Still, it could be argued that similar disparities abound in economic life – for example, between firms of different sizes and market power; or between countries with unequal resources and at different levels of development. A *general* theory necessarily has to abstract from such considerations, at least as a first approximation, if only to establish a theoretical base-line from which at a later stage to assess the significance of the initial abstraction, if any. Accordingly the exchange paradigm begins with the legal fiction of equality.

In a free labour market the hiring of employees is based on voluntary, contractual relations. Each party enjoys considerable discretion over whether to enter into or terminate a contract of employment. Within limits, employees are free to choose which employer to work for. Employers are free to choose from among the job applicants who present themselves the number and combination best suited to their needs. In practice these freedoms may be qualified. There may, for example, be jointly agreed or statutory provisions enjoining each party to observe a minimum period of notice before quitting the job or declaring dismissals or redundancies. Similarly, closed shop arrangements or seniority rules may restrict the range of candidates eligible for engagement in certain specified job classifications. But the labour market remains essentially free provided two conditions are met: (1) workers are not legally or in any other way bound to a particular employer or job; and (2) employers retain a high degree of latitude in deciding how much of what kinds of labour to employ and on what contractual terms without the need to defer to rules or directives issued by some superior authority.

Each party wants what the other has to offer, and each is prepared to give up something which the other values in order to get it. Employers want the right to make use of workers' labour power – their acquired bundle of skills, training, experience and other job-related attributes – for some specified period of time. To obtain this right they are prepared to pay wages, and possibly certain fringe benefits. What workers want primarily is a livelihood, wage earnings being for most employees easily their most important source of money income. But typically workers derive other kinds of gratification from employment too – companionship, social recognition, status, intrinsically rewarding work tasks, the enrichment of their life experience or the development of their personal potential. To obtain these *desiderata* workers are willing, on the right terms, to place their labour power at the employer's disposal.

On this view the labour market is an arena in which each party strives to achieve some approximate balance between the benefits they envisage from the employment contract and the cost or sacrifice incurred in realising them. When appropriately interpreted benefits and costs are balanced at the margin, the labour market is said to be in equilibrium. The study of the labour market can be defined as covering all aspects of the behaviour of workers and employers, the environment in which it occurs, and the institutions through which it is filtered, which have some significant bearing on the exchange of wages for labour-power and the process of market equilibration.

One of the standard complaints against neo-classical economics is that it takes an overly narrow view of the boundaries of the discipline. It might be thought that this summary definition of the exchange paradigm's object of study is sufficiently broad to encompass all kinds of social phenomena well beyond the traditional stamping ground of the neo-classical school. There is, for example, nothing in the definition which precludes the possibility that so-called 'institutional forces' – of which trade unions and collective bargaining are the leading, though by no means only, instances – might prove to be more important in determining the outcome of the exchange process than the forces of market competition and substitution, which are alleged to rule the roost in the neo-classical scheme of things. This is perfectly true. But the conclusion that follows is merely that the exchange paradigm can admit a variety of models. Whatever the disagreements between these models as to the relative weight of different determining forces, they concur in their definition of the phenomena which stand in need of explanation: namely, the mechanisms and results of labour market exchange. In this sense they inhabit the same universe of discourse.

If the exchange paradigm offers an unduly restricted view of the labour market, this has nothing to do with whether or not it can allow for 'institutional' explanations of market outcomes. It clearly can. Rather its boundaries are narrowly drawn for two quite different reasons. First, relations of exchange are only one aspect of an overall pattern of relations between employers and workers. This wider set includes, for example, their co-operative or conflictual relations within the process of production. It also includes their external relations as producers and consumers of specific bundles of goods and services which provide the materials for distinctive ways of life – systems of energy, transportation, housing, recreation, entertainment and so on. Second, in any actual society employer–worker relations are embedded in a social structure which also, and necessarily, contains *other kinds* of relationships between social agents – for example, between husbands and wives, parents and children, or between the 'working population' and 'economically inactive' financial dependents.

The reproduction paradigm, as we shall see, views labour market exchanges in relation to these other levels of what it insists on calling the *social formation*. (The significance of this term will appear presently.) Its object of study is the social formation as a whole. A preoccupation with just one of the levels of the social formation may be justified for certain limited, local purposes; but in the end these must be subordinated to a deeper, multi-levelled investigation.

Figure 1.1 below clarifies the boundaries of the exchange paradigm and also serves to highlight its other characteristic features. The two principal actors in the story depicted in the diagram are firms and individuals. As explained earlier, the former are not persons, but organisations which use and manage productive resources supplied by individual resource-owning traders. In more extended versions of the story other actors such as trade unions, employers' organisations or agencies of the state may put in an appearance. But they are not crucial to the core of the plot and are omitted from the brief synopsis which follows. The main elements of the plot are familiar and can be summarised under five headings.

8

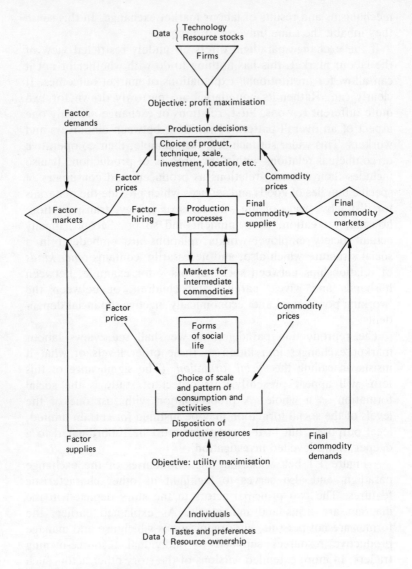

Figure 1.1 *The Exchange Paradigm. A Conceptual Map*

(i) Choice theory

The exchange story is choice-theoretic. It holds that in the final analysis all economic phenomena and behaviour are explicable in terms of choices made by individual agents. Of course, all kinds of institutional arrangements mediate choices on the way to the pure sphere of the final analysis. But institutions themselves are ultimately congealed choices – the embodiments of aggregated decisions made by social agents for conducting their affairs in one way rather than another.[2]

Choice theory entails a presumption that agents act rationally in the minimal sense that the reasons they have for selecting some particular course of action on balance outweigh any reasons of which they are aware against it. This formulation leaves open the possibility that their information may be imperfect. But no one can ever obtain all the knowledge relevant to any given choice. The consequences of decisions take time to unfold, and the future is inherently uncertain, the more so the further ahead lies the pertinent time horizon. Moreover, the improvement of an agent's knowledge imposes costs in terms of time, effort and expense. Rational, utility-maximising or cost-minimising behaviour consists, therefore, in making the best of this ineluctable 'imperfection' in the human condition.

The presumption that choices are rational sometimes has to be qualified. Behaviour which is individually rational may be socially pathological. A number of similarly placed, but isolated individuals may each rationally opt for a certain course of action. But the aggregate result of their decisions may turn out to be inferior to other feasible outcomes which they would all have preferred, but which are unattainable as long as they make their choices separately and without the benefit of a collective framework of decision-making. In this kind of case what has failed is not choice theory as a principle of social explanation, but the institutional structures for the expression of choice.

(ii) The fundamental data

Human beings are not creatures of pure spirit, but inhabit material bodies in a material world. Their choices are always constrained. At the level of the economy as a whole, the exchange paradigm postulates four sets of conditions which impose limits on the feasible range of productive and distributive outcomes. At any point in time the state of technology and the quantities of resources which their owners decide to make available for production are given. These two sets of conditions between them determine the economy's objective production possibilities. The precise pattern of resource allocation and output then depends on two other fundamental data: individuals' subjective tastes and preferences and the distribution of property rights. Which income-yielding resources and how much of each one individuals happen to own, set an upper limit on the amount of income they can in principle acquire if they decide to turn their given resource bundles into factors of production. The goals which inform these decisions depend on their tastes and preferences defined with respect to both resources and consumption goods. Tastes and preferences are here treated as unexplained data. It is not assumed that they are inexplicable; simply that however they come to be what they are is not the concern of economics.

(iii) Constrained maximisation

The choices made by individual agents can be analysed in terms of the principle of constrained maximisation. Firms are assumed to aim at maximising their profits on production and trade. The information they need for their production decisions is gleaned from the price signals continuously emitted by factor and commodity markets. By comparing commodity prices with factor costs firms calculate which commodities to produce, with what techniques, on what scale, and so on, in order to promote their over-arching objective. In an exactly symmetrical way individuals who are constrained by the prevailing pattern of resource ownership, conditioned by their given tastes and preferences, guided by market signals, and bent on maximising their utility, arrive at the various decisions pertinent to the disposition of their resources.

(iv) The process of exchange

Firms' production decisions give rise to a demand for the services of factors of production. Factor supplies in turn emanate from individuals' decisions regarding the disposition of their resources. Factor markets, including the labour market, are the arena in which the central actors in the story trade with each other. Firms pay out wages, interest and rent. In return they receive a flow of factor services which contribute to their production objectives. Individuals give up the use of (a portion of) their resources. In return they receive a compensating flow of income which contributes to their consumption objectives.

Markets for final commodities are simply the mirror image of factor markets. If we net out transactions between firms themselves involving the exchange of intermediate goods and services, then what is eventually delivered for final use are various supplies of final commodities. Similarly, using the income received from trading in factor markets, individuals express their demands for final commodities through the level and composition of their expenditure.

(v) The market as a control mechanism

There is no central agency to plan, organise, monitor and control the system of factor and commodity markets. Despite this a market economy exhibits order and not chaos. Resources do get allocated to various uses, and the social product does get distributed to individuals, in ways which are definite and tolerably predictable, and not in an unintelligible or random manner. This is because the market acts as a control mechanism. First, it issues signals furnishing firms and individuals with the information they need for decision-making. Second, through a ceaseless interplay between agents' decisions and actual market outcomes resources are continually reshuffled amongst different uses, and their products distributed among different users. The market functions, therefore, as a living laboratory in which decisions are tested, success rewarded and failure penalised. It yields objective criteria for making decisions *ex ante*, and for judging performance *ex post*. Third, since the market rewards success and penalises failure, it contains built-in performance incentives and corrective devices to eliminate mistakes or inadequate performance. Taken together these informational, guidance and feedback functions constitute a self-activating control mechanism.

Over the years economists have hotly debated the properties, strengths and weaknesses of this mechanism: for example, whether it is useful to define a general equilibrium state for a market economy, and if so, how to characterise it; whether, given some initial configuration of the four fundamental data, a system of competitive markets will, *ceteris paribus*, home in on an equilibrium state, assuming one to exist; whether this state, if realised, depends only on the fundamental data or is also affected by the path along which it is reached; whether the economy is stable in the face of departures from equilibrium; and so on. Important though these issues may be, my present concern lies elsewhere – with the silences and omissions of the exchange paradigm.

3 Blind Spots and Distortions

The conceptual framework outlined in the previous section gives rise to a number of blind spots and visual distortions. The former are indicated by the three 'black boxes' in the centre of the diagram. Consider first the boxes labelled 'Production Processes' and 'Markets for Intermediate Commodities'. Although exchange is inconceivable without production, the exchange paradigm is not primarily concerned with production as an activity. It acknowledges the technical and organisational aspects of the production process *within* the firm, and likewise the various backward and forward linkages *between* firms and industrial sectors formed by the economy's input–output structure. These processual and structural features of economic life may be of interest to students of other disciplines such as history, sociology or industrial relations. But they lie at the periphery of the economist's field of specialisation. Economists are not debarred from looking into them. But neither are they obliged to do so. The story they have to tell can just as well take as read the results of the process of production and the pattern of inter-industry input–output relations. It is a story which represents productive activity as a one-way flow running from original factors of production to final output with the intervening stages left out.

The quintessential economic activity is exchange. To be sure, the only example of a *pure* exchange economy is the celebrated, but rather bizarre case of the prisoner-of-war camp. Supplies of goods produced elsewhere are distributed to camp inmates through the good offices of the Red Cross. The prisoners then proceed to trade their initial allocations of parcels in order to improve their welfare. This basic conception, it is suggested, carries over to the case of an economy with production. Now, instead of taking initial holdings of goods as given, the data become initial holdings of productive resources. Individual resource-owning consumers trade with special intermediaries called firms, instead of directly with each other. Resources are exchanged against money payments; the incomes thus generated are in turn exchanged against final commodities. But the end result is the same as in the case of pure exchange.

Consider next the box labelled 'Forms of Social Life'. In the process of deciding on the disposition of their resources among different activities and consumption goods, individuals necessarily enter into certain distinctive social practices. Workers, for example, commit themselves to particular patterns of working time within organisations marked by definite hierarchies of responsibility, authority and status. In their work activities they perform certain prescribed tasks composed into specific job classifications. They may also take part in a variety of unofficial, informal activities during job-time. As producers they contribute to the creation of goods and services with specific features and intended to serve specific purposes. When eventually delivered to their final users these use-values become the ingredients for certain characteristic forms of consumption and ways of living. These forms and ways in turn progressively modify not only the natural and built environment, but also the capacities, opportunities and desires of its inhabitants. Moreover, on each of these sites of social life human beings find themselves involved in certain definite social relationships. In their homes, for example, workers are members of households and families which exhibit their own internal structures of authority and power.

None of this is denied by adherents of the exchange paradigm. It is simply dismissed as irrelevant to the primary purpose of economic analysis. Economists *may* investigate the forms of social life and the social relationships with which economic activity is imbricated. But they are not *obliged* to take account of people's social attributes in order to comprehend the economic process. All social divisions such as those of class, gender or race can simply be subsumed in the initial distribution of property rights, and thereafter need play no further part in the analysis. Considered in their common, economic role as resource-owning traders individuals are treated as undifferentiated, asocial atoms. And the point at which commodities disappear as they are used up is stipulated as the terminus of economic analysis.

In addition to these omissions from its visual field, there are two other areas in which the images produced by the exchange paradigm are flat, and therefore distorted. The first stems from what can be called the problematic of scarcity. Human wants are potentially unlimited, whereas the resources and technological possibilities for satisfying them will always be finite. It is, indeed, this pervasive and inescapable condition of human life which gives rise to the necessity for choice. The economic system is, in the end, nothing more than an elaborate device for coping with scarcity. Now it would obviously be foolish to *deny* the relevance of the scarcity theme for understanding the economic aspects of human society. But it is equally foolish to claim that scarcity is the *only* such theme, or even that it is always the most important. The commonest counter-theme arises from the fact that human and material resources are frequently, and sometimes heavily and persistently, under-used. But an even more fundamental problematic hoves into view once it is recognised that 'tastes and preferences' may not be exogenous, but endogenous to the economic system. What people want may not be independent of what is produced.

Mass advertising is merely one possible channel along which the pattern of production may influence individual preferences. Far more important are the various subterranean process of general cultural formation which shape society's values and standards. I shall have frequent occasion to refer to these processes in the course of this book. Here it suffices to point out that the notion of *the* economic problem as an eternal confrontation between unlimited wants and limited resources leads to two principal theoretical preoccupations: (a) with *optimising* the use of resources; and (b) with purely quantitative growth in order to push back the material constrains on want satisfaction. Suppose, however, that wants are shaped by the prevailing pattern of production, which sustains a particular way of life and furnishes a particular kind of social experience. Then a concern with optimising and growth appears far less compelling than the ethical question whether social production is organised so as to generate a *good* way of life, both for the individual and for society as a whole.

The second distortion consists of a double and misleading symmetry: both between the central actors, firms and individuals, and between the different factors of production. Firms and individuals are both treated as rational maximisers engaged in constrained optimisation. The critical point here is not the assumption of rationality or the assumption that agents strive to maximise some specified objective, though both are open to legitimate doubt. Rather it is the implicit supposition that the *objectives* of the two actors stand on the same footing.

In a capitalist commodity-producing economy the circuit of exchange followed by the activities of firms takes the form: $M - C - M^1$. An initial sum of money capital, M, is used to purchase commodities – means of production and labour power. These are then combined in the production process with a view to creating new commodities which can be sold at a profit and converted back into the form of money. Firms endeavour to ensure that the final term in the circuit, M^1, exceeds the initial term, M. If they succeed, they enlarge the money capital at their disposal waiting to be launched into a fresh circuit.

The exchange circuit in which workers participate is quite different. It takes the form: $C - M - C$. Workers begin with their own labour power, which from a certain point of view resembles other reproducible commodities. They exchange this commodity for a money income, M. But the purpose of the exercise is not in their case to accumulate capital. Rather they aspire to achieve or maintain a certain way of life. The commodities on which they spend their earnings are needed to support this way of life. These different patterns of goal-seeking can be formally assimilated within a uniform framework of constrained maximisation; but only at the price of obscuring the distinction between the purely quantitative goal of profit maximisation and the quality of life issues which confront workers.

A similar formal, but ultimately obscurantist, symmetry can be found in the way in which the exchange paradigm treats the different factors of production. For analytical purposes human and inanimate instruments of production need to be distinguished by nothing more than an algebraic subscript, as in statements of the form: $Q = f(X_1, X_2, \ldots, X_n)$, where Q is some produced output, and $X_1, X_2, \ldots, X_n$ are quantities of the various factors used in its production. But this procedure is highly questionable in the case of human labour power, and on grounds which in the first instance are analytical rather than humanistic or ethical. The argument is developed in detail in Chapter 5. In essence it amounts to the simple point that unlike other commodities, labour power is not separable from its owner and bearer, an individual human being endowed with consciousness and will. This fact makes human labour power simultaneously the most versatile and the most problematic of all agents of production.[3]

4   The Reproduction Paradigm

What we call 'society' is more than a mere aggregate of contiguous individuals connected like peas in a pod. It *is* an aggregate, but not so much of individuals as of the multiplicity of *relationships* which these individuals form in the course of their common life. These relationships in turn are not random, but systematic; or, more precisely, it is a presumption of any science of society that they exhibit sufficient internal coherence and order to justify talking about a 'social *system*'. The reproduction paradigm sets itself the task of discovering how this system works. In contrast to the self-imposed limitation of the exchange paradigm, its rival rejects conventional discipline boundaries and reaches out for whatever language seems appropriate to the grander scale of its ambition.

The central feature of the social system is that it is *self-reproducing*. This is a shorthand way of making three related points. First, although human societies continually interact with their natural base, their patterns of organisation are not imposed by nature. Natural conditions continue to influence their functioning, just as individual human beings cannot exist independently of their biological bodies and are subject to all the 'heartache and the thousand natural shocks that flesh is heir to'.[4] But the social organisation of homo sapiens has established a degree of autonomy from its natural origins. It is perpetuated by the system itself independently of the natural environment. Just how this is accomplished is explained in very general terms by the next two points. It has to be admitted, however, that these fail to do much more than gesture towards an explanation. A great deal more investigation is needed before anything like a satisfactory theory exists to explain how this self-organising property of social systems really works. In this respect the study of society is still in its infancy, comparable with the state of biology before the discovery of DNA and the microbiological revolution.

Second, society is self-replacing: it is able to maintain and renew itself as a going concern while still preserving the integrity of its structure. The composition of the population constantly changes as individuals die and new ones are born. Similarly, the members of society must continually replace their material means of subsistence by fresh productive efforts. Yet despite these permanent processes of molecular change, both the structure of social relationships and the structure of the economy exhibit a high degree of stability, though neither is totally rigid.

At the same time societies are self-transcendent. They are not condemned to a stationary state, but are able to push beyond the material and cultural limits on their scope for variation through learning, development and evolution. This is the third aspect of self-reproduction. Like living organisms and ecosystems which share this property, but unlike machines which do not, the progress of social systems through time is best understood in terms of processes of formation, growth and structural change. The order and regularity observable within society is different from that displayed by the interactions between the moving parts of a machine. A machine is constructed to perform specific tasks intended by its designer. Once built and kept supplied with an appropriate input of energy, the machine continues to operate in a predetermined way until either a malfunction causes it to break down or its components wear out. It then loses its orderly systemic quality and its constituent parts relapse into a state of rest. By contrast both human societies and other species of living organisms adapt to changes in their environment. They are also capable of self-regeneration in the face of varying degrees of functional impairment; and, if subjected to particularly heavy stress, can re-form their entire structure.

What differentiates human life forms from other self-reproducing systems is their capacity to understand and intervene in their own formative processes. Over millennia, but at a steadily accelerating pace, human beings have enlarged their material and cultural capital, gradually veering away from a blind, involuntary and uncomprehended path of evolution, and gaining the power to direct the course of social reproduction in accordance with ends of their own choosing. That these powers now include the capability of ending all life on earth certainly reveals the dark side of the human adventure. But it also indicates that the choice of ends is an inherently ethical undertaking. The expansion of our cultural horizons includes the growth of moral awareness and sensibility as well as the acquisition of scientific knowledge. Choices between alternative futures rest partly on informed judgements about the probable consequences of attempting to realise them. (Fatalism – the false belief that we are the slaves of destiny – is merely the limiting point at which freedom and prediction are abandoned in the supposition that nothing we might do can possibly make any difference.) But practical thinking (thinking about what to do) also calls for moral judgements. And the illumination for our moral decisions derives ultimately from ideas about what the good life consists of, both for the individual and for society as a whole.

In principle, then, the reproduction paradigm deals with all the interlocking processes by which society reproduces the material and cultural conditions of its existence, from procreation, agriculture and manufacturing to the most refined products of human consciousness. In practice economists working within this paradigm have tended to scale down their concerns to a narrow and often highly technical and formal set of problems arising within the theory of value.

This abridged theoretical focus began with Ricardo's attempts to find an invariable standard for measuing the value of reproducible commodities. Marx, it is true, did more than anyone to expound the principles of a reproductionist approach to political economy. But even his critical efforts remained imprisoned within the confines of the labour theory of value. Moreover, Marx never succeeded in moving by successive approximations from an abstract, stripped down model of the capitalist mode of production reduced to the barest minimum number of elements and relationships, to a richer understanding of capitalist social formations. Despite occasional flashes of insight and suggestive hints, subsequent reproduction-minded economists have rarely strayed from the realms of high theory and general principles. This tendency is revealed at its starkest in Sraffa's exclusive and deliberately restricted concern with the logical relationships between wages, prices and profits in a self-reproducing capitalist economy suspended in a state of long-run equilibrium.

These remarks should not be taken as impugning the status of pure ratiocination or casting doubt on the validity of its results. They are made simply to convey the point that, with two exceptions noted below, reproductionists have ploughed furrows well within the potentially broad boundaries of their paradigm's research agenda, leaving large tracts in a backward and undeveloped state.

One of these relatively neglected areas has been the labour market. The dominance of the exchange paradigm in this branch of mainstream economics has been little troubled by alleged demonstrations that under capitalism freely competitive labour markets co-exist with the exploitation of labour by capital. Not the least of the reason why such claims cut little ice was that Sraffa's disciples had undermined the traditional Marxist concept of exploitation couched in terms of the labour theory of value (see Steedman, 1977).

The two exceptions just referred to are the study of the labour process and the emergence during the 1970s of a diffuse, but influential feminist current of thought which was critical of political economy generally, and of both orthodox and Marxist treatments of the labour market in particular. The appearance of Braverman's pioneering book on the labour process under capitalism (Braverman, 1974) reopened a forgotten seam originally worked by Marx. But though welcome and long overdue, Braverman's initiative soon gave rise to Bravermania – a one-sided fixation on power relations *within* the capitalist enterprise. The relationships of domination and subordination embedded within the broader reaches of the social formation still remained out of view. The remedy for correcting this perceptual defect was supplied by feminists. It would be impudent to attribute this advance to the work of any single writer. What happened was more like a gradual growth of awareness that all schools of political economy were gender-blind. To overcome this blockage was going to require a paradigm shift rather than a marginal modification of men's studies. Or to put the point another way: the reproduction paradigm had hitherto been vastly underused and its slumbering powers needed to be roused.

Feminists reminded everyone of what should never have been

overlooked in the first place: that reproduction is simultaneously an economic, biological and social process. At the same time as they reproduce the materials and artefacts which they need in order to subsist and grow, human societies also reproduce their own biological substance and the forms of their social life. Social reproduction is always and everywhere a process of *joint* production. Its outputs – objects, people and social relations – are continually recycled as inputs into new creative activities. Once reproductionists have assimilated this elementary, almost banal truth, the scales which previously so restricted their vision fall away. They are in a much better position to explore the interconnections not only between class and gender, but among all the relationships of dominator to dominated which make up the texture of the social formation. This is what this book sets out to do in the specific context of the labour market.

5   The Plan of this Book

The itinerary of exploration is as follows. Drawing on the seminal work of Lukes (1974) Chapter 2 develops a three-dimensional conceptual framework for analysing social power relations, with particular stress on the processes of cultural formation. In Chapters 3 and 4 this framework is applied to the two basic paradigms of the labour market. As might be anticipated from the argument of this opening chapter, the exchange paradigm is found to be seriously deficient. It fails to take cognisance of any but the most blatant manifestations of social power, and lacks any language for handling its deeper and subtler forms. The reproduction paradigm is in principle better equipped in this respect, but remains woefully underdeveloped.

The next two chapters attempt to implement an appropriate development programme. Chapter 5 examines in some detail the peculiarities of labour power. The argument emphasises the special difficulties which confront all workers, as individuals no less than as collectivities, not just in prosecuting their interests in their relations with employers, but in deciding exactly where their best interests lie, and in articulating anything resembling a comprehensive conception of their interests. Chapter 6 takes this argument a step further by investigating the conditions in which these difficulties can be overcome. The key distinction here is between those social practices and projects which simply mesh with and tend to recreate the prevailing pattern of social relations, and those which self-consciously set out to transform them.

The second part of the book consists of an extended application of the theoretical ideas advanced in Part One. Chapters 7 and 8 are concerned with various aspects of society's work – the overall amount of time which people spend at work, paid or unpaid; the way in which this total is distributed among different social groups, especially, but not exclusively, between men and women; the forms of social life which rest on alternative social divisions of labour; and what work activities mean for those who perform them.

Chapters 9, 10 and 11 outline a new transformatory project for which, it is argued, the time is now ripe, and which has far-reaching implications for the organisation of society's work and the functioning of the labour market. The centrepiece of this project involves a transition from welfare state capitalism to basic income capitalism. 'Basic income' is the name given to the proposal that income and employment should be partially decoupled. Instead every individual in society should receive as an unconditional right a guaranteed income adequate to cover an agreed definition of subsistence and financed from the proceeds of taxation levied on everyone's other, earned or unearned, income.

These final three chapters explain why basic income is desirable and feasible. Desirable, first, because unrestrained output growth is no longer a sane objective of policy in the advanced capitalist countries, and employment policies need to be adapted to conditions of deliberately restrained growth; second, because basic income reconciles the maintenance of a regulated market economy with the enhancement of personal independence and security; and, third, because basic income tackles the contemporary crisis of the labour market and the welfare state in a way which unifies rather than fragments society. Feasible because of the advanced level of productivity bequeathed by capitalist development; and because it is implausible to suppose that work incentives would be destroyed by the increased taxes required to ensure that everyone's minimum subsistence needs are guaranteed.

In addition to considering the economic and ethical issues raised by basic income, Chapter 11 explores the political prospects of this transformatory project. The critical factor turns out to be the position of the organised labour movement, now in danger of submerging as a major political force. The labour movement may cling to an essentially conservative approach and leave unchallenged, or even uphold, the various relationships, of dominator to dominated which run through the labour market. Alternatively, it may commit itself to the basic income strategy and set its sights on an egalitarian re-formation of the structures of social reproduction.

Notes to Chapter 1

1. The analogy is borrowed from Wittgenstein (1969) who uses the concept of a 'world-picture' in the same sense as I am using the word 'paradigm'. A world-picture is the common ground that must be shared with others for communication to be possible. It constitutes the limits of the world for those who share that world-picture. But these limits are by no means fixed. New 'language games' emerge, others become obsolete as social practices change. For as Wittgenstein (1969, paragraph 23) himself puts it: '. . . the *speaking* of language is part of an activity, or of a form of life'.
2. Whether it makes sense to regard institutions as reflections of individual choice is open to doubt. Take racial discrimination in employment. Becker (1971) attempts to explain discriminatory practices in terms of employers' and/or employees' 'tastes'. But indulging such 'tastes' raises costs compared with non-discrimination. In a competitive market economy expensive indulgences should in the long run be selected out. It is difficult to explain the persistence and tenacity of discrimination without abandoning the individualistic premises of Becker's argument. See Marsden (1986, ch. 3).
3. A rather separate aspect of the misleading appearance of symmetry has to do with the definition and measurement of factors of production. Of the traditional trinity of factors – land, labour and capital – only the first two can be defined and measured in natural units – acres of equi-fertile land, and worker-hours of particular types of labour, for example. But the word 'capital' is ambiguous. It is used interchangeably to refer *both* to financial funds *and* to physical means of production. But only as sums of money or exchange-values can heterogeneous capital goods be made commensurable, whereas it is physical means of production which are actually used in the production process. However, the exchange-value of a given collection of physical capital goods depends on their relative prices, which in turn vary with the distribution of income between capitalists and workers. It is, therefore, difficult to attach any clear meaning to the idea of an abstract and

undifferentiated factor of production called 'capital' or 'capital in general' which yields up productive services and bestows on its owners entitlement to a compensating flow of income. This point formed the basis for a radical critique of the traditional neo-classical theory of factor pricing and distribution inspired by the work of Sraffa. As Steedman (1977) shows, the same critical insights also undermine Marxist theories of value and distribution based on the concept of value as a definite quantity of embodied labour time. What came to be known as the 'capital controversy' was at the forefront of theoretical debate amongst economists in the 1970s. It is relegated to a footnote here because it has no bearing on any of the issues raised in this book.

4. Hamlet does not seem too impressed by the compensating joys of physicality. Angels, ghosts and the like could never take pleasure in sex, yoga, dancing or other forms of muscular-skeletal exertion.

2
The Concept of Power[1]

1 Preliminary Definitions

'Power', as has often been noted, is an essentially contested concept – one of those concepts which inevitably involve endless disputes about their proper uses on the part of their users. I shall take it that the chief situations in which we wish to use the concept of power are those in which there is actual or potential conflict between agents whose interests in the outcome of one or more issues diverge. The term 'agent' here refers to any unified locus of decision and action, and thus embraces both human individuals and organisations with or without legal personality. The definitions of 'issues' and 'interests' are taken up below. I shall also assume, for convenience, that there are only two agents in any conflict situation.

The primary meaning to be attached to the concept of power can be stated as follows: A is said to exercise or enjoy power over B when, with respect to some specific issue, or set of issues, A's interest in the outcome conflicts with that of B, and, for reasons to be investigated, A's interest prevails over B's. Three points need to be noted in connection with this formulation. First, an 'issue' is any matter which either is currently, or could become, an object of decision and action by either agent. The hypothetical phrase 'or could become' is, as we shall see, significant. It is important not to restrict the domain of the concept of power to those matters which at a given time happen to be the objects of conscious choice, decision and action. If our definition of power is to embrace all the phenomena which can plausibly be argued to fall within its scope, it must be wide enough to include that class of cases in

24

which agents possess some significant advantage over their antagonists even when this advantage cannot be attributed to any intentional action on their part. It follows that the anaysis of power relations involves more than identifying winners and losers, and explaining the conditions of victory or defeat, in battles over what both the contending parties regard as key issues. Power consists not only in its exercise: an agent may also enjoy power without, so to speak, having had to work for it; indeed, without being aware of its source at all.

The second point to be stressed is that the above definition serves merely to fix a linguistic usage. It explicates sentences of the form 'A has the power to achieve outcome x' or 'A has power over B (or more power than B) with respect to issue i'. To attribute power to A does not in itself explain why outcome x occurs, or why A triumphs over B: it simply gestures towards an explanation. This is why our definition contains an open-ended reference to 'reasons to be investigated'. In social contexts it is usually a mistake to conceive of power as a kind of resource which will always yield its holder a determinate return whenever it is set to use. If an agent's power is defined as a set of pre-given capacities to realise results that accord with its interests, then it has to be admitted that the relationship between power and fortunes is highly variable. This is most apparent when a disputed issue is settled by an overt power struggle. The statement that A was the more powerful party at best provides a sufficient answer to the question: 'Why did A win?' in a context where it is understood that the disparity between A and B was so gross that the outcome of the contest was never in doubt: the initial conditions of the struggle were so stacked in A's favour that its victory was a foregone conclusion. But, as Hindess (1982) argues, it is misleading to adopt this case as a paradigm of power struggles. In general the connection between initial conditions and final outcome is uncertain and unpredictable. Hindess cites the military and political defeat of the USA in Vietnam as an exemplary illustration.

It sometimes happens in bargaining encounters that the division of payoffs in the final settlement can be seen in retrospect to reflect the initial relative strengths of the bargaining partners. 'Strength' in this context might be measured by comparing the sanction costs each side is able to inflict on the other relative to the costs each would itself sustain by resorting to sanctions in order to enforce its demands. If A obtains the superior payoff, it might then be argued that this *is* sufficiently explained by A's relative strength. But usually this verdict can be pronounced only after the event: *ex ante* it is rarely certain what the outcome of bargaining will be. For even leaving aside the influence of bluff, deception and negotiating skill, the whole purpose of exchanging threats, commitments and information during the course of negotiations, and, if need be, taking the issue to a trial of strength – a revealing phrase – is to eliminate the two sides' initial uncertainty about their relative strengths. The distribution of bargaining power is not known in advance of the bargaining process itself. Moreover in many models of the bargaining process a unique outcome is not determined once initial conditions have been specified: the character of the final settlement depends on the path by which it is reached (see Coddington, 1968). Thus statements attributing power to social agents are synoptic and inherently stand in need of further elaboration.

The third comment to be made about our definition concerns the use of the term 'interests'. It should not be presumed that interests are attached to agents independently of the particular struggles in which they are engaged, as if agents possessed certain 'essential' interests by virtue of their social attributes – class, sex, age, ethnic identity, etc. Interests are indeed what the fighting is about (or would be about if it occurred). But it does not follow that the interests at stake come first and the fighting second. For in almost all situations there are several, possibly contradictory, interests which agents might select as the basis for action. In what follows the process of goal selection is treated as part of the study of power relations, not as a datum of that study.

2   The Three Dimensions of Power

With this definition it becomes possible to identify three dimensions along which social power is distributed. First there are those contested issues with respect to which the rival agents both hold consciously articulated interests, *and* are both capable of bringing to bear various instrumentalities – constitutional prerogatives, propaganda, activation of alliances with third parties, damaging sanctions and so on – in order to influence the outcome within some more or less regularised and acknowledged decision-making procedure.

Second, there are issues with open outcomes which will be settled within some established decision-making procedure, and with respect to which, as in the first dimension, both A and B hold conscious and conflicting interests. In these cases, however, A's interests prevail over B's because B is denied access to the relevant decision-making process. This may happen *either* because B's attempts to pursue its interests are systematically frustrated by prior actions on A's part to ensure that the issue remains non-negotiable; *or* more importantly, it may happen because B simply fails to press its claims, judging the chances of success to be so slim as not to be worth pursuing. The latter is the notorious case of 'anticipated reactions'. Here, in contrast to the first dimension of power, no overt conflictual behaviour can be observed. Instead the disadvantaged party surrenders in advance and, however reluctantly, acquiesces in the status quo.

The third dimension of power presupposes a distinction between 'interests' and 'wants'. There are cases where the interests of agent A come into conflict with interests which agent B could in principle come to hold, but where A's interests prevail by default because B's potentially opposing interests remain latent and undefined. Here, in contrast to dimensions one and two, B simply does not entertain the possibility that A's differential advantage could be challenged: indeed, may not even recognise that A enjoys any advantage.

Social scientists and philosophers have traditionally been reluctant to grant the distinction between interests and wants which underlies this third dimension of power. If people suffer some disadvantage from existing social arrangements, why do they not do something about it? And if their inaction cannot be explained by a careful study of two-dimensional power, what is the empirical basis for the claim that they stand on the unpleasant end of an unequal power relationship? Surely, it is argued, to depart from the observable reality of what people say or believe their interests to be, is to grant a charter for unbridled metaphysical speculation based on some alleged divergence between people's subjective interests and what are claimed to be their 'real' interests of which they happen to be unaware?

However, the distinction between latent and perceived interests need not commit those who make it to claiming any special insight into other people's 'real' interests. It is true that Marxist and other doctrines of 'false consciousness' do indeed lay claim to such insight. They single out certain interests – for example, that of the working class in overthrowing capitalism, or that of women in overcoming male privilege – as ontologically privileged. But it is not necessary to insist that one set of interests is more 'real' than another. All sincere expressions of interest are equally real, however ethically unappealing or perverse they may appear to external observers.

It does not, however, follow that potential or latent interests which an agent fails to perceive are irrelevant to the study of power. What is required to validate the third dimension of power as a legitimate domain of inquiry are three propositions, put forward here as reasonable working assumptions. The first is that agents' subjective conceptions of their interests change over time. Second, that the ways in which agents structure the potential issue space in their environment and select a particular set of interests to act upon, are not neutral in their consequences for the distribution of advantage. Third that there are systematic, and in principle knowable, social processes which tend to reinforce and reproduce the subordinate status of the inferior agent in some power relationships; that is, tend to predispose these agents towards conceptions of their interests which are disabling compared with alternative conceptions which would incline them towards challenging their subordinacy. The first, and most unexceptionable, of these propositions allows for the possibility of empirical checks on alleged instances of the second and third.

An example will help to clarify these points. It is taken from John Stuart Mill's famous essay, *The Subjection of Women* (Mill, 1983). Mill argues that women's social relationship to men is that of a subject class to their masters. It stands, he says, as a glaring exception to the central principle of

modern institutions, social ideas and life, that human beings are not born to their place in life, and chained down by an inexorable bond to the place they are born to, but are free to employ their faculties, and such favourable chances as offer, to achieve the lot which may appear to them most desirable.

Mill attributes the long survival of women's servitude compared with other relations of bondage to three factors: first, the sheer number of beneficiaries from the relationship – the entire male sex – greatly exceeds the numbers privileged by other kinds of power relations; second, any powerholder's desire for power is strongest over those who are nearest to him and with whom his life is passed; and third, male powerholders possess greater facilities to prevent any uprising against their power because their subjects live constantly under the eye of their master, in isolation from their sister subjects, and with the strongest motives for seeking his favour or avoiding giving offence.

In our terms, so far, Mill's account of men's power over women operates in dimensions one and two. Mill goes on, however, to point out that women's masters desire more of them than actual service. 'Men do not want merely the obedience of women; they also want their sentiments.' Thus women are mentally, as well as physically, enslaved. Their socialisation tends to repress independence and spirit, to inculcate submissiveness and self-denial, and to have no life but in their affections for the men to whom they are connected or the children who constitute an additional tie between them and a man. Because these attributes are linked with sexual attractiveness, and hence with material security, 'it would be a miracle if the object of being attractive to men had not become the polar star of feminine education and formation of character.' To the standard response that the condition of women is explained and justified by 'women's nature' Mill replies that

What is now called the nature of women is an eminently artificial thing – the result of forced repression in some directions, unnatural stimulation in others . . . a hot-house and stove cultivation has always been carried on of some of the capabilities of their nature, for the benefit and pleasure of their masters.

And later he notes the corrupting effects of male supremacy on boys who grow up believing in their superiority to half the human race.

What this example makes clear is that the subjection of women cannot be entirely understood in terms of dimensions one and two. Women's subordination is secured not only by force, but also by the pervasive effects of child socialisation and the institutions of marriage and the family in shaping women's character, attitudes, beliefs and wants. If women fail to complain of their lot this is not simply because resistance would entail great risk, hardship and self-sacrifice; it is also because they are willing accomplices in the prevailing apportionment of roles and resources. Mill is drawing attention to this consensual aspect of the power relations between men and women. His essay is a forceful plea for a redefinition of the boundary between the 'natural' and the 'artificial' realms of the social order.[2] What is also clear from the history of feminism since Mill's day is that this boundary is shiftable and has shifted: the area of social life which is immunised against the very possibility of critical scrutiny by large numbers of women has undoubtedly shrunk. It is precisely this boundary shift which has revealed the full extent of women's oppression and has vindicated Mill's social analysis.

3 Issues, Interests, Decisions and Non-decisions

It may be useful to depict the preceding discussion in a diagram (Figure 2.1) which divides up the issue space confronting any agent. The rectangle represents the agent's issue space. This is the total set of issues with respect to which the agent may in principle come to form definite interests. Given this set there are three junctures at which power relations may come into play. First, they may be at work in the formation of the agent's *interest field*, represented by the larger of the two concentric circles; that is, they may influence which subset of issue space the agent selects as the focus of his interests. By definition the area of the issue space outside this circle contains the set of issues with respect to which the agent's interests remain latent and undefined. Not all the issues to be found within the complement set of the interest field will be so located for reasons stemming from the distribution of power. Some of the

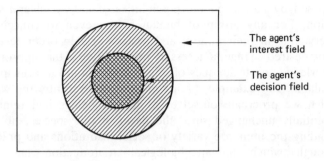

Figure 2.1 *Issue space. The unshaded area of the rectangle represents the set of issues with respect to which the agent's interests remain latent and undefined.*

issues towards which the agent remains indifferent will have no implications for the division of advantage between the contending sides. Nevertheless, it has been argued above that we need to be alert to the possibility that power relations play some role in fixing the boundaries of the interest field.

Second, power relations may determine the extent of the agent's *decision field* represented by the smaller of the two circles; that is, they may demarcate a region of the interest field within which the relevant decision-making processes lie beyond the agent's access. Issues within this non-decision field are excluded from any agenda of joint decision making, and the agent lacks any direct means of advancing his interests in their outcome.

Third, power relations may determine the outcome of those issues which lie within the agent's decision field. This is the arena of what are normally thought of as power struggles.

The three junctures identified above correspond in reverse order to the three dimensions of power. It is not necessary to be precise about the boundaries of the agent's issue space. The set of issues from which the agent selects an interest field is clearly less than infinite. It will change as human beings learn to manipulate their environment and slowly accumulate a common cultural capital which allows them to roll back the constraints imposed by nature on the possibilities of individual and social action. For any group of human beings even to conceive of intervening in their natural and social world in order to effect some desired change, a necessary precondition is that appropriate knowledge and techniques of intervention should in principle be available. For example, until comparatively recently the way in which we procreate ourselves as human beings had remained essentially unchanged since the dawn of our species, notwithstanding the immense variety of social institutions and practices through which human biological reproduction has been accomplished. Developments in procreative technology over the past quarter of a century – improved methods of contraception and abortion, techniques of fetal monitoring, artificial insemination and the emerging technology of extra-uterine gestation – have now set in motion the transition from a quasi-natural, spontaneous process to a consciously controlled process of production. This in turn has created the material base for the women's movement to take up reproductive rights as public issues in a way which could not have occurred before. There is an obvious sense in which women's control over their own fertility, bodies and sexuality could not have become objects of political thought and action as long as reproductive techniques remained at an essentially palaeolithic level. It is hardly surprising that the feminist movements of the late nineteenth and early twentieth centuries failed to take up these issues, concentrating instead on the struggle to gain access to areas which had hitherto been a male monopoly: the vote, education, skilled work, the ownership of property, political office, and participation in artistic and cultural life.[3]

For our purposes it is unimportant to fix the limits of issue space. What matters is that issues which lie unambiguously inside those limits may fail to figure within the agent's interest field, and that this suppression of potential interests may be due to the structure of power. It is also important not to misconceive the general nature of interest suppression. There is a strong temptation to think of the area of issue space within which an agent's interests remain undefined as a kind of blind spot in the agent's field of vision caused by some perceptual impairment. Such a diagnosis suggests that the fault – for this is how the visual block will appear to a concerned outsider who holds this conception – can be cured by an operation of a purely mental kind, whether directed at the intellect or the emotions. The indicated therapy will consist of some theoretical or sentimental (re-)education designed to expand the victim's consciousness and confer enlightenment. Thus it is assumed that latent interests are simply waiting to be (re-)discovered and could be so discovered by anyone with a sufficiently emancipated mind.

But in general it is a mistake to model the processes of interest formation and suppression as purely cerebral activities. As we shall have frequent occasions to observe throughout this book, an agent's interest field is embedded in a particular configuration of social institutions and practices, which exist independently of the agent and possess a certain inertial momentum. Hence as a general rule an agent cannot simply decide to pursue a new set of practical interests. The re-ordering of the interest field, and even more of the decision field, can occur only as part of an overall process of active social construction. Education – in its broadest sense – has its part to play in this process. But unless new ideas, perspectives and values acquire some purchase on social practice, which includes the practice of others, the agent's interests will tend to continue to run along the channels carved out by *current* practice. Moreover, whereas individuals can change their ideas and outlook relatively quickly, the pace of *social* transformation, though not always steady, is necessarily slow by comparison.

In practice the distinctions we have drawn are too sharp to do justice to the subtleties of real world power relations: it may not be easy to assign particular cases to one or other of the three sub-sets of issue space. Consider, for example, the riot or other acts of direct civil disobedience by groups who are debarred from the opportunity to influence decisions through regular, legitimate channels. Such actions can often be a highly effective way of achieving favourable outcomes for oppressed groups. Conceivably a group may fare better from a strategy of extracting concessions as a defiant outsider than it would if it allowed its representatives to step across the threshold between the interest field and the relevant decision field. On the other hand if the group's principal grievance is precisely that it is excluded from participation in its own governance, no amount of material concessions will in the end be an adequate substitute for an extension of the franchise. It is probably less misleading to describe this kind of case as an exceptional instance of the non-decision set. Its very exceptionality will in the normal course of events lead to its incorporation in an enlarged decision field. On the other hand, for exactly the same reasons the case could immediately be assigned to the decision field as a primitive and embryonic form of negotiation and joint decision-making. To the extent that the threat of mass disobedience is credible, those who hold nominally exclusive decision-making authority will tend to anticipate the reactions of their subordinates and frame their policies so as to avert displays of disaffection.

The boundary surrounding the interest field is similarly blurred. Latent and actual interests shade into each other according to the clarity with which distinct interests are perceived. For example, an oppressed group may recognise in a general way that it occupies an inferior, subordinate place under existing social arrangements. It may as a result feel generalised discontent with the prevailing order and a generalised aspiration towards a more satisfactory one. It may even develop a vague conception of the broad principles on which an alternative order might be built. A group in this position is evidently poised on the edges of the interest field. However, as long as its discontent and yearnings remain unfocused and amorphous, they will normally have little practical effect on the running of social affairs. An opportunity for the group's interests to emerge from the shadows is likely to arise only at comparatively rare moments when the system of government has been responsible for some gross deficiency – say, an unmitigated failure to protect its subjects' lives and safety, or a flagrant abuse of authority – and its complete overthrow appears likely or immediately practicable. And even then, unless the formerly oppressed interests rapidly acquire a sharper definition, the destruction of a discredited *ancien régime* scarcely guarantees that the new order will fulfil the group's dreams. In the ordinary course of events diffuse oppositionist attitudes may actually inhibit the transformation of a subject-group's outlook and practice, and thus perpetuate its subordination. Utopian belief-systems from Christianity under the early Roman Empire to the anarchist, socialist and communist movements of the nineteenth and twentieth centuries have frequently, and paradoxically, served to sustain the status quo by providing their adherents with spiritual compensation for present suffering and impotence.[4]

The essence of the argument of this chapter can be stated starkly as follows: A has power over B not only (1) when A's interest prevails over B's despite B's resistance; but also (2) when B's interest is denied access to the relevant decision-making process; and (3) when B has potential interests which conflict with A's but of which B is currently unaware.

Notes to Chapter 2

1. The analysis of power set out in this chapter is adapted from Lukes (1974).
2. For an extended discussion of the distinction between the 'natural' and the 'artificial', and of the attempts by claimant groups to redraw the boundary between the two see Peattie and Rein (1983).
3. This argument is developed by Fernbach (1981).
4. For a discussion of this phenomenon in the British labour movement see Hobsbawm (1964) and Nairn (1965).

3
Power in the Exchange Paradigm

1 Introduction

The prevailing view of mainstream economists on the role of power in the labour market, and in the economy generally, probably differs little from the assessment pronounced over sixty years ago by Alfred Marshall (Marshall, 1920, pp. 521–2).

> 'alliances' and 'counter-alliances' among employers and employed, as well as among traders and manufacturers . . . present a succession of picturesque incidents and romantic transformations, which arrest public attention and seem to indicate a coming change of our social arrangements, now in one direction and now in another; and their importance is certainly great and grows rapidly. But it is apt to be exaggerated; for indeed many of them are little more than eddies, such as have always fluttered over the surface of progress. And though they are on a larger and more imposing scale in this modern age than ever before; yet, now, as ever, the main body of movement depends on the deep, silent, strong stream of the tendencies of normal distribution and exchange; which 'are not seen', but which control the course of those episodes which are seen.

In this passage Marshall eloquently contrasts organised attempts by sectional interest groups to secure advantageous economic outcomes with 'the tendencies of normal distribution and exchange', or market forces. Two main points stand out:

one implicit and the other explicit. The first is that these contrasting sets of determinants are distinct and mutually exclusive: if the one set is effective, the other is ineffective. We shall take up this point later.

Second, Marshall is emphatic that the hidden hand of the market, conceived as impersonal because it aggregates the decisions of many individual agents, dominates the course of distribution and exchange, if not in the short run, then certainly in the long run. It may reasonably be inferred that all, or at least the overwhelming majority of cases of organised action to resist or nudge the hidden hand in some preferred direction fall into one or other of the following categories:

(1) Those which are ephemeral and are more or less rapidly negated by market forces;
(2) those whose effects, though enduring are of comparatively minor magnitude;
(3) those which countervail some other extra-market force working in the opposite direction, and thus merely serve to reproduce the approximate outcome which would have obtained anyway if the hidden hand had had the field to itself;
(4) those which are nothing more than epiphenomena, merely registering the conjuncture or movement of underlying market forces, which provide both necessary and sufficient conditions for their existence.

This classification of what it seems natural and convenient to refer to as 'power forces' leaves a residual set whose effects are neither ephemeral, negligible, mutually self-cancelling nor illusory. The conventional judgement, supported by Marshall in the passage cited, is that this residual set is either empty, or at most contains a few deviant and exotic curiosities.

In this chapter I make no attempt to survey the various empirical studies which may be adduced to uphold or rebut the conventional judgement.[1] Rather I shall explore the way in which power is conceptualised in the exchange paradigm of the labour market particularly in its dominant neo-classical version. For by and large this conceptualisation tends to be vague, inexplicit and unrefined. Accordingly part of my purpose is to lay bare a view of power which exists only in a practical, intuitive and untheorised state. But I shall also point out some of the limitations of this view.

Until Section 5 the discussion is confined to the role assigned to power forces which impinge directly on exchange itself. When they operate at this level power forces can be considered as part of the economic process, however much they 'distort' its 'normal' flow. But the exchange paradigm does not rule out the possibility that economically relevant power forces may also be at work *outside* or (logically) *prior to* the market exchange of commodities and factors of production. Pre-economic power, which influences economic outcomes indirectly, belongs to the political realm of society. The way in which exchange models handle power forces at the political level is taken up in Section 5 when the focus of discussion shifts from power *within* to power *outside* the process of exchange.

2   Power as Capacity and Power as Relationship

In any discussion of power emphasis may be placed either on power as a capacity, facility or ability, or on power as a relationship between social agents. This distinction corresponds to the locutions 'power to' and 'power over'. The definition of power presented in Chapter 2 was couched in terms of power as relationship, though power in the sense of capacity was also discussed. In ordinary usage these two aspects of power are logically related. This is because most of the contexts in which we wish to talk about power are of the zero-sum type. In a zero-sum situation, if A has the power to achieve x (power as capacity), where x represents some positive gain for A over and above the outcome which would have prevailed in the absence of this power, then necessarily there is some B at whose expense x is achieved.[2]

The exchange paradigm treats these two aspects of power in two related but quite separate stages, corresponding to the hallowed distinction between positive and normative economic analysis (see Lipsey, 1983). Power as capacity belongs to the realm of positive analysis. This consists of accounts of how agents may acquire and retain the ability to shift the terms of exchange in their favour by comparison with the 'fully competitive' outcome. Power as relationship enters the picture only at a second stage. This consists of normative analysis of the repercussions for social welfare which flow from the exercise of power as capacity.

Consider, for example, the standard partial equilibrium account of the impact of a trade union on the relative pay of a particular grade of labour. From a microeconomic standpoint the main cost of a high wage settlement is the possibility that some of the union's members will become unemployed. By definition a union has less to fear on this score, the lower is the elasticity of demand for the grade of labour it organises, *ceteris paribus*. Following Marshall's famous analysis of the determinants of this elasticity (Marshall, 1920), we can say that a union will enjoy greater power to raise its members' relative pay:

(1) The less elastic is the final demand for the product.
(2) The lower is the elasticity of substitution in production between unionised labour and other factors of production (including non-union labour belonging to the grade in question).
(3) The smaller is the grade's share in total production expenses (the so-called 'importance of being unimportant' rule).[3]
(4) The lower is the elasticity of supply of co-operant (substitute or complementary) factors.

Addison and Siebert (1979) add to this list a fifth condition relating to the effectiveness of the union's control over alternative supplies of labour to the union's members within the relevant grade. For a given degree of internal cohesion, this control will be positively related to union density – the proportion of the labour force within its jurisdiction which the union has succeeded in recruiting. By raising the density of its membership the union can reduce the threat of competition from non-union firms in the same product market, and the threat from the substitution of non-union labour in the production process. In other words by pursuing an expansionist policy the union can alter conditions (1) and (2) in a manner which enhances its wage-raising power.

The partial equilibrium setting of this kind of analysis can be modified by allowing for the possibility of spillover effects whereby union pay rates influence the pay of non-union workers. Non-union employers, for example, may choose to match union pay scales in a bid to avert the unionisation of their workers (see Rosen, 1969). But the main point to be emphasised here is that the focus of the paradigm's positive analysis is on power as capacity. Assuming that power in this sense can be demonstrated to exist, the question: 'Over whom is this power exerted?' is construed to mean 'At whose expense are such sectional gains achieved?' This question is then investigated in terms of standard social welfare analysis. The final assessment will depend on what assumptions are made about the optimality of resource allocation prior to intervention, and about the reactions of employers and other workers to any change in the union/non-union wage differential. On most assumptions it is concluded that a rise in the relative pay of a group of union members either reduces total job opportunities or depresses the absolute level of non-union wages. If we further assume: (1) that workers who remain or become unemployed, or experience a fall in their wages, would prefer not to suffer these consequences, if they could possibly avoid them; and (2) that these preferences deserve as much respect as those of the unionised group; then we can conclude that whatever gains the union makes are at their expense. Union power thus turns out to be power over other sections of the labour force.

There are only two major exceptions to this statement. One occurs when the union's wage gain galvanises employers into reorganising the labour process and raising productivity (the so-called 'shock effect'). In order for costs and prices to *fall* as a result of a wage rise it must be assumed that the induced change woud have been profitable before, but employers either did not realise it or were complacent. Moreover, self-financing wage increases can only be a once-for-all or once-in-a-while phenomenon. For both these reasons the empirical importance of this case is unlikely to be great. The second exception occurs when a union is formed amongst the employees of a firm which enjoys monopsony power in the labour market. As is well known, in this special case the union can succeed in raising *both* wages *and* employment up to the level of employment that would be associated with the competitive market wage. This is the countervailing power case noted earlier.

The conceptual separation of the positive analysis of power as capacity from the normative analysis of power as relationship stands out clearly in this treatment. If we were to confine attention to the former, the latter would drop out of sight. It is probably true to say that most of the studies which have used this conceptual framework to investigate the consequences of collective organisation for various facets of the labour market have been motivated by a concern to *pass judgement* on regulatory intervention, and that this judgement has usually been hostile. Nevertheless, the point remains that, within this framework, in order to understand 'brute' power forces, independently of how they are evaluated, only power as capacity is relevant.

Not only this; a purist who insisted on shunning all value judgements and remaining strictly within the confines of positive analysis, would find no language in the lexicon of the exchange paradigm for specifying power relationships. Logically, as we have seen, where power as capacity exists, there must be certain definite affective relationships between specified agents. But to move from the statement that A's actions affect B in some significant manner, to the claim that A wields power over B, requires some reference to B's interests. It is not sufficient to know that B's behaviour is consistent with the proposition that B loses from A's actions; or even that B believes himself to be the loser. We also need to know whether B actually *is* the loser; and this requires some additional premise: for example, that B is the best judge of his own interests, or that B's interests are worthy of respect. But admitting this extra premise takes us out of the realms of positive analysis. In the exchange model's *primary* analysis of how power forces may alter the terms of exchange, there is no room for a 'power over' vocabulary.

3 The Identification and Measurement of Power

A closely related feature of this treatment of power is the assumption that in a fully competitive economy, if it existed, power forces would be absent. The fully competitive market system constitutes a base-line from which deviations can be identified and measured and traced to their source in various frictions and imperfections which permit power forces to intrude. The impact of trade unions, for example, is measured by comparing actual labour market outcomes with what would have happened under fully competitive conditions. This kind of comparison is not intended to be interpreted historically. There is no suggestion that labour markets before the advent of trade unions and collective bargaining conformed to the competitive model. Rather, what is intended is a purely notional comparison with a hypothetical labour market which has probably never existed historically, and certainly cannot now be directly observed.

Now there can be no objection in principle to the use of convenient logical fictions as a method of analysis.[4] But this method does carry a cost in the present context. For by construction, what students of power call 'the relevant counterfactual' – a statement indicating what would happen in the absence of some alleged power force – is not open to observation. This poses considerable problems for empirical attempts to test and estimate the influence of power forces, as we shall see in the next section.

Recent neo-classical literature on labour markets has stressed that they contain an irreducible minimum of frictions and imperfections due to the existence of information and adjustment costs.[5] In this newer vintage of models competition remains atomistic, but less than perfect: labour market participants lack complete knowledge about the whole array of wages and prices in the economy; firms can administer wages; and labour mobility is a costly and uncertain activity. As a result trading can take place at disequilibrium prices, and market participants are forced to bear the costs of adjustment to disequilibrium themselves. The traditional theory of competitive markets adopted the logical fiction of the omniscient auctioneer or central coordinator. The auctioneer's functions were: (1) to issue costless price information to all transactors; and (2) to ensure that all bids and offers remained provisional and no exchanges were actually effected until, by an iterative process of trial and error, a consistent set of market-clearing prices had been identified. Competitive factor and commodity markets were supposed to behave 'as if' they were directed by such an auctioneer. In the new microeconomics of the labour market this logical fiction is abandoned.

Unavoidable market imperfections arising from natural information and adjustment costs create openings for localised power forces to emerge. For example, suppose a firm faces a shortage of labour in a particular grade. The adjustment emphasised in traditional models would be for the firm to increase its wage offer in order to induce recruitment into that grade from the external labour market. However, the firm cannot be certain of the number and quality of the job applicants who would be attracted by this inducement. It may, therefore, choose to fill its vacancies by arranging to transfer and train workers in other grades who are already on its payroll. But workers who have received specific on-the-job training know that they could inflict significant turnover costs on their employer by threatening to quit and seek jobs elsewhere. Equally the prevalence of on-the-job training raises the costs to workers of invoking the quit sanction or pushing their luck to the point where their employer is forced to declare redundancies. If they join the outsiders within the general pool of unattached labour in the external labour market, they become less eligible than insiders as candidates to fill vacant job slots.

Thus even in atomistic labour markets each employing unit will extrude islands of bargaining power above the sea of market forces. Of course, it could still be maintained that the level and changes in the level of the ocean tightly circumscribe the islanders' autonomy, particularly in the long run.

Whilst this class of models certainly represents an advance in realism over the old perpetual market-clearing fairy-tale, it does complicate the problem of identifying and measuring power forces. For these forces now fall into two types: those which are thrown up by natural impediments to the movement of the hidden hand; and those which are contrived, and, in principle, removable. But the boundary between these two types is hazy. Natural pockets of bargaining power create a potential for conflict. And where this potential exists, institutions are likely to emerge to regulate it. But once they have sprung up institutions tend to undergo a process of organic growth and acquire a considerable degree of autonomy from the environment in which they first germinated. As Kerr (1954) argued over thirty years ago, when firms and workers envisage an enduring, though indefinite attachment to each other, the labour market tends to become 'balkanised': each employing unit forms an independent fiefdom with its own idiosyncratic customs and rules. The boundary between 'natural' and 'contrived' power forces is also elastic. By definition it will shift with every change in the objective structure of information and adjustment costs. Hence in place of the theoretical absolute zero of perfect competition, we now have only an imprecise and relative zero.

One way out of this difficulty is to interpret *all* so-called institutional or power forces as rational, cost-minimising or utility maximising, responses to market imperfections.[6] Consider the use of comparisons with external reference groups in wage negotiations. This is often presented as a self-evident example of an intruding power variable. But the practice of adhering to some customary pay relationship can be rationalised as a particular type of market adjustment process. Instead of undertaking *search* activities (advertisements, interviews, job sampling, etc.) in order to improve their knowledge of labour market conditions, employers and workers find it more efficient to engage in *monitoring* activities (wage surveys, use of specialised data consultancy services, etc.). Similarly instead of adjustment occurring through voluntary job quits with feedback effects on employers' wage offers, firms and workers prefer to negotiate wages directly, and in their negotiations will take explicit account of the wage levels which their monitoring activity indicates prevail elsewhere.

On this view so-called institutionalist and market force theories offer not competing, but complementary explanations of wage determination within a unified theory of rational choice. Power forces become an integral feature of real world labour markets. Measuring their incidence becomes a matter of assessing the balance between different types of information gathering and adjustment strategies. The zero point on the scale of power can be equated with *real* markets in which one particular type predominates. 'Market' and 'power' remain exclusive categories: but there is no presumption that atomistic adjustment mechanisms are normal, or indeed preferable to any other.

This synthetic approach certainly overcomes the problem of the unobservable counterfactual. Its central claim is as yet speculative: it remains to be seen whether all those facets of labour market behaviour which defy explanation in terms of models of atomistic competition, can be subsumed within a more general theory of rational choice. But even if this were the case, the very fact that the synthesis rests squarely within the rational choice paradigm exposes it to serious criticisms as an analysis of social power. These will be pursued in the final section of this chapter.

4 Power Forces as Supplementing Market Outcomes

So far I have argued that the primary meaning of power in the exchange model of the labour market is that of power as the capacity to distort the pattern of economic outcomes and the distribution of rewards away from those which would prevail in competitive conditions. As long as the question at issue is: 'How can such distortions arise and persist?' it is neither necessary, nor indeed possible, to be *specific* about the relationships of power in society. To put it crudely: instead of Lenin's famous question: Who Whom? the exchange paradigm asks Who, What and How Much? Power is treated by analogy with a scarce resource which may be acquired and set to work to satisfy whatever objectives its owner happens to set himself. All instances of power are depicted as deriving from some impediment in the competitive process. Embedded in all the multifarious manifestations of power is a common substratum. Power as capacity is essentially the same no matter who holds and uses it. This explains, for example, why adherents of the exchange model persist in regarding trade unions as the labour counterparts of the monopolistic firm. Both are conceived as having cornered a scarce resource, at least over a certain neighbourhood.

This notion of power as a scarce resource fulfils an important conceptual function in the neo-classical version of the exchange paradigm. The central concept in the neo-classical theory of distribution is that of marginal productivity. In a competitive economy, given the supplies of the various factors of production, the distribution of the social product among them is determined by the market valuation of each factor's contribution to production at the margin – the value of each factor's marginal product. The distribution of income amongst persons then depends on how much of each factor each person happens to own. This principle is held to be universally applicable: it governs the rents accruing to landowners no less than the wage differential of skilled over unskilled labour.

The primitive idea underlying this theory of distribution is that income sources-cum-recipients which are apparently quite dissimilar, nevertheless derive their incomes in essentially similar ways. The notion of power as a scarce resource associated with natural or contrived flaws in the competitive mechanism, allows this primitive idea to survive outside the theoretical body in which it was originally lodged, and to migrate from the world of perfect (or simply atomistic) competition to the world of imperfect competition. It is as if power-holders possessed an extra factor endowing them with a distraint on the division of economic rewards. By definition this factor vanishes under competitive conditions. But when these conditions fail in some respect, the power factor comes into play, yielding its owner a private return, even though it is socially unproductive.

Starting from the notion that power gains access to the economic process through gaps and malfunctions in the organisation of markets, it is natural to treat the influence of power forces on economic outcomes as essentially *supplementary* to those 'normal tendencies of distribution and exchange' which Marshall saw as decisive. In a sense the orthodox judgement about the marginality of power forces is built into the conceptual framework of the exchange paradigm.

The *manner* in which power forces supplement the outcomes which would otherwise be thrown up need not be a simple additive one: the intrusion of power forces in one section of the economy may modify market behaviour elsewhere, thus creating both direct and indirect channels of influence. These points can be illustrated by considering the standard approach adopted in one of the growth industries of the economics profession over the past thirty years – the testing and estimation of aggregate wage equations.

In an economy with a significant non-unionised segment of the labour force the aggregate level of money wages can be defined as follows:

$$W = TW_u + (1 - T)W_n \qquad (1)$$

where W is the aggregate money wage level; W_u is the union wage level; W_n is the non-union wage level; and T is the proportion of the labour force belonging to trade unions, which, for the purpose of the argument, we assume to be identical to the proportion of the labour force paid at union-negotiated wage rates. If we define

$$\lambda = \frac{W_u - W_n}{W_n}$$

as a measure of the union/non-union wage differential then

$$W = W_n (1 + T\lambda) \qquad (2)$$

It follows that:

$$\dot{W} = \dot{W}_n + \left[\frac{\lambda}{1 + T\lambda} \right] \frac{dT}{dt} + \left[\frac{T}{1 + T\lambda} \right] \frac{d\lambda}{dt} \qquad (3)$$

where a dot over a variable denotes that variable's proportional rate of change over time.

Equation (3) brings out clearly that there are in principle three channels by which unions can influence the movement of money wages. First, they may increase the size of λ, the union/non-union wage differential. Second, they may increase T, the density of trade union organisation. Third, they may influence money wages indirectly by causing W_n to rise more rapidly than it would otherwise have done. It is easy to see that in the absence of this third, spillover effect the direct union impact on the rate-of-change of money wages is likely to be small.

In the first place, although all empirical studies indicate that λ is positive, they also reveal that λ does not rise continually, and, indeed, in certain periods registers a fall. There is therefore unlikely to be much *persistent* union impact on $\dot{W}$ through this channel. Second, changes in T over the length of time interval of interest in studies of money wage movements – typically a year – are comparatively small. Hence the purely automatic effect of union expansion on the aggregate wage level cannot contribute much to the overall explanation of money wage changes. Third, the order of magnitude of the coefficients on dT/dt and $d\lambda/dt$ is unlikely to be much in excess of 0.2 and 0.5 respectively if we make plausible assumptions about the typical average values of λ and T.

Hence unions can have a major impact on $\dot{W}$ only if their effects on wage determination spread beyond the area of direct union influence and become part of some dynamic process affecting the whole economy. Ignore for the moment any such spillover effects whereby W_u becomes one of the determinants of W_n. Assume, as is customary, that $\dot{W}_n = f(E, p^e)$ where E is excess demand in the labour market and $\dot{p}^e$ is the expected rate-of-change of prices over the relevant time horizon adopted by labour market transactors, which, again for the sake of argument, we assume to be shared by both employers and workers alike. With these assumptions the aggregate wage equation has the general form:

$$\dot{W} = f(E, \dot{p}^e) + g(M) \tag{4}$$

where M represents the direct influence of unions on negotiated wages.

Now none of the arguments of the two functions f and g can be directly observed. Hence a typical estimating equation might be:

$$\dot{W} = a_0 + a_1 U + a_2 \dot{p} + a_3 Z \tag{5}$$

where U is the percentage unemployment rate, taken as a proxy for unobservable excess demand; $\dot{p}$ is some proxy for the expected rate of inflation, constructed, say, out of past and current values of the actual rate of inflation; and Z is some proxy for independent trade union influence on money wages, constructed, say, out of strike statistics or union membership data.

Equation (5) illustrates clearly the general point of this section: that in the exchange model of the labour market power forces – represented in this example by the 'intruder' variable Z – merely supplement the operation of market forces – represented by the variables U and $\dot{p}$.

Matters become only slightly more complicated if we allow spillover effects to modify the market behaviour encapsulated in the form of the function f. The effects of power forces are now divided between the direct power variable Z, and any indirect spillover from union wage negotiations to non-union pay. These indirect effects might in principle be estimated by measuring changes over time, or across different segments of the labour market at a given time, in the coefficients a_0, a_1 and a_2 of equation (5). There is, of course, the difficulty we noted earlier that there may be no satisfactory way of estimating the pure form of the function f which would prevail in the absence of the spillover process. But this practical problem does not affect the central principle of conceptualisation employed in the exchange paradigm: that social power can and should be understood as an external encroachment on the competitive market mechanism, which supplements its results.

It is always possible that empirical tests of wage equations such as equation (5) may indicate that in the labour markets of advanced capitalism, power forces have supplemented the operation of the market to the point of supplanting it. Disputes over the relative importance of power and market variables in the aggregate wage equation have been a major line of dissension between 'institutionalist' and neo-classical theories of wage determination. What is interesting, however, is that both sides in these disputes have adhered to a common conceptualisation of power and market: whilst appearing to be fundamental their quarrel has been essentially empirical.

A far more profound objection to this whole approach to the explanation of money wage movements is that the attempt to isolate market and power forces is wholly artificial and misleading. As will become clearer in the following section, it is possible to separate these forces into watertight compartments only at the expense of seriously restricting the range of phenomena to which the language of power can be legitimately applied. By adopting an alternative, broader and, I shall argue in subsequent chapters, superior conceptualisation of power, it becomes possible to view market forces as operating within a matrix of social power relations. The full meaning of this statement cannot be clarified at this stage in the exposition. But its general flavour can be conveyed by briefly reflecting on the type of aggregate wage equation considered in this section.

It is critical to the enterprise of estimating the relative impact of market and power forces that the variables which purport to reflect the working of the market should not themselves be significantly affected by the distribution of social power. In equation (4) above the arguments of the function f are supposed to be interpreted in this way. Suppose, however, that the average level of U over some historical period has been influenced by the state's macroeconomic policy stance which has made the maintenance of a low average unemployment rate a major priority.[7] Suppose further that this policy stance owes less to any change in economic ideas and fashions, and much more to an implicit contract between the state and the trade union and labour movement. Under the contract the state agrees to maintain, as far as it can, a full employment regime in return for trade union moderation in wage bargaining and a general willingness to cooperate with, or at least not obstruct, the state's objectives and priorities for the national economy.

The unions have an obvious interest in such an arrangement both to improve their members' material security and to enhance their own institutional power and status. The state for its part is likely to be aware of the risks and costs of a full employment regime – a chronic, though perhaps manageable, inflationary tendency, and a fundamental shift in the balance of strength between employers and workers on both the wage bargaining and the job control fronts. But it may plausibly reason that these corollaries of full employment are outweighed by the corresponding dangers of social disaffection and potential instability which could attend a failure to satisfy popular aspirations for greater job and income security.[8]

Where the level of unemployment has been underpinned by such a ramified social settlement it can hardly be regarded as an unadulterated market variable. Of course, this kind of arrangement is unlikely to last forever: the matrix of power relations which gave birth to it will eventually be restructured, though only in the course of long-term social changes and possibly also political upheavals.[9] The state's commitment to full employment may wane as the balance between the costs of alternative strategic choices is perceived to shift. But the general point is that the re-emergence of mass unemployment as a disciplinary regulator of the labour market, no less than the full employment regime which preceded it, can be interpreted as the market outcome of a new alignment of social power relations. In a sense Marshall's judgement of the dominance of market forces over the long run can be turned on its head. Or perhaps it would be better to say that the notion of an invariant and normal tendency of distribution and exchange exists only in the imagination of those whose understanding of the development of society is suspended within a historical vacuum.

5 Exchange Models and the Three Dimensions of Power

At various points in the argument of this chapter I have noted that in exchange models 'power' and 'market' are mutually exclusive categories. It is now time to take issue both with this assumption and with another, closely related to it: namely, that in analysing power it is sufficient to consider only the *decisions* which agents make in situations of social conflict. These two assumptions stand or fall together. This is because, from the standpoint of an exchange model, any claim that agents possess power (in the sense of capacity) can be judged only by the degree to which they actually succeed in altering the terms of exchange in their favour. A necessary (though not sufficient) condition of such success is that agents should consciously deploy whatever power source they possess in pursuit of their interests as they see them. They may exploit pre-existing defects in the competitive mechanism, or they may 'artificially' create and perpetuate new ones. But, in either case, for an outcome to qualify as the product of power it has to be attributable to some intentional action on the part of the powerholder. If there is no evidence that a beneficiary agent consciously sought to bring about some outcome which happens to be particularly favourable to him, then his fortune derives from the lottery of the market, not from the exercise of power.

In this section I shall challenge these assumptions by fulfilling my earlier promise to analyse the way in which the paradigm deals with *indirect* economic power operating outside the exchange process proper. Simultaneously I shall show that exchange models cannot accommodate the third dimension of power distinguished in Chapter 2; and that they can admit only a limited class of cases belonging to the second dimension: namely, those in which it can be demonstrated that the more powerful agent engages in various kinds of manipulation and chicanery to exclude his opponent from decision-making. For most practical purposes the paradigm's concept of power is one-dimensional.

It will help to clarify the discussion if we consider an imaginary economy. Suppose that there is no monopolistic influence on the terms of exchange in any market: universal competition ensures that every economic agent is a price-taker in every factor and commodity market. Suppose nevertheless that the configuration of the four basic parameters of supply and demand[10] is particularly favourable to one particular group of resource-owners. Imagine, for example, that the factor 'land' is scarce relative to other productive resources; that under existing technical conditions 'land' happens to be used intensively to produce commodities which are highly valued by society given its current tastes and preferences; and that 'land' ownership is restricted to one (minority) class in the population. Let it be assumed, however, that there is no collusion amongst the members of this class to force up the average level of land rents: competition between landowners is sufficiently strong to equalise the rent per unit of equifertile land.

It is evident that the conditions we have postulated will generate relatively high land rents. The personal distribution of income will be skewed in favour of the landowning class. Hence the landowners will enjoy a superior voting weight in the expenditure decisions which determine the allocation of resources among different productive uses. If their consumption preferences diverge from those of the rest of society, the composition of social output will differ from that which would obtain under a more egalitarian pattern of land ownership.

The question is: Could the landowners in our imaginary economy be described as enjoying or exercising power over the rest of society? Now, as we have seen, exchange models are wedded to a *behavioural* concept of power: A has power over B when their interests conflict and A's actions cause his interests to prevail over B's, each agent's interests being ascertained only by reference to their overt behaviour. It follows from this that the landowners in our example could be described as powerholders only if it could be demonstrated that they are actively preventing a redistribution of income by successfully resisting popular demands either for a reform of the system of land tenure or for the introduction of a tax on land rents. In other words the attribution of social power would be appropriate and justified only if the landowners were demonstrably able to enforce their 'class monopoly' of a scarce and valued resource against the express wishes of other sections of society. They might, for example, bribe or intimidate electors or members of the legislature; attack and harass the reform movement; or threaten rebellion or disruption if the government attempts to implement a reform programme.

But suppose that the landowners have committed none of these acts, and that there is no popular demand for reform. Then the most that could be said would be that the prevailing pattern of land ownership was a source of social inequality. This might or might not be morally regrettable. But whatever the ethics of the case, an adherent of the exchange paradigm would have to conclude that the inequality derived not from the exercise of power, but from a particular constellation of the four underlying conditions of market exchange. Regardless of the natural and historical origins of this state of affairs, its contemporary beneficiaries would not be responsible for creating or maintaining it.

Now this answer to the question posed above excludes two kinds of cases which might be thought to cast doubt on it. The first is the possibility that the landless majority are cowed into submission to the prevailing system of property rights. They may be aware at some level of their consciousness that an alternative system could be devised in which their interests would be better served. But they refrain from challenging the landowners' dominant position because, realistically or not, they are inclined to discount their prospects of success. They resolve to put up with their lot. If asked, they declare themselves to be perfectly satisfied with the way things are, though they might, perhaps, harbour some deep resentment which could be detected by a careful observer.

Alternatively the landless majority may simply be ignorant of any possibility that the system of land tenure might be changed. The idea does not even flicker in the deepest recesses of their minds. They acquiesce uncritically in the existing system. They may even uphold prevailing property rights with the sanction of moral authority, regarding them as part of the natural, and therefore inevitable, order of the world.

The exchange paradigm's behavioural concept of interest and power excludes these instances of the second and third dimensions of power from its purview. It allows power forces to affect the terms of exchange in only two ways. *Within* the exchange process individual agents or coalitions of agents may take advantage of weaknesses in the competitive mechanism or may mobilise to suppress competition over a certain area. If we rule this out, as in our imaginary economy, then the only other possible site of power lies *outside* or *prior to* the exchange process; that is, at the political level of society.

Agents may organise within the political sphere to secure some favourable distribution of property rights or to countervail market outcomes under the existing distribution. But the exchange paradigm recognises as belonging to the domain of power only those actions which are consciously directed at maintaining or altering property rights and the associated division of economic rewards. Where no such actions are to be observed, the pattern of property rights and rewards is free from the influence of social power. Given any initial set of natural and historical conditions, the working out of market forces will determine each agent's fortunes. But, if no agent can be held responsible for creating or sustaining these conditions, no agent can be described as the beneficiary or victim of a power relation.

Now the two counter-examples to this claim presented above both involve what might be called failures of interest representation. In the first example some agents' interests remain politically null because of an adverse balance of political forces. In the second potential interests remain suppressed as a result of the cultural formation of the agents in question. It might be argued that exchange models *can* provide for such lapses of interest representation. What is needed is to apply to the political process a conceptual device analogous to universal competition as a standard for identifying instances of power within the process of market exchange. Imagine a political regime under which every agent has equal access to the political process and, on average, an equal chance of influencing the results of that process. In such a regime agents would be equally able to formulate and promote whatever interests they deemed to be most important. No (important) interest would be systematically ignored or overridden. Conversely, evidence that some well defined and numerous interest had been excluded from the political process, could be traced to departures from the ideal standard of political equality, just as power within exchange derives from a breakdown of the conditions of market equality.

There are two problems with this argument. The first is that it is not at all easy to specify the characteristics of the requisite political regime. Stated abstractly what is needed is a polity in which political power is sufficiently dispersed both as between state and civil society and as between the various agents in civil society to ensure approximate equality in the conditions of political contestation. As a bare minimum we might say that this general requirement will be met when government is routinely compelled to attend to the interests of the governed, and when, in deciding who is to be entrusted with governmental authority, each (adult) person counts for one, and none for more than one.

But just what set of specific rules for assigning governmental authority will meet the bill? One standard answer would probably approximate to Dahl's characterisation of polyarchical systems of government (Dahl, 1971).[11] Lindblom (1977), summarising Dahl's discussion, offers the following list of rules guaranteeing rights and prerogatives: freedom to form and join organisations; freedom of expression; the right to vote; eligibility for public office; the right of political leaders to compete for votes and support; alternative sources of information; free and fair elections (open, honestly conducted, one person one vote, etc.) which decide who is to hold top authority; institutions for making government policies depend on votes and other expressions of preference.

It might be thought that where these rules are scrupulously observed, the political system will afford equal and open access to all distinct social interests, and no interest group will be able systematically to block a redistribution of assets or benefits which has succeeded in attracting widespread support. Actually even if we restrict ourselves to the first dimension of power, the rules of polyarchy are at best necessary, but not sufficient conditions for achieving a degree of political equality which would parallel the levelling effect of competition amongst market participants. To mention but two of the problems: nothing within the specified rules excludes the possibility that a permanent majoritarian interest will oppress and discriminate against a minority; furthermore, different political groups may be unequally endowed with the resources and skills needed for political success.[12]

However, it is not necessary in the present context that a system of government under which all distinct interests enjoy equality of political influence, should actually exist; or even that it should be a realisable possibility. It merely has to be conceivable. If its concept is coherent, then, just as perfect competition defines a theoretical zero, so, it can be argued, the ideal polyarchy provides a base-line for assessing actual political power, and, in particular, for analysing failures of interest representation.

Even if we grant this line of argument and leave aside the problem of devising a plausible and coherent political system with the requisite properties, there remains a second, more serious problem. The behaviourist model of power is necessarily compelled to adopt a very narrow view of what is to qualify as a breakdown or deficiency in the system of interest representation. To revert once more to our imaginary economy: if the only interests considered as legitimate objects of study are those which agents currently manifest in their observable behaviour, then cases such as that in which the landless section of society is culturally incapable of challenging the position of the landowners cannot even be acknowledged.

The behaviourist model's scope in the second dimension of power is not much greater. Suppose that the interest of the landless in achieving reform has become conscious. It is only when the conditions of the ideal polyarchy are overtly violated that the landowners can be said to wield power over the rest of society. The landowners may engage in preemptive action to frustrate the expression and advancement of the landless interest; or, if, despite this, the landless succeed in pushing their interests on to the political agenda, the landowners may enjoy a preponderant influence over the policy-making process. But if the landless interest simply remains mute, the landowners will neither want nor need to take any action at all. There will be no conflict of interests to be observed, and hence no basis for any attribution of social power.

6   The Central Claim of the Exchange Paradigm

It might be useful to summarise the discussion of this chapter with a brief statement of the central claim of the exchange paradigm's analysis of power in the labour market. The paradigm defines the primary meaning of power as the capacity to win the lion's share of the payoffs in the zero-sum games of social conflict. As far as the labour market is concerned, the more the sway of competition extends within the economy, and the more nearly the polity approximates to the conditions of polyarchy, the smaller the total incidence of power in this sense. In a fully competitive economy supported by a polyarchical system of government, the labour market will be more or less free from the influence of power forces. Relations between the parties to employment contracts will be relations between free and equal traders. The terms of contracts will involve the exchange of approximately equivalent values for each party; for the employer the cost of employing labour will be balanced at the margin by the value of labour's contribution to production; for the employee the cost of supplying labour services will be equal at the margin to the value of the compensation received. Costs and benefits in each case will, of course, be those perceived by the parties themselves.

There can be no guarantee that the terms of exchange in such a system will not be associated with (substantial) inequalities between individual resource owners. Indeed, some individuals may be so poorly endowed with the productive attributes which employers require that their market rewards fall short of bare subsistence. Ethics or expediency may then prompt charitable or welfare initiatives to redress market outcomes. But the primary distribution of rewards between winners and losers would simply be inherent in the underlying conditions of supply and demand. Provided that political action to alter these conditions or to remedy their effects is not permanently frustrated by heavy concentrations of political power, the situation could not be attributed to anyone's action or design.

It follows that if the concept of power is restricted to cases in which agents consciously act to promote their own interests at the expense of others with whom they are in conflict, the politico-economic system outlined above would exhibit a negligible incidence of social power. No agent would exert or enjoy any significant power over any other: all would be equally powerless to affect the terms of market exchange, even if these terms happened to result in wide disparities of income. In this sense all agents would be equal.

Notes to Chapter 3

1. See, for example, the studies by Lewis (1963). Ashenfelter and Johnson (1972), Pencavel (1974), Johnson (1975), Mulvey (1976), Metcalf (1977), Layard *et al.* (1978) and Mulvey and Abowd (1980).
2. Some writers (e.g. Parsons, 1969, ch. 14) object to the treatment of power as a zero-sum phenomenon. Parsons proposes a redefinition according to which power as capacity is a feature of all cooperative human activities working on a resistant environment and requiring leadership without there being any necessary conflict between leaders

and led. Such activities are said to generate power in the sense that they produce results which would otherwise be unattainable and from which all may benefit. On this definition it becomes possible to speak of 'power to' without necessarily implying any 'power over' relationship. However, as Lukes (1974, p. 26) points out, this revisionist approach is out of line with ordinary usage, and simply defines the problems associated with power conflicts out of existence.

3. Hicks (1963) demonstrates that in wage negotiations it is sometimes 'important to be important' rather than the converse. This is when the elasticity of substitution is high relative to the elasticity of final demand. For a discussion of the meaning of this condition, see Maurice (1975).

4. Compare, for example, the way in which Sraffa's *Production of Commodities by Means of Commodities* (Sraffa, 1960) can be interpreted as re-enacting Marx's 'logical-historical' method. In order to highlight the essential characteristics of the capitalist mode of production, an initial, largely imaginary, system of simple commodity production is postulated into which capitalist social relations then supervene. See Meek (1973), Preface, pp. xxxii–xliv.

5. See, for example, Phelps *et al.* (1970) and Burton and Addison (1977 and 1978).

6. See the suggestion put forward by Addison and Siebert (1979, pp. 483–8) for synthesising market and institutionalist explanations of wage determination.

7. The means by which the state exerts this influence need not involve any close and direct linkage between the government's budget deficit and the level of economic activity. The policy commitment to 'full employment' may itself be sufficient to boost the long-term state of business expectations component of the marginal efficiency of capital. As a result buoyant levels of investment in fixed capital may be sufficient to sustain high activity rates without the need for much direct and detailed fiscal stimulation. That is the 'safety net' argument for the role of Keynesian policy in underpinning the full employment boom of the 1950s and 1960s. See Matthews (1968).

8. For a more extended development of this argument in the context of post-war Britain see Purdy (1976).

9. For a suggestive analysis of the British labour movement's loss of political influence after the high point reached during the Second World War and its immediate aftermath, see Hobsbawm (1978).

10. See the discussion in Chapter 1, pp. 9–10.

11. 'Polyarchy' means literally 'rule by many'.

12. For further discussion of the problems of achieving political equality amongst diverse interest groups see Lively (1975, ch. 2).

4
Power in the Reproduction Paradigm

1 Introduction

This chapter has two main purposes, both of them sympathetically critical of the classical Marxist version of the reproduction paradigm. The first, pursued in Sections 2 and 3, is to examine the traditional Marxist response to what I called at the end of the last chapter the central claim of the exchange paradigm. I shall show that whilst this response has a certain force, it remains enmeshed within the same conceptualisation of power as its rival. Moreover it fails to exploit the potentialities inherent within the reproduction perspective for embracing an extended, three-dimensional view of the power relations between labour and capital. In Section 3 I illustrate some of the ways in which these relations may be structured by power in the second and third dimensions.

My second purpose developed in Sections 4, 5 and 6 is to re-examine the reproduction cost theories of wages, sketched, though never elaborated in any detail, by Ricardo and Marx; to re-interpret their central idea that there is at any given time a historically determined equilibrium real wage; and to draw out the implications of this re-interpretation for the analysis of power in the labour market. This account indicates the rich vista of issues which are potentially at stake in the relations between labour and capital, and prepares the ground for a more detailed analysis of how labour's interest field and decision field are formed. This will be the subject matter of Chapters 5 and 6.

2   The Labour Process and the Critique of the Exchange Paradigm's Central Claim

Ever since Marx wrote 'Capital' Marxists have strenuously denied the claim that a competitive system of exchange between agents who are free and equal in the sense discussed in the last chapter, would constitute a social power vacuum. The basis for this denial resides in the analysis of the capitalist labour process. Let it be granted that the process of exchange is free from any direct social control over the terms of market contracts, and from any indirect control over the underlying parameters of supply and demand. Even so, Marxists argue, in a *capitalist* economy, the labour process within the enterprise is the site of enterprise despotism.[1]

In the labour process the interests of wage workers and capitalists are in conflict, perhaps not on *all* issues, but certainly on a wide range of issues thrown up in running the enterprise as a going concern. It can, therefore, be expected that each side will strive to persuade or coerce the other to submit to its will. In the course of this continual struggle those who direct the government and administration of the enterprise will normally gain the upper hand. For the structure of enterprise authority and power has to be functionally adapted to the externally imposed imperatives of market survival and success. These imperatives will normally dictate that dysfunctional claims and pressures exerted by workers against the enterprise's resources and organisation be subordinated to the primary need for cost reduction and profitability. Thus, for example, the interests of workers in maintaining established and preferred work rhythms and routines,[2] or in composing the tasks associated with a particular technical process into interesting and fulfilling jobs, will in the long run be defeated.[3]

Now the argument that enterprise despotism will inevitably throw up outcrops of dominance/subordination even in an otherwise flat, competitive terrain, is difficult to refute, though a sophisticated essay in refutation is explored below. But whatever one thinks of the argument, it does not in itself really challenge the conceptualisation of power at work in the exchange paradigm. Merely to emphasise the ineluctable confrontation between capital and labour within the labour process, and to trace the

shifting fortunes of war along the 'frontier of control',[4] is still to
remain within a one- or at best two-dimensional discourse.

It may even be possible for the committed and ingenious
adherent of the exchange model to reinterpret the *concept* of the
act of exchange in such a way that it subsumes the phenomena
of labour process conflict. Consider some initial set of contractual
terms of employment. Then let contingencies arise within the
labour process which were not foreseen in the original contract,
and to which workers are reluctant to adapt as management
wishes. Or suppose that management issues rules and commands
which workers regard as illegitimate, or at least of doubtful
authority, under the specified contractual terms. It might then
be argued that workers in effect momentarily re-evaluate the
detailed exchange of effort for reward, and decide whether to
comply with management's will, press for a revision of the
contractual terms, or quit the job. On this view the exchange of
labour services for a right to receive compensation, is not a
discrete, periodically repeated act, but a more or less continuous,
rolling sequence of acts.

It is true that workers' options during these moments of
tension in the labour process will be constrained by the
management's power to sack, the general state of the labour
market and various other factors. (Similar considerations will
bear on management's calculations.) But, in the end, whatever
the distribution of (one-dimensional) power, the employment
relation is necessarily one in which workers are paid to obey
some sub-set of the possible range of management commands.
This applies not just to capitalist employers, but to *any* employing
agent, including a self-governing producers' cooperative. It may
be that management enjoys wide discretion in fixing the terms of
workers' obedience. Or it may happen that workers comply with
some management commands to which they do not consent,
since expedient calculation, as well as legitimation, is a motive
for obedience. But, it could be argued, the *potential* for unequal
exchange merely demonstrates the need for care in applying
exchange models. One should avoid over-hasty conclusions about
the equality of market participants. But this is no reason for
abandoning the paradigm itself.

Certainly for *some* of the cases in which control over the
labour process is disputed, this extended notion of exchange as

an open-ended and dynamically evolving process, has some plausibility. In the archetypal exchange relation A surrenders or offers something of recognised value in order to induce some response by B from which A will benefit. Sometimes disputes over the labour process will lead to a variation in the benefits each party offers the other, and can, therefore, reasonably be viewed as a resumption of some previous negotiation over the terms of exchange. Whether the same can be said when the 'benefit' A holds out takes the negative form of an offer to refrain from injuring B in some specified way if B complies with A's will, is perhaps more problematic.

But regardless of whether events within the labour process can or cannot be accommodated within the exchange model, the point is that either way the operative concept of power is one-dimensional. Discourse at this level fails to do justice to the full ramifications of the reproduction paradigm for the analysis of social power. We saw in Chapter 1 that from the reproduction perspective labour market transactions are one aspect of the ensemble of processes through which a particular pattern of social life is reproduced. It is, therefore, pertinent to ask whether the relations between capital and labour, both in the labour process and in the external labour market, may not be conditioned by the culture embedded within this wider context. More specifically, we need to investigate whether *systemic* social processes are at work which tend to press these relations into a mould of dominance and subordination.

The word 'systemic' here signifies that our concern is with those features of a given social order which are 'of human creation but not of human design'.[5] These features are definitely not part of the natural base of human society. Nor, on the other hand, have they been intentionally designed or consciously activated by anyone. They operate blindly and 'behind the backs' of social agents. We need to investigate this obscure region of the social formation because, as I have repeatedly pointed out, conscious action to secure some advantage in conflict situations, is merely the visible tip of the iceberg of social power. Below the surface of social life may lie a concealed domain of social forces which generate systematic tendencies for certain interests to triumph over others.

3 The 'Social Bases of Obedience'

The basic premise of this investigation into the systemic sources of social power is that available cultural definitions of social reality limit the range of possible responses to that reality. If the lower ranks within any hierarchy of authority and power are convinced that there is no alternative to the way things are, or that, however disagreeable their lot, things could still be worse, they will tend to make the best of their straitened circumstances. As a result the hierarchy will be stable and enduring. Hence if we are to explore the potency of any systemic forces which act to inhibit workers' efforts to identify and resist the causes of disadvantage and deprivation in the employment relationship, we shall have to examine the cultural formation of workers in capitalist societies. This task is taken up more fully in subsequent chapters. Here I wish first to consider what *kinds* of social processes are likely to be involved. My account draws heavily on the approach developed by Barrington Moore (1978).

Barrington Moore addresses a more general version of the question I have posed about the employment relationship: namely, how has it come about that oppressed social groups have frequently submitted to their oppressors without any show of resistance, and have even legitimised their sufferings? He distinguishes four main types of social conditions which establish what he calls the 'social bases of obedience'.

First, there are pressures to group conformity. Traditionally, solidarity amongst workers has been seen as a positive source of strength, reducing competition between individual workers and enhancing their ability to prosecute their collective interests against their employers. But the solidaristic cohesion which ostracises the blackleg, the non-unionist or the rate-buster, may also work to the advantage of the employer. It may be turned against individual 'deviants' who by defying norms imposed by the boss risk provoking unlooked for conflict which threatens the group as a whole. The archetype of this situation is the 'malcontent' prisoner who resists abuse or brutality by the warders and exposes his fellow-prisoners to the danger of reprisal.

Instances of this phenomenon in the industrial context abound, particularly where the labour process depends on collaborative teamwork. Consider the skilled manual worker who takes pride in his craft. He attempts by example and persuasion to bring his workmates to take time and care over their product and to ignore pressure from their superiors to complete the job as rapidly as possible and to 'slobber it o'er'.[6] He will almost certainly encounter work group pressure to drop his fastidious ways, particularly where immediate monetary rewards or future job security are at stake.

The case is similar for the worker in a nuclear power plant who discovers that the company is not only skimping its safety precautions, but actually falsifying its records of statutory safety checks. Her attempts to mobilise her fellow workers on the issue meet a hostile reception. Though naturally anxious for their own lives and health, they prefer the risk of contamination to the prospect of losing their jobs if the plant has to be closed down. They even obstruct her efforts to compile a dossier on the company's practices.[7] Or, finally, take the case of the worker in a large bureaucratic organisation whose ideas for changing established routines in the interests of clients, and for developing a more client-oriented service, are rebuffed by her colleagues as disruptive of 'professional control'.

In contrast to group solidarity directed against external opponents, the victims of introverted solidarity are likely to suffer a loss of dignity and an erosion of their sense of personal integrity. Workers who are driven to conform to practices which they find morally repugnant, however much these may be explicable in terms of market pressure or organisational logic, are likely to lose any sense of their ability to control the labour process and its product. These consequences may also spill over into other aspects of their lives, creating a generalised loss of self-esteem and feeling of powerlessness. And since this state of mind is hard to live with, they will be strongly tempted to remove the cognitive dissonance between their own standards of conduct and the norms required at work and internalised by other employees. Ready relief is available in the variety of 'common sense' formulas by which we all suppress the pain of the truth: 'There is no point in making a fuss'; 'There is nothing anyone can do about it'; 'We all have our crosses to bear', etc.

The second process inhibiting workers' capacity to articulate and pursue their interests effectively Barrington Moore calls 'atomisation'. At its most extreme this involves the destruction of prior social ties and habits to the point where individuals are left without the support of other human beings. The disintegration of the pre-capitalist economy and culture in England during the Industrial Revolution is a prime example. It was experienced by the uprooted and dispossessed as a catastrophe. Their power and will to resist were sapped, notwithstanding the rearguard actions of artisans and others in defence of their ancient rights (see Thompson, 1963, *passim*).

There is a mass of historical and experimental evidence that whilst a vigorous kin and communal life disciplines individuals and stifles their freedom of action, it also nourishes the strength and self-confidence needed to stand up to external authority.[8] Exceptional persons may be capable of retaining the courage of their convictions without the security of knowing that behind them stands a united community which will uphold their judgements and deeds. But without this moral and psychological prop, most of us, in the face of our superiors, have difficulty in self-assertion, are inclined to yield before the most immediate source of pressure and try to avoid giving offence and provoking an unpleasant confrontation. Regular repetition of such experiences is the breeding ground of submissive personalities and attitudes. For a series of similarly placed, but isolated individuals certain goals and actions are precluded by comparison with a cohesive group which is conscious of a common identity and shares a common way of life. Thus in the modern nuclear family women engaged full time in housework and childcare are isolated and dispersed. Informal friendship networks with sister houseworkers may offer some comfort and support. But where, as Mill put it (see Chapter 2, p. 29), subjects 'live constantly under the eye of their master' who has the strongest material and psychological motives for perpetuating their position of segregated dependence, it is hard for women even to acquire the notion that a redefinition of the sexual division of labour might be possible, desirable and feasible, let alone to act on it.[9]

Barrington Moore's third disabling condition, which he calls 'fragmentation' is the opposite of atomisation. Fragmentation describes the situation of an oppressed or subordinate group whose historical formation has left it divided into two or more competing sections with their own divergent sub-cultures and perceived interests. Ethnic rivalries amongst industrial workers in the USA provide the outstanding example, though one that is repeated to a greater or lesser degree in most countries.[10] Whereas atomisation *destroys* prior social bonds, fragmentation *intensifies* them.

It is important to understand that what is involved in fragmentation is not simply, nor even mainly, the tendency of princes, commanders, officials and bosses throughout the ages to play on the mutual enmities and suspicions of their subjects in order to divide and rule. The point is that even if their rulers disdain this time-honoured tactic of domination, each fragment of a subject class perceives its grievances and the remedies for them from within the blinkered perspective of an 'in-group, out-group' culture. The in-group defines gain and loss, success and failure primarily in relation to the setbacks or advances of the out-group. Other relations of privilege and oppression lie outside their range of vision. Indeed, rulers may feel impelled to arbitrate and resolve disputes among their warring subjects for the sake of social peace. If this happens, each subordinate group's allegiance to the prevailing social order may be strengthened. Those who stand at the summit of the social hierarchy may be gratefully acknowledged as a source of protection and justice.

For example, when black sharecroppers and farm labourers migrated from the declining rural areas of the American South to take jobs opened up in the industrial North by the boom of the First World War and the 1920s, they encountered a wall of hostility from the white workers. Hemmed in by racial prejudice and violence they came to see their industrial opportunities as the gift of their employers, and willingly accepted harsh factory conditions. Their industrial submissiveness and conservative attachment to the employers in turn intensified the exclusivist and segregationist policies of the white trade unions (see Brody, 1980, pp. 14–20).

Rulers may sometimes foment discord among their subjects for their own ends. But to do so is to risk incurring the charge of abusing their authority. Normally their rule will rest on more secure foundations if they bend their main efforts to the business of managing and mitigating civil conflict. They will then be seen to fulfil the general expectation that rulers ought to perform services which are essential to their subjects' well-being – the dispensing of justice, the maintenance of personal security and the prevention of social strife. If they acquit themselves of these duties they may legitimately invoke their subjects' obligation to acknowledge their authority and obey their commands. The *principle* of hierarchy will be consolidated in the popular consciousness.

The fourth condition which may dispose subordinates to consent to their position is co-option. The heads of an organisation may, either on their own initiative or under pressure from below, concede to their subordinates a limited responsibility for managing the collective enterprise, whether this is a nation state, a prison, an educational establishment or an industrial firm. Whatever the stated purpose of such collaborative exercises, it is a common observation that one of their predictable consequences is to provide the lower ranks with a source of self-esteem, whilst at the same time safeguarding the interests of their superiors.

Human beings have a (possibly innate) need for their own importance and worth to be socially recognised. To disappoint this need is to court disaffection. This risk is averted if the rank and file acquire pride in occupying a humble, yet acknowledged, place in the social order of the organisation. Individual and group psychology come to be adapted to the sustenance of the prevailing power structure. Subordinates learn to behave in ways which are pleasing to those in charge of their environment. They internalise their masters' social codes and standards. Once this tendency has taken hold it becomes very difficult to disengage from it. Critical rejection of a system so apparently gratifying to all concerned becomes almost impossible.

On the other hand, co-option is rarely a straightforward, unambiguous strategy for domination by containment. There is always the possibility that what begins as a limited devolution of decision-making power, intended to promote loyalty and obedience to those who retain supreme authority and control, may turn out to be the thin end of a democratic and egalitarian wedge. A good example is the militant Factory Councils movement which sprang up in Turin and other industrial centres of northern Italy in the closing stages of the First World War. The Councils were hailed by Gramsci and other socialist intellectuals as organic expressions of proletarian democracy and as the embryonic form of revolutionary soviets. Yet the Councils had their origins in the shop committees (*commissione interne*) fostered by leading Italian industrialists in order to handle shop-floor disputes in a period of labour shortage and social unrest (see Cammett, 1967).

Moreover there are definite limits to the adaptive potential of co-option. Factors ranging from the physical constraints of space and time to cultural definitions of the boundary between public and private life, curtail the number of situations in which it is feasible for large masses of people to participate directly in collective decision-making. For the most part co-option is forced to work through *representative* channels. Only those from amongst the lower ranks who are, or can hope to become, representatives themselves, are available to be mentally captured for the organisation. How far a system of representation succeeds in winning a greater commitment from the remainder, depends on what are often unpredictable political interactions between representatives and their constituents. And there are few more hated figures in the sub-culture of oppressed groups than the turncoat, the copper's nark or the boss's man. Co-option is thus the most problematic of Barrington Moore's social bases of obedience. It is interesting that of the four types of cultural stultification he distinguishes, co-option is the one which comes closest to being a deliberate strategy for domination, as distinct from an unplanned sub-system of the social formation.

In this section I have suggested that in any unequal power relationship a number of social, cultural and psychological forces are likely to be at work, either separately or together, which instil into the minds of their victims a sense that both the relationship and its consequences are morally proper, practically unavoidable, and, perhaps, existentially inevitable. People whose emotions, perceptions and modes of reasoning are thus 'enthralled', cannot even begin to mount a struggle around those of their interests which are denied an outlet within the prevailing social order. For if they were to formulate and act on demands embodying these interests, they would necessarily challenge some aspect of the structure of authority, the division of labour or the distribution of the social product. This is possible only if they can overcome the feeling that the existing system is unalterable, and dispute its moral authority.

4 The Reproduction Cost Theory of Wages

In Section 2 I argued that if the reproduction paradigm is to fulfil its promise to offer a more thoroughgoing account of the capital–labour relation than that of its principal theoretical rival, its adherents need to raise their sights beyond a fixation on the labour process. I suggested that this could best be done by exploring the ways in which power in the second and third dimensions circumscribes workers' horizons and claims and perpetuates their subordination to capital. In Section 3 I illustrated the kinds of systemic processes which produce this crippling effect. So far, however, I have not established any clear connection between these processes and the specific transactions by which workers exchange their labour power against money capital in order to reproduce themselves both as biological beings, economic agents and social actors. In order to make this connection it is necessary to review the reproduction cost theories of wages first propounded by Ricardo and Marx.[11]

Both Ricardo and Marx maintained that in the long run real wages would tend towards a fixed level which Ricardo called 'the natural price of labour', and Marx 'the value of labour power'.[12] This fixed level was historically determined by forces external to and independent of the balance of labour supply and demand. It corresponded to the 'necessary costs' of reproducing the class of labourers both from day to day and from one generation to the next. Neither theorist examined in any detail what these 'necessary costs' were nor how they were determined. Both regarded them as being, at any historical stage in any particular society, practically known, and both took them as given in their analyses of the determination of profits and prices.

The two writers differed in the mechanisms which they postulated for restoring real wages to the equilibrium level. Ricardo relied on a Malthusian population growth principle to keep the supply of labour adjusted to the demand over the long run. Marx scathingly rejected the notion that the *capitalist* labour market was regulated by an ahistorical, natural law. In his view wage levels were determined by the respective bargaining strengths of workers and capitalists. These in turn depended primarily, though not exclusively, on the prevailing level of unemployment. For a given labour supply unemployment would fluctuate with the pace of capital accumulation and the pace of labour-displacing technical change. Capitalism thus generated its own internal mechanism for regulating the labour market. Since our concern here is with the equilibrium real wage level itself rather than the mechanism of equilibration, this difference is unimportant.

Both Marx and Ricardo emphasised the element of habit and custom in the necessary costs of reproduction. Thus Ricardo (1951, p. 97) states:

> An English labourer would consider his wages under their natural rate, and too scanty to support a family, if they enabled him to purchase no other food than potatoes, and to live in no better habitation than a mud cabin; yet these moderate demands of nature are often deemed sufficient in countries where 'man's life is cheap', and his wants easily satisfied. Many of the conveniences now enjoyed in an English cottage, would have been thought luxuries at an earlier period of our history.

In a similar vein Marx writes:

> [The labourer's] natural needs, such as food, clothing, fuel and housing vary according to the climatic and other peculiarities of his country. On the other hand, the number and extent of his so-called necessary requirements, as also the manner in which they are satisfied, are themselves products of history, and depend therefore to a great extent on the level of civilisation attained by a country; in particular, they depend on the conditions in which, and consequently on the habits and expectations with which, the class of free workers has been formed. In contrast therefore with the case of other commodities, the determination of the value of labour power contains a moral and historical element. (Marx 1976, p. 275)

Now this clear admission by both Ricardo and Marx immediately destroys the elegant simplicity of the notion of the value of labour power as a fixed point to which market wage levels must return in the long run. If the value of labour power contains a (slowly) variable moral and historical element, it is indeterminate.

Occasionally Marx offered hints as to how determinacy might be restored. One suggestion was that the value of labour power progressed along a kind of historical ratchet. During periods of prolonged economic boom and tight labour markets, market wage levels would be bid up above the prevailing level of the value of labour power. Workers would experience a hitherto unaccustomed level and range of consumption. If this relative affluence lasted long enough, habits, expectations and standards would be transformed. The value of labour power would undergo an irreversible upward displacement, possibly assisted by the efforts of trade unions in resisting wage cuts when the boom eventually subsided. In formal terms the value of labour power could be determined as a weighted average of past realised real wage levels. But this suggestion was never really followed up, though, as we shall see, some such ratchet process is broadly consistent with nineteenth-century English experience.

Subsequent writers in the Classical/Marxist tradition of political economy have tended to conceptualise the value of labour power as the sum of two separate and additive components: a fixed and naturally determined subsistence minimum, and a variable and historically determined extra – the moral and historical element. Thus Sraffa (1960, pp. 9–10), writes:

We have up to this point regarded wages as consisting of the necessary subsistence of the workers and thus entering the system on the same footing as fuel for the engines or feed for the cattle. We must now take into account the other aspect of wages since, besides the ever-present element of subsistence, they may include a share of the surplus product. In view of this double character of the wage it would be appropriate, when we come to consider the division of the surplus between capitalists and workers, to separate the two component parts of the wage and regard only the 'surplus' part as variable; whereas the goods necessary for the subsistence of the workers would continue to appear, with the fuel etc., among the means of production.

It should be added that Sraffa refrains from following this precept and, in deference to the traditional unitary concept of wages, treats the whole of the wage as variable, adding, however, that his discussion could be easily adapted to 'the more appropriate, if unconventional interpretation of the wage suggested above'.

This conceptualisation seems to be at work in Marx's account of capitalist industrialisation in late eighteenth and early nineteenth-century England.[13] In summary, Marx argues that the protracted and far-reaching economic and social transformation wrought by the Industrial Revolution created a gross disparity of power between the industrial capitalists and the emergent class of free proletarians. Capital was able to acquire the labour power it needed on terms which did not even permit the maintenance of the standard of life attained prior to the epoch of rapid industrialisation.

Whether and how far popular living standards *did* decline between roughly 1780 and 1830 in England has been keenly debated by economic and social historians ever since. This debate is not at issue here, though some important methodological points raised by E. P. Thompson (1963) will be taken up presently. What I wish to stress is that implicit in Marx's description and denunciation of the decline of popular living standards is the *analytical* notion that real wages were, for a period, reduced below the value of labour power. The moral and historical element was progressively squeezed towards the *ne plus ultra* of what was needed simply to enable the labourers to survive from one day to the next. This minimum standard enabled labour power to be 'maintained and developed only in a crippled state' (Marx, 1976, p. 277).

Eventually this phase of 'superexploitation' came to an end. The rapid progress of capital accumulation which superexploitation permitted, gradually narrowed the gap between the demand and supply of exploitable labour power, and reduced the power imbalance between capitalists and workers. At the same time political forces were aroused and drawn into struggle over the extension of state power to regulate the activities of private capital through factory legislation and the factory inspectorate. (The immediate objects of state intervention were, of course, the employment of women and children and the length of the working day, but these issues may be taken as symptomatic of the entire range of issues bearing on the standard and quality of life of the factory proletariat and their families.) Once these processes were completed, Marx implies, the integral value of labour power, including its restored moral and historical element, became the pivot around which real wages would henceforth revolve as capital accumulation settled into a more normal rhythm.

Strictly speaking, one should not think of the moral and historical element being 'restored' since this suggests a return to the way of life prevailing before the Industrial Revolution. It would be more accurate to speak of new living patterns emerging as industrial capitalism extended its sway over more and more sectors of the economy. These patterns provided a new fixed reference point in wage determination. Thus Hobsbawm (1969, p. 164) notes that:

> between 1870 and 1900 the pattern of British working class life which the writers, dramatists and T.V. producers of the 1950s thought of as 'traditional' came into being. It was not 'traditional' then but new. . . . It was neither a very good nor a very rich life, but it was probably the first kind of life since the Industrial Revolution which provided a firm lodging for the British working class within industrial society.

On the preceding two pages Hobsbawm cites the following significant innovations in living patterns during this period:

— Between 1870 and 1896 meat consumption per head rose by one third, with the proportion of imported meat in total consumption trebling.
— New fruit – first jam and later the banana – came to supplement or replace apples as the only fresh fruit eaten by the urban poor.
— Fish and chip shops were established.
— Food, clothing and footwear came to be purchased from

new retailing outlets, particularly the 'Co-ops' and the rapidly growing multiple and chain stores.
— Sewing machines and bicycles appeared as the first comparatively cheap consumer durables.
— The tram was developed as the first means of public transport specifically aimed at the working class.
— Popular entertainment and sport were transformed by the advent of the music hall and the rise of football as a national institution.

To Hobsbawm's list should be added the rather more fundamental development in the relations between men and women *within* the working class which became entrenched during this period. As the male dominated trade unions achieved increasing security, public respectability and official recognition, they worked to eject women from the labour force or to segregate jobs by gender in the name of protecting craft skills and status. The 'family wage' – that is, a wage sufficient to enable a working-class man to support a wife and children confined to the domestic economy outside paid employment – gradually secured acceptance as a 'natural' social arrangement (see Coote and Campbell, 1982, ch. 2).

This brief digression on the experience of the English working class in the nineteenth century indicates how Marx and Ricardo's reproduction perspective ramifies through every pore of social life, and vindicates their insistence on the role of moral and historical factors in fixing just what are to count as the 'necessary' costs of reproduction. Nevertheless their conceptualisation of the moral and historical element in the value of labour power is inadequate, as I shall argue in the next section.

5 The Moral and Historical Element

We have seen that the Classical/Marxist tradition regards the value of labour power as the sum of two separate but additive components. The bare subsistence minimum, which Marx suggests was approached during the phase of superexploitation, is normally topped up by a flexible moral and historical supplement.

The problem with this view is that even the concept of a 'basic' subsistence minimum is not a natural but a social product. Suppose we take 'subsistence' to be defined in terms of certain specified minimum needs: for example, to meet minimum standards of nutrition, health, sanitation, education, etc. Two points immediately arise. The first is that no minimum standards can ever be specified except in relation to a particular set of *purpose: for what* is any particular bundle of use-values, b_1, b_2, ..., b_n, needed? In the case of labour power, even on a very narrow view of the relevant purposes, we have to specify the concrete labouring activity to be performed – navvying or machine-minding, for example. Now it is certainly true that the relationship between, say, required human energy inputs and outputs, or between the technical skills demanded in the performance of particular work tasks and the capacities of the workers who are to perform them, has an obvious natural basis. A malnourished labourer cannot perform heavy manual work for long periods of time,[14] and an innumerate person cannot add up accounts.

But only in *society* is it determined which activities are to be performed, on the basis of what techniques, and how the work tasks associated with a given technique are to be combined into jobs. There were indeed binding physiological reasons why navvies needed a minimum calorific intake, a minimum intake of liquids etc. But there are other technically feasible ways of digging canal trenches or laying down railway track, ways which involve less expenditure of energy per worker. This point exemplifies the general truth that from a given set of natural facts no social facts whatsoever can be deduced.[15]

Second, the actual way in which any specified minimum standards are met (i.e. the precise composition of the 'subsistence' bundle of use-values), is also socially determined. Thus, as Ricardo's comment quoted above (p. 70) suggests, the substitution of potatoes for bread or oatmeal in the working-class diet during the Industrial Revolution, was generally perceived as a degradation. The nutritional content of these goods was irrelevant. If anything, the cheaper potato was nutritionally superior to the white, and increasingly adulterated, bread which the working class regarded as their birthright. Yet throughout the period the white loaf remained a symbol of social status and the price of bread was regarded as the first index of living standards. For fifty years from 1790 to the repeal of the Corn Laws '. . . a regular dietary class war took place . . .' (see Thompson, 1963, p. 315).

Over a century later George Orwell observed the same phenomenon in his investigation of the weekly food and fuel expenditure of an unemployed miner's family living on the dole. After noting what an appalling diet the family ate, and commenting that a more wholesome diet could in theory be purchased at a much lower cost, Orwell pointed out that

> the ordinary human being would sooner starve than live on brown bread and raw carrots . . . a millionaire may enjoy breakfasting off orange juice and Ryvita biscuits; an unemployed man doesn't. . . . When you are unemployed, which is to say when you are underfed, harassed, bored and miserable, you don't *want* to eat dull, wholesome food. You want something a little "*tasty*". (Orwell, 1962, p. 86).

Again, these examples point to a general truth: except *in extremis*, human beings never have needs or wants in the abstract. They do not want, say, food in the abstract, but food of particular, socially determined kinds, prepared and eaten in particular, socially determined ways.[16]

These considerations do not make the concept of subsistence meaningless or arbitrary: merely historically and morally relative. It follows that it is incorrect to think of the value of labour power as having a fixed natural – and a variable, social component. The full range of elements it contains, together with the size of each one, are socially determined, and may, as the case of bread versus potatoes shows, become the objects of social action, decision and conflict. Thus it was not that the moral and historical element of the value of labour power was compressed towards a natural limit beyond which no further erosion was possible. Rather, the specific forms and consequences of early capitalist industrialisation in England called forth increasingly widespread and vociferous moral outrage and social resistance. Eventually these reactions succeeded in re-stabilising a capitalist economy which, left to itself, threatened to destroy the material and moral conditions of its own existence.

What I am arguing, then, is that the value of labour power has a *pervasive* moral and historical aspect. There are two important implications of this proposition. The first is that the value of labour power has an irreducibly *subjective* dimension. Thompson (1963) makes this point forcefully with reference to the debate on living standards during the Industrial Revolution. No judgement on this issue is adequate, he argues, which ignores the question of how contemporaries of all social classes experienced and perceived the great transformation in which the nascent working class was caught up. Thompson's history of the agricultural labourers, urban artisans and handloom weavers – selected because their experience seemed to colour most the social consciousness of the working class in the first half of the nineteenth century – leaves no doubt that these groups were perceived, both by themselves and by others, as having suffered a marked deterioration in the overall quality of their lives. This was true both in a narrow calculus of dietary change, mortality and morbidity rates, and in a broader assessment of environmental brutalisation, restrictions on personal freedom and the destruction of the pre-industrial family and domestic economy. It is, as he says,

> perfectly possible to maintain two propositions which, on a casual view, appear to be contradictory. Over the period 1790–1840 there was a slight improvement in average material standards. Over the same period there was intensified exploitation, greater insecurity and increasing human misery. By 1840 most people were 'better off' than their forerunners had been fifty years before, but they had suffered and continued to suffer this slight improvement as a catastrophic experience. (Thompson, 1963, p. 212).

In other words, a standard of life does not exist except as a standard which is actually lived and experienced by flesh and blood men and women capable of reflecting on and evaluating their experience. In the present context what this means is that the necessary costs of reproduction depend not just on the range and size of the physical constituents of the real wage, but also on how worker-consumers feel about the way of life in which these physical constituents enter as inputs. Within the reproduction perspective the real wage can be said to be at its equilibrium level only when the way of life it sustains is felt to conform to certain standards of acceptability.

The subjective dimension of the value of labour power is closely related to the second point. Traditionally, as we have seen, the term 'moral and historical' has been taken to be equivalent to 'customary, habitual or traditional'. This connotation is certainly present in Marx's definition. Now it is easy to see how it might be thought that this was the *full* meaning of the term if what I have just called 'standards of acceptability' were always, as Marx implies, determined by past experience, by what people have come to expect out of life. Nevertheless it is useful to retain a degree of freedom in fixing meanings here. To say that y is determined by x is not to say that y and x mean the same thing.

Moreover, it might not always be true that standards of acceptability depend *only* on past experience. People might, for example, come to judge their current situation by reference to conditions which they have never experienced, but which they hope and expect to enjoy in the future. Or it might be considered culturally unacceptable and socially disabling to lack certain goods, not only because these have been widely possessed for a long time past, but also because, regardless of what people might ideally prefer, they have become indispensable aids to effective participation in social life. Standard examples are the use of a private motor vehicle in areas without adequate public transport; a fixed abode – not just shelter – in a social system reliant on regular, fast and efficient communication in which a residential identity is an everyday necessity; a telephone in communities with mobile populations whose networks of kinship and neighbourhood support have been attenuated; the money, equipment and skills required to enjoy recreational activities in a society where waged and unpaid domestic labour preempt a less overwhelming share of people's time budgets; and so on. To lack these things is to be condemned to exile as a social outcast.

Thus, the proposition that a certain real wage prevails over the long run when it supports a way of life which meets certain subjective standards of acceptability, does *not* mean that workers have become habituated to this way of life, and regard it as the most probable outcome of their transactions as owners and traders of labour power. These standards of acceptability are more than 'habit and custom': they are standards deemed to be legitimate and proper. They may be so deemed *because* they are customary. But the source of their legitimacy is a secondary issue. The important point is that the value of labour power has a fundamental, *normative* significance. Attached to its various elements, so to speak, are a series of uncodified civil rights. Taken together, these rights constitute a multi-faceted 'just price' for the sale of labour power.

It was precisely the normative claims inscribed in the value of labour power which were trampled and denied during the phase of superexploitation. And it was precisely because they saw their struggle as one to retrieve their rights in the face of a ruthless and implacable enemy that the early working class fought back with such determination and violence.

6 Systemic Power and the Moral and Historical Element

The revisionary view of value of labour power developed in the previous section enables us to appreciate the role of systemic social power in shaping the standards to which workers lay claim in their interchange with capital. We have seen: (1) that in the reproduction paradigm the long-run equilibrium real wage rests on conditions external to the exchange process; and (2) that these external conditions include the normative order to which the working class subscribes. The existence of perceived rights to certain dietary standards, hours of work, holidays, opportunities for recreation etc. sets limits to the claims which capitalists and workers may legitimately make against each other. During the Industrial Revolution it was capital which overstepped these limits.

It is equally conceivable that in a different historical context the limits might operate on the other side to restrain workers' demands, retard the growth of real wages and hence facilitate capital accumulation. Thus a working class with no special attachment to a pre-industrial way of life might well be prepared to endorse Keynes's reasoning that they would benefit far more in the long run from the forced abstinence which a profit inflation imposes on them, than they would lose in the first instance in the shape of diminished consumption . . . so long as wealth and its fruits are not consumed by its nominal owner, but are accumulated, the evils of an unjust distribution may not be so great as they appear. (Keynes, 1930, pp. 162–3).

In this passage Keynes envisages that workers might be brought to consent to the rule of capital as the speediest and the most reliable route to material prosperity provided only that capitalists fulfil their role as trustees of society's resources by reinvesting, and not squandering, their profits.

But this is to consider only the way in which the state of the normative order conditions the *quantitative* distribution of aggregate income between wages and profits. More important for our purposes is the *qualitative* question whether the detailed and disaggregated elements of the normative order are consonant with existing social relations and tend to reproduce and reinforce them; or whether, on the contrary they contain tensions and incongruities which are subversive of the prevailing order. 'Subversive' normative standards provide workers with a cultural resource enabling them both to conceive alternative social practices and to act on this conception.

There is no *a priori* way of determining whether the normative order lodged within the value of labour power will tend either to confirm or to undermine existing social hierarchies, and in particular the dominance of capital over labour. Both tendencies may coexist in different combinations. All that needs to be noted for the time being is the possibility that in the course of capitalist development the moral and historical element may be reshaped to fit a pattern of use values and an associated way of life which celebrate and sanctify the norms and practices of capitalist civilisation. If this adaptation occurs, labour's conflicts with capital will flow along channels which drain off any fundamental challenge or threat to the social system as a whole. Imposing displays of militancy in struggles over the division of a social product of given composition and methods of production, will coincide with an uncritical and subaltern acquiescence in the conventional definitions of what are to count as 'goods'. The successful mobilisation of power in the first dimension will be a misleading indicator of the total constellation of three-dimensional power.

I have already several times alluded to the 'subversive' face of the moral and historical element which was most prominent in the 'heroic' phase of working-class history during the Industrial Revolution. What was at stake in the ferocious class struggles of this period were alternative principles of social organisation. The legitimate claims embodied in the value of labour power, grounded as they were in an enduring way of life which stretched backwards into the pre-capitalist past, were radically incompatible with capitalist social relations. Arguably, throughout the nineteenth century workers' economic struggles continued to be conducted within a framework of reference which was independent of the rising capitalist civilisation. Marx and Engels' famous description of the tendency of capitalism to erode all pre-capitalist, organic systems of social order and stability, may have been correct, but only on a long-sighted, telescopic view of the historical process.[17] The tenure of pre-capitalist practice and belief proved to be stronger and longer than they allowed for. For example, the British labour movement's patriarchical *démarche* at the turn of the nineteenth century, referred to earlier (p. 74), can be seen as a successful attempt to shore up a system of domestic relations which would otherwise have been destroyed by the gender-blind process of proletarianisation.

Over the long run, however, capitalist industrialisation steadily commodified economic activity; personal and social mobility were enhanced, self-contained communities dissolved, and extended family groupings replaced by simplified husband–wife, parent–child relations; attitudes to work, time, labour discipline and immediate versus deferred gratification were transformed. Gradually a working class emerged which was divorced from the conditions in which it was first formed. Even if survivals from the pre-capitalist past continued to inform some aspects of popular culture, the mature working class did not – indeed in many respects *could* not – look backwards to find models for defining its rights and interests.

In principle maturation would, as the socialist and Marxist movements believed, liberate workers' mental horizons and energies for a decisive struggle against capital and capitalism.

And certainly the mature working class possessed superior intellectual, organisational and political resources with which to assert and defend its claims than its forerunners. On the other hand, there could be no guarantee that the underlying objective of workers' claims would be social innovation and reconstruction. Workers had shaken off archaic inhibitions against using and seeking to strengthen their market power.[18] But there was nothing to ensure that the points at which they chose to give battle, would not be those on which the captains of industry and state were least vulnerable and most amenable to negotiation and compromise, however much the latter might prefer to avoid any engagement at all. But this is to run ahead of the story.

Notes to Chapter 4

1. For a clear and cogent exposition of the classical Marxist view on this question see Rowthorn (1974).
2. On the importance of *rhythm* at work, particularly in manual jobs, the suffering caused by its disruption, and the general nature of the 'effort bargain' between management and workers, see Baldamus (1961).
3. Braverman (1974) provides the standard account of the deskilling and degradation of labour alleged to be one of the central tendencies of the capitalist mode of production.
4. The phrase 'frontier of control' was coined by Goodrich (1975) to denote the disputed boundary between the 'territorial' space occupied by management and workers respectively in the running of the enterprise and the disposition of its resources, on the analogy of the systems of trench welfare used in the First World War. In our terms the frontier comprises the boundary between the workers' interest field and decision field, as well as disputed issues lying within their decision field.
5. This useful phrase is taken from Hayek (1967). Hayek, of course, emphasises the generally *benign* consequences of that body of rules of conduct which has evolved in the course of human development, and which enables each member of society, without knowing it, to act within an orderly social environment. But there is no *a priori* presumption that the unconscious observance of these uncodified norms will be an unqualified social gain from which all members of society derive equal benefit. Hayek argues that any social order rests on a complex, but robust system of social practices which have proved themselves over a long period of time through the

social equivalent of natural selection. But there is no necessity to accept his conservative preference for exempting this spontaneous order from social criticism, nor his belief that dire consequences for human freedom will inevitably attend the use of conscious human agency to re-order our collective social inheritance.

6. The phrase and the example come from Robert Tressell's (1955) famous novel *The Ragged Trousered Philanthropist*.

7. The example is adapted from the film *Silkwood* (1984), Rank Film Distributors, USA.

8. For a survey of this evidence see Barrington Moore (1978), ch. 3.

9. For a poignant account of the oppressions suffered by the housewife in contemporary North America see French (1978).

10. For a careful commentary on the complex processes by which during the USA's rapid industrial expansion in the late nineteenth and early twentieth centuries Protestant was mobilised against Catholic, white against black and native against immigrant, see Davis (1980). As Davis points out, it was not mass immigration *per se* which created ethno-religious and racial conflict within the American proletariat. Rather, ethnic solidarities were forged as conscious survival strategies in a defensive reaction against exclusion and victimisation in the new country.

11. Ricardo's and Marx's ideas are perhaps better described as an *approach* to wage theory, since neither writer developed them much beyond a fairly rudimentary stage.

12. Strictly speaking, the 'value of labour power' is the vector product of the various physical elements of the equilibrium real wage and the labour time required, directly and indirectly to produce each one of these elements. Since I am not concerned with the labour theory of value, the labour time component can be ignored. The term 'value of labour power' can then be used simply to refer to the equilibrium real wage. This usage makes the term synonymous with Ricardo's 'natural price of labour'.

13. See Marx (1976), Chapter 10, 'The Working Day', Chapter 15, 'Machinery and Large Scale Industry' and Chapter 25, 'The General Law of Capitalist Accumulation'.

14. Though, obviously, if the available supply of malnourished labourers is for practical purposes unlimited, each one who collapsed in exhaustion could be replaced by a fresh 'hand': a method of labour organisation which is not unknown in human history, and which reinforces the point being made here: that human needs can be specified only by reference to some *ethical* standard.

15. For a lucid exposition of the nature of the distinction between the material/natural and the social properties of society, and of the impossibility of deducing the latter from the former see Cohen (1978, ch. 4).

16. The qualification *'in extremis'* is intended to cover such desperate cases as non-ritual cannibalism – once the frequent fate of sailors shipwrecked on the high seas, and not unknown in our own day

among the survivors of air disasters in remote regions. It is interesting to note that even in these stark conditions, apparently, a rough ethical code tends to be used to determine who gets eaten!

17. See Marx and Engels (1962). The key passage is as follows:

> The bourgeoisie, wherever it has got the upper hand, has put an end to all feudal, patriarchal, idyllic relations. It has pitilessly torn asunder the motley feudal ties that bound man to his 'natural superiors', and has left remaining no other nexus between man and man than naked self-interest, than callous 'cash payment'. It has drowned the most heavenly ecstasies of religious fervour, of chivalrous enthusiasm, of philistine sentimentalism, in the icy water of egotistical calculation. It has resolved personal worth into exchange value, and in place of the numberless chartered freedoms, has set up that single unconscionable freedom – Free Trade. In one word, for exploitation, veiled by religious and political illusions, it has substituted naked, shameless, direct, brutal exploitation.

18. Several writers have advanced explanations of the upsurge of British working-class wage militancy in the late 1960s and early 1970s in terms of the prior attrition of long established cultural inhibitions on the crude assertion of market power. See Goldthorpe (1978) and Phelps Brown (1975)

5
The Peculiarities of Labour Power

1 Introduction

In order to apply the concepts of the social bases of obedience and of systemic power imbalance to the specific conditions of the labour market, it will be helpful to analyse in some detail those features of labour power and of the labour market which distinguish them from all other commodities and markets.

The first two of these peculiarities, discussed in Sections 2 and 3, taken together constitute the foundations for what it is convenient and suggestive to call the human interests of labour in the employment relation. In Section 4 I criticise the classical Marxist view of the formation and destiny of labour's human interests under capitalism. The problem with this view, I suggest, lies not so much in its insistence that workers' human interests are necessarily denied in a system which treats their labour power as a commodity like any other; nor in its failure to imagine that a capitalist economy could alleviate the grosser forms of working-class deprivation and provide the majority of its labour force with a high level of material prosperity. Rather, classical Marxism fails to recognise (1) that the interests of labour are problematic; (2) that this is a necessary, nor merely contingent feature of the world; and (3) that in consequence there is no such thing as the essential or general interest of labour which can be invoked as a touchstone for thought and action. The special feature of labour power underlying these propositions and neglected in the classical Marxist view, gives rise to what I call labour's existential problem.

85

Finally in Section 5, I consider the way in which trade unions impinge on workers' perceptions of their interests. I conclude that although collective organisation goes some way to resolving the difficulties workers face in deciding where in any given context their best interests lie, in practice it falls a long way short of achieving any strategic integration across the diversity of labour's actual and potential objectives.

2   The Inalienable Character of Labour Power

The first distinctive feature of labour power is that, unlike all other commodities which may become the objects of contract and exchange, labour power is not separable from its owner and bearer: it is, as the jurist has it, inalienable. Plots of land, buildings, machines, fuel supplies, computer software and inanimate commodities in general literally change hands when they are bought and sold: human 'hands', in a free labour market, can only ever be hired.

Several major consequences flow from this inherent restriction on property rights in labour contracts. The subject of the contract – an individual person – is at the same time its object. Employers may be interested only in those qualities of their employees which are strictly pertinent to the job in hand – punctuality, reliability, diligence, dexterity, honesty, charm, etc. But workers remain integrated personalities. Willy-nilly they are endowed with the immense capacity for thought and feeling which the human species with its large brain size relative to that of other primates has evolved in the course of a million-and-a-half years of social development. This simple fact makes labour power simultaneously the most versatile and the most problematic of all the agents of production. Workers do not require to be precisely programmed or regulated for the full potentialities of their productive services to be delivered up. Equally they may use their autonomy of thought and action to evade managerial control and impose their own ends on the labour process. Employer–employee relations are conducted in an uneasy symbiosis with the wider field of human purpose and endeavour: the market for labour services can never be purified of contagion from this source.

The fact that wage workers *legally* surrender (partial) control over something that *physically* remains under their control has a particular corollary: the labour process is always to some degree affected by workers' willingness to perform their work. Inanimate means of production will regularly and without the need for coaxing or coercion do whatever is required of them within the limits of their natural properties. Whatever artificial intelligence they may incorporate, the factor that distinguishes them from labour power is their complete indifference to the purposes they are made to serve and the ways in which they are treated.

Human beings, on the other hand, possess consciousness. And their consciousness is polarised between states of good and bad feeling. No doubt there is enormous variety in the objects and situations which may elicit good and bad feeling respectively. But with the possible exception of certain unusual and degenerate cases, there is for every human being a limit to the accumulation of negative feeling which he or she will tolerate before seeking remedial action of one sort or another.[1]

In the context of the labour process this implies that wage workers care, and cannot help caring what happens to them as their productive skills and capacities are set to work. Nor is the threshold of tolerance determined solely by the requirements of material metabolism: even at quite low levels of social development, people judge their work by the degree to which it answers their distinctively human, culturally determined needs – whether it makes full use of their talents, enables them to acquire new ones or enriches their experience; whether their product serves ends which they believe to be socially useful; whether they are able to perceive some significance in their own individual contribution to the collective enterprise; and so on. Moreover, even the most menial and repetitive tasks allow some scope for discretion over the pace and methods of work; and human ingenuity continually creates free space even under the most vigilant supervision. It follows that sooner or later the mental act of caring will materially affect the labour process.[2]

3 The Reproduction of Labour Power

The second peculiarity of labour power lies in its conditions of reproduction. In common with other non-natural productive inputs labour power is a *produced* agent of production. But unlike other commodities which, as capitalism develops, tend to be produced under capitalist relations, labour power is not capitalistically reproduced. Indeed, this would be impossible in a free labour market. One can imagine a system of commodity producing slavery in which the supply of new human infants is controlled by firms specialised in the production of labour power. These firms would make profits by selling or leasing mature adult workers to other firms whose property they would then become. Such systems have certainly existed historically.[3] But they clearly violate the condition that workers remain free to deploy their own labour power as and when they see fit.

In our own society the reproduction of labour power is carried out through an enormous variety of activities from the basic act of procreation to formal education and training programmes. What follows is one way of imposing order on this variety, freely adapted from Murgatroyd (1983). In Engels' classic formulation the production and reproduction of immediate life '. . . is of a twofold character: on the one side, the production of means of existence, of food, clothing, shelter and the tools necessary for that production; on the other side, the production of human beings themselves, the propagation of the species' (see Engels, 1972, pp. 71–2). Whether and in what sense these twin processes of social reproduction are, as Engels claims, in the final instance the determining factors in human history, need not detain us here. What matters for our purposes is that this passage suggests a very basic way of classifying the ensemble of activities through which human beings reproduce themselves biologically, economically and socio-culturally.

These activities can be divided into two types according as their end result is primarily the production of objects or the production of people. In 'object production' human beings act on the external world – the natural environment as this has been progressively modified during the pre-history and history of our species – in order to adapt and manipulate it. 'People production', on the other hand, involves acting on our own biological material and promoting the various capacities – cognitive, affective, physical, aesthetic and spiritual – which human beings need to acquire and master if they are in their turn to play an effective part in the activities of production and reproduction. Evidently the most basic people-producing activity is pro-creation itself. But there are many other activities whose main purpose and end-product is to stimulate and expand certain human capacities, and, conversely to inhibit and contract others. These take place not only when schools and employers impart formal instruction and training; but also when parents informally (and, as often as not unconsciously) socialise their children as they feed, clothe, clean, nurse and care for them; or when the mass media seek to inform, entertain, persuade and mobilise their viewers, listeners and readers.

Many activities combine *both* kinds of production. The armed forces, for example, not only deploy means of violence in order to produce certain services on behalf of the state – protection for (and sometimes control over) the population under the state's jurisdiction. They also train their (overwhelmingly male) personnel in military skills, which sometimes have civilian applications, and cultivate appropriate mentalities: for example, unquestioning obedience to commands, and the readiness to injure and kill other human beings. In particular cases it may be difficult to decide whether the object- or people-producing aspect of an activity is primary. But an element of arbitrariness is present in any way of classifying social production. Consider the analogous problem of discriminating between 'goods' and 'services'.

The activities of object- and people-production may be further subdivided according to their social location. In advanced industrial societies each kind of activity can be found in both the 'public' and the 'private' domains. By 'public' here I do not mean those areas of formal employment conventionally referred to as 'the public sector': that is, the nationalised industries and the services provided by central and local government. Instead the term covers the whole span of production organised on the basis of formal contractual relations between enterprises and their wage-earning employees. Whether these enterprises are publicly or privately owned is irrelevant to the present discussion. By contrast, the 'private domain' consists predominantly of household units of production and consumption. Typically within each household a married woman – sometimes assisted by other blood relations of her husband, including children – undertakes various kinds of domestic labour but receives no contractual payment for her services. Her work in this domain is not formally regulated at all, being governed by historically evolved custom and practice and informal negotiation with her husband.

Finally, the products of both kinds of activity in both social locations may either be destined for sale on a market, or may pass directly into some further use, such as consumption, without the mediation of any market transaction. Thus a small family farm may produce milk, meat, vegetables etc. for the market or for its own domestic consumption. In traditional Marxist terminology the use-values produced by the farm assume the status of commodities in the first case, but remain plain and simple use-values in the second.

These three distinctions – according to the primary purpose of (re-)producing activities, their social location and whether their output passes on to a market – are drawn together in Table 5.1 below, generating eight types of activity, examples of which are given below the table.[4]

The distribution of the total set of socially reproductive

Table 5.1

| | Social location of production | | | |
| | Public domain | | Private domain | |
	Commodity	Use value	Commodity	Use value
Objects	1	2	3	4
People	5	6	7	8

1. Manufacturing industries.
2. Military defence; local authority refuse collection.
3. Family businesses such as shops and small farms producing marketed goods and services.
4. Home cooking; dress-making; domestic laundry; do-it-yourself repairs and maintenance.
5. Independent fee-charging schools; private hospitals; management consultancy services.
6. State schools; state medical care provided free at the time of use; local authority personal social services.
7. Mothers paid fees for looking after other people's children.
8. Unpaid home-based care of family dependants.

activities will alter over time as some types of production expand whilst others shrink. Thus the rise of industrial capitalism enlarged cell 1 at the expense of cells 3 and 4, whilst the growth of the state's public welfare and social control functions enlarged cell 6 at the expense of cells 5 and 8. But whatever the precise pattern of social reproduction at any given time, two points stand out clearly from this system of classification. First, there is no single organising centre for the reproduction of labour power. For one thing, many of the activities assigned to cells 1–4 are also, directly or indirectly, responsible for shaping the skills, values and attitudes of the workers involved either as producers or consumers. For example, the business of rearing, transporting and butchering livestock both promotes and is sustained by an ethical code which denies or devalues the rights of non-human animal species. The labour force employed in farms, road haulage, abattoirs and retail food distribution learn to harden their hearts against the undoubted pain and suffering which their activities inflict on their means of production. Neatly packaged joints of meat and poultry help to suppress consumers' awareness that their dinner was once a sentient creature, and atrophy the inclination and skills needed to maintain a vegetarian diet.[5]

But even if we leave aside the 'externalities' of object-production, the primary activities of people-production are not concentrated in any one site, but extend across the very different kinds of sub-systems of social reproduction contained in cells 5–8. The second point is that the greater part of these sub-systems are not under the direct control of capitalist employers, and only some of them (those in cell 6) are organised by the state and thus in principle susceptible to indirect political pressure. It is reasonable, then, to conclude that although capital may from time to time seek to influence particular aspects of the reproduction of labour power – standards of childcare, educational curricula, methods of student finance, industrial training schemes, etc. – the process as a whole is substantially autonomous.[6]

This conclusion woud be banal were it not for the importance of its corollary: the various activities involved in reproducing labour power can all be thought of as cases of joint-production. Their end-product is not just labour power in just those quantities and with just those qualities which employers require:

it consists of whole human beings. As integrated personalities everyone acquires some capacities which are relevant only or mainly outside the sphere of market relations, and indeed may have no marketable value at all. Thus only a tiny fraction of those people who display athletic prowess, moral or physical courage, selfless devotion or a facility for telling jokes, ever makes any money out of these aptitudes, or would even dream of doing so.

Correspondingly, those activities which *are* directly relevant to the job market, invariably contain some *extra*-market significance and purpose as well. Schooling provides a major example. From the standpoint of orthodox economics the formal education system can be regarded either as the producer of those productivity-augmenting skills and characteristics which individuals acquire as their 'human capital'; or, alternatively, as a large-scale job-market screening and signalling device.[7] But in performing these functions the system simultaneously transmits prevailing cultural patterns and norms.[8] Alongside other institutions of socialisation – principally the mass media, but also, in so far as they function as instruments of social control, the health and other personal social services – schools exert a standardising influence on children drawn from millions of diverse family backgrounds. One particular aspect of the cultural formation of each new generation is its induction into a society marked by the hierarchy of gender. In countless subtle ways children come to appreciate that those attributes and qualities associated with males are also the ones that are valued, whereas becoming a woman means learning to accept second place. The classroom encounters and experience of boys and girls diverge. In general girls learn to limit their ambitions, devalue their own achievements and cultivate a passive, dependent self-image. Even those with outstanding academic records are encouraged to enter conventionally feminine occupations, and, unlike boys, to immerse themselves in domestic commitments. Preparation for entry into the job market continually regenerates the gender hierarchy.[9]

Thus the reproduction of labour power, both from day to day and from generation to generation, is inextricably intertwined with the reproduction of social relations in general. The various activities involved may develop in particular shapes and directions in response to the force of capital; but their roots and growth potential remain autonomous.

4 Classical Marxism and Labour's Existential Problem

In the previous two sections I argued that labour power is distinguished from other commodities by two features: its inseparability from its owner, and the fact that its reproduction is a diffuse and autonomous social process which cannot be capitalistically controlled. What these two features have in common is that each is the source of a very broad variety of potential aims and interests which wage workers may bring to bear on the employment relation. Because labour power cannot be detached from agents who are socially constructed as whole persons, the interests which these agents could in principle choose to define and act on are drawn from a wider and more varied spectrum then those of other owners and traders of commodities. It is useful to register this point by calling these interests the 'human interests of labour'. If workers actually assert their human interests and demand that their terms of employment or the organisation of the enterprise be adjusted to accommodate them, there is a high probability of conflict with their employers, in so far as the latter must, on pain of competitive failure, follow the principles of market rationality. The next question is whether labour's human interests are likely to coincide with express wants, and, if so, whether these wants are likely to find an outlet in some kind of *action*.

Now classical Marxism had no doubts about the answers to these last two questions. It might be admitted that at any given moment workers showed no particular awareness of their 'real' interests and their underlying antagonism with capital; or, even when workers possessed some minimum sense of class identity and membership, this class consciousness might still fail to eventuate in any significant, let alone successful, economic or political action. Nevertheless, classical Marxism held that over the long run independent working-class interests, wants and action would coalesce. Then, once an autonomous workers' movement had emerged, it would initiate a progressive transformation of capitalist society, either by revolutionary or evolutionary methods depending on the prior establishment of political democracy.

Ultimately the reason why classical Marxism reposed such confidence in the historic mission of the working class as the grave-diggers of capitalism, stemmed from the third peculiarity of labour power. This is that once capitalist relations of production have spread across the greater part of the economy, labour power becomes relatively useless (i.e. has little use-value for its owner) unless it is hired out to some employer or other. *Before* capitalism has taken over most spheres of material production – as, say, in North America from the seventeenth to the late nineteenth centuries – there remains space to gain an independent livelihood as an artisan or small farmer outside the capitalist sector. And even under advanced capitalism there are still marginal opportunities for self-employment as an alternative to wage labour. It is for this reason that 'useless' was qualified by 'relatively' in the last sentence but two. None the less it is safe to say that once capitalism becomes the economically dominant mode of production, the vast majority of the labour force depends on continual success in selling their special commodity. Admittedly, with a developed social security system, the penalty for failure is not outright starvation, appeals to charity or the rigours of the workhouse. But for most 'primary' workers prolonged unemployment still means a stigmatised, marginal and underprivileged existence which precludes full participation in the prevailing pattern of social life.

For classical Marxism this third feature of labour power played a dual role in determining labour's destiny. On the one hand it underpinned workers' dependence on capital and ensured that their human interests would in the end be subordinated to the maintenance of acceptably high rates of profit and accumulation. Thus during a phase of rapid expansion when the demand for labour power temporarily outstripped the growth of supply, there would be headroom for workers to compel attention to their demands and extract piecemeal concessions from capital. But such short-term success in improving the terms on which they supplied their labour power, would itself generate a reversal in the balance of labour market advantage by inducing either a fall in the rate of capital accumulation or a quickening in the pace of labour-displacing changes in technique. The threat of precipitation into the ranks of the unemployed would periodically curb the 'pretensions' of the working class. Organised efforts by trade unions to advance workers' human interests would be relatively ineffective in the face of this impersonal market coercion.

On the other hand, as workers experienced the limitations of purely trade union struggles, they would become schooled in socialism. They would learn to identify the systemic causes of their common deprivations and frustrations, and raise their sights towards the higher goal of mounting a political challenge to the power of capital.

It has long been commonplace to dismiss this classical perspective of a workers' movement rising ever onwards and upwards to a socialist destiny. Socialist intellectuals themselves from Lenin onwards came to abandon the early optimism of Marx and Engels about the learning curve running from trade union struggle to socialist politics. *Ad hoc* reservations based on the alleged corruption of union leaders or the privileged position of a labour aristocracy gave way to more systematic sociologies of trade unionism. These pessimistic interpretations variously stressed the conservative consequences of the competitive-sectional structure of trade union organisation; the oligarchic cast of the union bureaucracy; the role of collective bargaining procedures in institutionalising and sanitising labour–capital conflict; and the calculated attempts of professional managers and national statesmen to incorporate labour leaders as junior partners in the governance of enterprise and state.[10]

It is noteworthy, however, that none of the twentieth-century socialists who reappraised the consequences of trade unionism for the social cohesion and political stability of capitalist societies appears to have pushed his 'pessimism' to the point of doubting that it *was* the historic mission of the workers' movement to be the agent of social transformation. Indeed, their arguments took this premise as axiomatic: what had to be explained were the practical obstacles to its realisation. It was acknowledged that the development of appropriate political strategies, programmes and tactics for the workers' movement was a 'science'. This 'science' did not spring spontaneously out of raw class experience; it could only be created within the framework of an organised political party. Accordingly the political tasks of bridging the gaps between interests, wants and action were complex and arduous. But it continued to be assumed that the underlying human interests of labour which formed the foundation and starting point of the whole socialist project were themselves clear, distinct and unproblematic.

This assumption ignores or glosses over a fourth peculiarity of labour power: namely, that the interests which workers have at stake in the employment relationship are multiple, heterogeneous and ultimately non-commensurable.[11] There is never a straightforward, unambiguous definition of what workers' interests are in any given context. At root this peculiarity stems from the fact that the owners of labour power are real human individuals – precisely the characteristic that classical Marxism relied on to orient the workers' movement in a socialist direction. By contrast, the owners of other commodities sold to enterprises are overwhelmingly other enterprises. Except for small family concerns and self-employed persons, the interests of these other commodity traders are relatively easy to reduce to quantitative/monetary indicators of costs and benefits. This is because capitalist production is production for exchange-value. As Alfred P. Sloan (one-time head of General Motors) put it: 'the business of the automobile industry is to make money, not cars.'

It is true that enterprises face tactical problems of a business strategy nature; there may be disputes between different sections of enterprise management about the best means of expanding the exchange value under the enterprise's control; and the interplay of sectional interest may have some influence on corporate policy. But these are second-order issues. The enterprise confronts no first-order problem about the *criteria* by which alternative policies and actions are to be evaluated and ranked: no problem, that is, about ends.

The owners of labour power, on the other hand, are continually faced with the problem: 'What is it that we want to get?' Moreover whereas the market provides the enterprise with a ready-made laboratory in which decisions can be tested and errors detected in a relatively short space of time,[12] it is much more difficult for workers to decide what is to count as an erroneous conception of interest. Tactical actions can be tested out, but the lessons taught by experience about underlying objectives are much more opaque.

In short, labour faces an existential problem which other commodity traders do not have to bother with. The impersonal imperatives of market rationality cut through the complexity of the questions: 'What ought we to do?' and 'What shall we do?' Productive activity is assessed purely in terms of its extrinsic value.[13] This drastic simplification of its purposes greatly enhances the power and efficiency of the enterprise as an agency for mobilising and deploying resources. Admittedly individual human beings too may exhibit a 'market mentality', forever searching out ways to use the resources and opportunities at their disposal to expand the sum of exchange value in their possession. But market transactions are only part of the totality of human interactions. This principle of behaviour could never provide a self-sufficient ethical and practical code: to attempt to make it so would be regarded as pathological. Furthermore, someone who tried to combine one set of principles for the marketplace with a completely different set outside it would be liable to severe logical inconsistency and psychological tension.[14] Human beings cannot avoid the necessity to come up with some sort of answer to questions about the ends of action.

Labour's existential problem has both an individual and a collective aspect. Each individual worker has interests on several fronts at once. There are, first, their interests as commodity traders concerned to obtain the best practicable terms in the process of exchange. This category of interests – the exclusive focus of the exchange paradigm – embraces such issues as the absolute and relative levels of wages, security of tenure, provisions governing layoffs and redundancies, fringe benefits, and so on.

Second, workers are producers and participants in the labour process. In this sphere they are concerned with working conditions, health and safety rules, the detailed division of labour within the enterprise, job satisfaction, etc.

Third, outside, but adjacent to, the immediate employment relation and place of work workers are consumers of the goods and services to which their wage labour affords access. The *real* wage (for which the economists' ratio of money wages to the cost of living is merely a more or less adequate *index*) consists literally of a bundle of material use-values. These use-values in turn, having been acquired on the market as commodities, enter as one kind of input, alongside domestic labour and whatever portion of the household time budget is surplus to necessary toil, into the ensemble of social activities generically known as 'consumption'. As Henry Ford, in somewhat sentimental vein, once put it: 'There is something sacred about wages – they represent homes and families and domestic destinies. On the cost sheet wages are mere figures; but in the world wages are bread boxes and coal bins, babies' cradles and children's education – family comforts and contentment.'[15]

The 'domestic destinies' to which Ford refers are lived out for the most part in family units, and this defines a fourth distinct area of workers' interest formation. The conventions surrounding the employment relation – for example, custom and practice governing the length and pattern of the standard working day/week/year/lifetime – are intimately connected with the distribution of roles and privileges between husbands and wives, parents and children. The forms of employment and the forms of family life are mutually conditioning elements of an overall system of social relations. Consider the concept of 'the family wage' introduced in Chapter 4 (p. 74). To uphold this concept is to assign men to the pre-eminent public domain of employment and money, and women to the subordinate, private domain of housework and the care of dependants. It is evident that the conceptions of interest likely to prevail under this sexual division of labour will be very different from those associated with a more balanced distribution of time and activities between men and women.

A vivid illustration of this point is contained in Bea Campbell's account of the history of the pithead bath issue among Britain's coalminers (Campbell, 1984, pp. 103–7). Despite the fact that under the 1911 Coal Mines Act pithead baths had to be provided if two-thirds of the miners in each pit voted for them, by the time of coal nationalisation 35 years later only one-third of collieries possessed this facility. The issue was just not given priority by most members of the Miners' Federation. Campbell suggests that the explanation for this failure to take up their statutory entitlements lies in the miners' patriarchal control over the labour and time of their womenfolk. Most miners preferred to have pit dirt cleaned from their workclothes and bodies by the unpaid labour of their wives, notwithstanding the paucity of their domestic washing facilities and the pollution of their homes by coal dust and sulphurous fumes.

Finally, whether they realise and care about it or not, workers have interests as demiurges: they are enrolled by their employing enterprises into activities which continually reconstruct the natural and social environment. Both the processes and results of all the activities of social reproduction set in motion long chains of social and ecological consequences. Some of the links in these chains are invisible or disputed in our present state of knowledge. But many others are known to science, and popular awareness of the resource depletion and the environmental and social damage caused by particular patterns of production has expanded in recent years. The workers employed in any branch of production bear responsibility for these consequences, no less than soldiers engaged in the destructive work of war may be held in varying degrees accountable for the war aims of their state, and even more for their methods of warfare.

The individual worker's interests on each of these five fronts will frequently be in conflict. Pride in the exercise of skill or the execution of high quality work may conflict with the demands of supervisors or pressure to qualify for production bonuses. A woman's domestic responsibilities may rule out acceptance of jobs offering superior pay, training and promotion prospects if these jobs also require long hours of work at inconvenient times and an uninterrupted commitment to her employer. Doubts about the social benefit conferred by the products a worker is employed to make may be tempered by anxiety over job security, or simply by fear of appearing to be eccentric. Discontent at deskilling and the erosion of job autonomy may clash with the felt need to maintain culturally acceptable and socially compulsive levels and modes of consumption.

All these divergent interests are present within each individual worker. The problems of interest diversity are compounded when we consider workers collectively. The historical formation of the labour force leaves in its trail a variety of cross-cutting divisions of interest within the working class. The gender system and ethno-religious cleavages have already been alluded to. In addition the restructuring of the labour process during the twentieth century has created new variations on the ancient theme of the division between mental and manual labour.[16] Scientific management and work study have continually altered the mix between the planning/conceptual and executive/manual components of jobs. The reconstituted division of labour has intensified the demarcation between white- and blue-collar jobs, and fostered new rivalries of power, status and reward within each segment of the enterprise labour force.[17] And far from unifying the various fragments, the trade unions have, as often as not, perpetuated and amplified the antagonisms of gender, ethnicity and occupation.[18]

Outside the immediate employment relationship itself workers' interest affiliations diverge according to their relationship to the means of consumption. Divisions of interest between different groups of worker-consumers have become increasingly prominent with the decay of old, cohesive working-class communities. These communities, concentrated in residential areas close to their sources of employment, shared a rough equality of life experience, and maintained strong traditions of solidarity, mutual aid and communal self-discipline.[19] Post-war material prosperity and deliberate public policy, especially towards transport and housing, have created new stratified and segregated class formations. On the one side, stand affluent, working-class owner-occupiers with their own private vehicles and sufficient job security and personal savings to banish immediate financial anxiety from their horizons. On the other are the new urban poor, trapped within local authority housing estates which have long since lost whatever lustre they once had as monuments of municipal socialism, and degenerated into refuges of the oppressed. They depend heavily on public transport and the rest of an array of increasingly cramped and deformed social services. And not only are these new strata distanced from each other by spatial and social gulfs; each is internally disintegrated by the dominant privatised and consumerist vision of the 'good life'. The blinkered and egotistical values and motivations encouraged by this vision are manifested on the one hand in 'legitimate', albeit irritant, sectional wage militancy; and on the other, in 'criminal' acts of looting, theft and personal violence.

Finally, the most obvious divisions within the labour force of any economy follow the contours of economic organisation itself.

Whatever the other forces at work to unify or fragment the class of wage workers, workers' immediate and strictly economic interests as commodity traders are necessarily bounded and shaped by the organisational logic of production. Disputes with employers over jobs and pay rarely present themselves in the first instance as class-wide issues.[20] Rather they are perceived as the concern of specific sections of workers belonging to specific work groups, departments, occupations, plants, divisions, enterprises, industries or localities. And against a background of scarce resources and economic interdependence, it is inevitable that the sectional interests of workers in a particular organisational or adminstrative unit will collide not only, or even mainly, with the interests of their immediate employer; but also, and perhaps most saliently, with the interests of other workers in other units, or with the interests of workers in general.

These kinds of intra-class conflicts are highlighted by sectional strike activity, though the problems are quite general and exist even in the absence of strikes. Internecine strife may break out because other workers are employed in units which have customer or supplier links with the strike-bound unit, as when strikes in one department, firm or industry lead to secondary layoffs elsewhere; or because the other units concerned are in competition with the striking unit, and stand to gain or lose by the outcome of the primary dispute; or, finally, because all workers are also consumers, and, other things being equal, stand to lose both from the immediate withdrawal or shortage of the product or service affected by strike action, and from any increase in its price resulting from the offer of preventive inducements to minimise disruption to supply. This last type of conflict between sectional interest groups is particularly acute in those public services where there are few or no substitutes and where public health or safety is at risk when supply is disrupted by strike action. Moreover in this sector the strain of cost-raising dispute settlements is borne by taxes, rates or the level and quality of the service and cannot be avoided by the exercise of consumer discretion.

In so far as trade union organisation and activity tend to mirror the logic of production, these internal divisions will assume a permanent institutional form. It remains to be seen in the final section of this chapter how far trade unions can supply an answer to labour's existential problem.

5   Trade Unions and the Logic of Collective Action

One of the principal functions of trade unions is to transcend or ameliorate conflicts between workers arising from competition over scarce resources and economic interdependence. They seek to do this by harnessing the interests and motivations of each labour force unit (individual or group) to some agreed, common objective or set of objectives. Indeed, it is a mistake to view unions as coalitions, which merely aggregate *given* interests and attempt by concerted, collective action to attain *desiderata* that would otherwise lie beyond the reach of the isolated individual. Trade unions are themselves agents of interest formation. They strive to redirect or transform the perceived interests of workers as separate individuals; to give expression to interests which would otherwise remain inchoate; to provide an institutional forum for resolving divergent interests; and to maintain amongst their numbers a workable consensus about which issues should be included on the agenda of negotiation with employers and what degree of priority should be attached to each. Trade unions are one of the main vehicles available to workers for constructing a coherent, stable, collective interest out of what would otherwise be an uncertain, fluctuating or contradictory congeries of particular views.

The creative role of trade unions can be illustrated by considering the archetypical case of the job queue. Imagine an employer faced with a finite queue of equally competent and qualified workers who exceed in number the jobs he wishes to fill. The employer proposes his hiring terms and enquires which workers are willing to accept a job on those terms. Assume that the rules of the game require each individual to decide whether to accept the employer's offer without knowing for certain in advance how the others will respond, and without being able to communicate with them. To simplify the analysis assume also that each worker's preferences as between obtaining a job and remaining unemployed are initially identical; and that each worker expects that whichever way the others respond to the employer's offer, their response will be uniform.

In these conditions each individual can see that there are four possible outcomes according as s/he accepts or refuses the offer, and as the others accept or refuse the offer. In order of preference self-interest dictates the following ranking of these four outcomes:

(1) Everyone rejects the offer; there is then deadlock and the employer must improve his offer or suffer an interruption of his business.
(2) The individual accepts the proposed terms whilst the others reject them; the individual is then certain of a job.[21]
(3) Everyone accepts the offer; the employer then hires randomly and each individual has a probability less than one, but greater than zero of being picked.
(4) The individual rejects the offer, whilst the others accept; the individual is then certain to remain jobless.

What is the individual's optimum strategy in this situation? If s/he refuses the offer, the outcome may be (1), but could be (4). If s/he opts to accept, the worst that could happen is (3), and there is a chance of (2), both of which are better than the worst outcome of a refusal. It follows that if the individual is concerned to minimise the worst outcome, acceptance of the proposed terms is the indicated strategy. But if everyone reasons in this way the actual outcome will be (3). Everyone's most preferred outcome, (1), is simply unattainable as long as each individual is compelled to act in isolation.

Collective organisation brings outcome (1) within reach. The workers' response to the employer's offer can then be coordinated and centralised. So far the union is merely aggregating the workers' given interests. But now suppose that a collective refusal of the employer's terms has been orchestrated so that there is, for the time being, no agreement on hiring terms. The employer is not bound to improve his offer immediately. He must decide his next move by comparing the costs of resisting the workers' pressure for improved terms with the costs of conceding their demands.[22] Let us suppose that his resistance costs are lower: he holds out against raising his offer and there is deadlock.

The union is now obliged to back down or declare a strike. Assume that it elects to take strike action. In the ensuing trial of strength it is essential that there be no breaking of ranks on the union side. As the strike continues there may be individual workers whose purely self-interested calculations lead them to conclude that a job on the employer's terms is at least better than no job or pay at all. In other words, some individuals may begin to alter their original ranking of the four outcomes and elevate (2) above (1). They will then be tempted to destroy the united front and place their own individual interests above the union's definition of the collective interest. In acting in this way they would be following the logic of individual action.

But the logic of collective action demands that this kind of dissident behaviour be prevented – by consensual means if possible, but by coercion if persuasion and argument fail. Picketing, for example, combines both these methods of influence. It is intended, partly, to demonstrate the degree and intensity of support for a strike and to urge waverers and dissidents to set aside their doubts in the interests of unity and loyalty. But it is also intended to place physical obstacles to the movement of goods and labour to and from the employer's premises.

In other words the union must preserve group solidarity in one of two ways. It may endeavour to change the perceptions of its individual members as to where their best interests lie, causing them to sublimate any purely self-interested standpoint, and instead to see themselves as members of a collective which deserves their overriding allegiance. To the extent that the union's efforts to cultivate a collective ethic succeed, its members will not even entertain the thought that outcome (2) might be preferable to outcome (1). Alternatively, if some individuals fail to internalise the group code, then the union, acting in the name of what it has defined as the collective interest, reserves the right to invoke coercive sanctions against recalcitrants (through intimidation, ostracism, discipline and, ultimately, expulsion). In this way the union restricts the freedom of individual workers to do whatever suits them best at any particular time.

In practice neither educative/transformatory nor organisational/coercive means of averting disunity ever work completely smoothly. All kinds of tensions persist: (a) between what individuals perceive as their best interests and whatever definitions of the higher group interest emerge out of the processes of internal union government; and (b) between individual freedom and organisational effectiveness. Nevertheless the general point is clear: the logic of trade union action differs from that of individual action; in following this logic trade unions necessarily tend to reshape or repress individuals' conceptions of their interests.

This transcendent logic of collective action does not, however, go far towards resolving labour's existential dilemmas. Quite apart from the fact that trade union success in redefining workers' interests is usually incomplete and fragile; the redefinitions themselves remain limited and distorted by all the sources of interest diversity and conflict discussed in the previous section.

Thus trade unions tend to express and confirm the various intra-class relations of privilege and domination which have become inscribed within the historical formation of the labour force. It is significant that some of the most militant episodes of trade union history have centred around the most conservative of objectives. A classic example is the shop-floor movement which developed in the munitions and shipbuilding industries on Clydeside during the First World War. The movement came out in open defiance of the official union leadership's collaboration with employers and state to promote the war effort. In the course of bitter and violent clashes with the authorities, the movement's revolutionary leaders adopted a programme of opposition to the war, nationalisation of their industries and workers' control of production. Yet the basic issue which had unleashed this revolt was the resistance of the élite craft workers in the engineering industries to the dilution of craft skills by the introduction into the factories of unskilled workers, most of whom were women (see Hinton, 1973).

At the organisational level the unions' principal activity, collective bargaining, is dispersed and decentralised across a large number of autonomous bargaining units. On most issues for most of the time there is little *ex ante* coordination of policy: sectional defensive concerns tend to be given priority over any strategic integration of the various fragments of the working class and the various aspects of their lives. The logic of collective action flourishes *inside* the boundaries of corporate organisation and union jurisdiction; beyond these limits its force is soon spent.

In short, those forms of industrial action and consciousness which classical Marxism saw as the royal road to socialism, may not only happily coexist with both class and non-class relationships of dominance and subordination; they may also become implicated in maintaining them. Normal trade union activity provides no reason to amend our major conclusion: that both as individuals and as groups workers confront a host of potential interests which will often be incompatible, and amongst which there is no compelling, over-arching principle of choice comparable to the univalent standard employed by the enterprise. Labour's existential problem has no fixed or pre-given solution: the complexity of workers' human interests cannot be collapsed into any single 'essential' or 'representative' interest of labour.

It follows that the teleological view of the workers' movement as heading towards a long-run socialist destiny is without foundation. And even assertions of broad sociological tendency are open to grave doubt. There may be reasons to expect that workers will incline towards conceptions of their interests which involve a wholesale reconstruction of state and society. But the grounds for holding the opposite expectation – that workers will embrace interests which consolidate the existing social order – are just as strong.

Nevertheless there is a certain sense in which we can meaningfully speak of the general interest of labour; or, to be more precise, the *meta*-interest of labour. The specific shapes of the interest – and decision-fields surrounding workers' relations with their employers are socially determined. In particular, these fields are truncated by various social forces and conditions which deny, inhibit or distort workers' freedom to choose between alternative goals. The very complexity of labour's human interests makes them vulnerable to two- and three-dimensional power. Now, if freedom of choice and self-determination are desirable states (whether or not they are actually desired), it will always be in workers' interests that their ability to articulate and pursue specific interests should, as far as is practicable at any given time, be liberated from this kind of pre-conscious limitation and bias. The enlargement or relocation of the fields of interest and decision will not in itself determine any specific agenda and set of priorities for action: labour's existential problem cannot be abolished. But it will at least ensure that certain issues are not excluded from the agenda or downgraded in importance by the hidden structure of social power.

From the argument of this chapter it appears likely that the struggle to realise labour's higher order interest in liberation will require internal rehabilitation, growth and unification as much as, if not more than, the defeat of any external 'class enemy'. Exactly what is involved in rescuing issues from the limbo of the second and third dimensions of power, so that they become the focus of thought and action in the first, is explored in the next chapter.

Notes to Chapter 5

1. Apparent exceptions to this generalisation were the 'zombies' or 'walking dead' observed in Nazi concentration camps. The listless and apathetic behaviour of these inmates was invariably a prelude to their death, whether prematurely at the hands of bewildered camp guards, or naturally as a result of their own self-neglect. However, these and related cases of nervous breakdown and suicide could be interpreted as desperate remedies for extreme deprivation and stress. To choose one's own death or removal from 'normal' social intercourse as a lesser evil than the pain of living under intolerable conditions, would not be an exception to the statement in the text.

2. For a review of the literature (as it existed up to the late 1960s) investigating whether, how and how much various types and degrees of direct workers' participation in planning, organising and monitoring their own job tasks, affected workers' morale and were accompanied by directly consequential changes in such indicators of labour performance as productivity levels, time-keeping, absenteeism, sickness and accident rates, see Blumberg (1968, chs 5 and 6). See also Hodgson (1984, pp. 135–9).

3. As noted earlier in the text (p. 32), by comparison with the immense advances in techniques for reproducing material use-values since the neolithic agricultural revolution, the technique of human biological reproduction has remained virtually unchanged from the dawn of our species up to the present. This fact, together with the relatively long period of infantile dependence in humans, has severely limited the scope for external social manipulation of

and control over the procreative and infant development stages of the reproduction of labour power. Normally, apart from any natural increase in their slave populations, slave systems have relied on military conquest and kidnapping to replenish their supplies of labour power.

4. It will be observed that a few activities are not included in any of these eight categories: notably commodity production undertaken by self-employed persons whether primarily to produce 'objects' (e.g. jobbing window cleaners) or 'people' (e.g. private tutors, professional nannies). Use-value production by the self-employed appears to overlap on the one side with domestic labour, and on the other shades off into hobbies and other financially unrewarding pursuits. It would be simple to extend the table to cater for these marginal cases.

5. For a powerful philosophical critique of these and other kinds of species supremacism see Singer (1976).

6. This point, and indeed much of the argument of this chapter, can be regarded as an elaboration of the contrast, noted in Chapter 1, between the circuits of exchange of labour power and of other commodities: $C - M - C$ and $M - C - M^1$ respectively.

7. For the human-capital approach see Becker (1975); for the job-market signalling approach see Spence (1973).

8. For an economic-theoretical elaboration of this perspective on schooling see Bowles and Gintis (1975).

9. See Stamworth (1981), and for a more general discussion of how girls learn to be women, Sharpe (1976).

10. For a review see Hyman (1971).

11. This formulation and the discussion which follows is inspired by Offe and Wiesenthal (1980).

12. Can be detected *ex post facto*, that is, *Ex ante* the firm has to learn to cope with uncertainty about the future. In particular, when undertaking investment in fixed capital, the firm must decide whether, when, in what direction and on what scale to enter into long-lived and costly commitments in situations for which past experience may provide little guidance. But this does not alter the point that once a specific commitment has been made, the market will reveal whether the expectations on which it was based were well founded. When the firms turns round to face the future, it will again find a new prospect of uncertainty before it.

13. Naturally, employers seek public legitimation and self-reassurance by stressing that this criterion does not contradict humanitarian principles; or, alternatively, that humanitarian postures will be found, on close inspection, to have worse social consequences than business realism. For a fascinating study of how Quaker employers in the early twentieth century sought to reconcile the logic of the market with the avowed values and beliefs of their faith, to the detriment of the latter, see Child (1964).

14. Cf. Brecht's double-life character Shen-Teh/Shui-Ta in 'The Good Person of Szechuan', Brecht (1985).
15. See Ford (1973, p. 163). The passage from which this quote is taken makes it clear that Ford *also* saw wage reductions as poor financial policy. High and stable wages were essential to the mass production of mass consumption. On the supply side they were needed as incentives to secure acceptance of methods of work organisation yielding high productivity. On the demand side they sustained the purchasing power required to absorb the ever expanding output of consumer goods which rolled off the assembly lines. Ford's grasp of the interrelations between the various facets of the wage workers' central life interests, and his vision of how his technical and organisational revolution would transform the working class psychologically and culturally, are highly instructive. For a classic study of the social consequences of the Fordist revolution see Lynd and Lynd (1929).
16. Fernbach (1981), following Bahro (1978), argues that the socially constructed division between mental and manual labour was the first *class* division in human history. He suggests that it developed with the transition from the hunter-gatherer mode of production to settled agriculture, and was brought to perfection by the riverine civilisations of Egypt and the near-East. 'Class' thus antedated the emergence of private property in the means of production by thousands of years. The division between mental and manual labour survived as a geological stratum in subsequent social formations. Although still overlaid by the division between capital and labour in the West, it is exposed on the surface of society in those countries of 'actually existing socialism' where the upper, and more recently formed, layers of class division based on private property have been forcibly removed.
17. See Braverman (1974), especially Chapters 15–18.
18. See for example Rubery's (1978) critique of dualist and radical theories of labour market segmentation. It is, she argues, wrong in principle to consider only the motivations and actions of capitalists in accounting for the development of the economic structure. The stratification of the labour force results not from any technological imperative or capitalist strategy of divide and rule. Rather it arises as groups of workers attempt to control the supply of labour and preserve niches of bargaining power as defensive reactions against the threat of competition and substitution.
19. For a graphic description and analysis of the social, political and moral consequences of the decay of these traditional, close-knit communities see Seabrook (1978).
20. The rare exception occurs when the dispute is universally recognised as having symbolic or strategic importance in determining the future balance of bargaining strength between all employers and their respective workforces. In this case each group's own self-

interest reinforces the appeal to moral sympathy as a motive for class-wide solidarity.

21. Where, as in most situations, the labour process involves some specialisation of job tasks and production depends on teamwork, a critical minimum number of workers would have to accept before anyone could be set to work. This would not debar the employer from taking individuals on to his payroll *before* the threshold of operational viability had been passed, as an incentive to those remaining in the queue to accept the terms offered. The anaytical case in the text ignores these niceties of industrial bargaining.

22. The employer's resistance costs will consist primarily of the profits, if any, which he will directly forego, when production is halted for the duration of a deadlock over hiring terms; plus, the profits he will indirectly lose in the future if some of his frustrated customers permanently transfer their orders to rival suppliers. His concession costs will consist of whatever reduction in profits results from any increase in pay and other terms he is prepared to offer.

6
Labour's Goals and the Reproduction of Unequal Power

1 Introduction

In the previous chapter I argued that there are no universal substantive interests which can be attributed to workers in their various individual and social roles. On the other hand, if freedom and self-determination are important values, then it is always possible to postulate a formal and negative interest in overcoming conditions which cause potential or actual interests to remain silent. Such silencing occurs when the social practices attached to workers' various roles systematically generate an interest field which excludes significant issues (dimension 3), or disqualify some consciously held interests as candidates for action (dimension 2).

In this chapter I shall examined the ways in which social reproduction may condition workers' substantive interests and divide up their issue space into zones of differential eligibility. This is a large and uncharted subject. The discussion must be regarded as a preliminary reconnaissance rather than an exhaustive mapping.

The method of exploration is as follows. Since the processes we are concerned with operate at a pre-conscious level, it is useful to begin the analysis with a choice-theoretic model of goal selection as a reference point. Section 2 presents the ingenious model devised by Crouch (1982), which incorporates the phenomenon of unequal power in the second dimension.[1] Then,

111

step by step the limitations of this model as a framework for explaining goal selection are pointed out. The critique of the rational choice model simultaneously provides insights into systemic bias and distortion affecting labour's goals, and the conditions in which these influences may be counteracted. These insights are developed in Section 3 by way of an extended discussion of goal conflict drawn from the experience of the workers' plan movement which flourished briefly in Britain in the 1970s.

Throughout Sections 2 and 3 two simplifying assumptions of the choice-theoretic model are maintained: (1) that goal selection can be modelled by positing just two conflicting goals; and (2) that the values workers attach to these goals, together with the costs of achieving them, can be quantified and made commensurable. As the argument of Section 3 unfolds it becomes apparent that these simplifications are radically inappropriate in complex choice situations where the alternatives consist of total packages of interrelated elements with ramifications extending into many facets of social life. Such holistic alternatives are better handled from a social reproduction perspective. This is naturally suited to analysing the socio-cultural consequences of economic structures and the ways in which particular patterns of economic organisation enlarge or contract human possibility and choice. To draw out these consequences not only enables us to probe the roots of social power and trace the full extent of its influence on social action; it also highlights the *ethical* aspects of any assessment of an entire way of life, when the issues at stake cannot sensibly be reduced to any single, purely quantitative yardstick of valuation.

Section 4 steps outside the narrowly utilitarian world of choice theory and examines the nature of transformatory social action. The objective of a tranformatory project is precisely to re-order oppressive socio-economic structures on the basis of some explicit ethical ideal. It is creative rather than reactive in character, value-rational rather than instrumentally rational, holistic rather than segmented. Workers, or any other subordinate social group, who initiate a transformatory social practice may countervail the forces tending to reproduce the unequal power relations in which they would otherwise remain enmeshed.

2 A Choice Theoretic Model of Goal Selection

Strictly speaking, in the discussion of the peculiarities of labour power in Chapter 5, I established only that workers possess multiple and conflicting interests in the employment relationship: I asserted, but did not prove, that these various interests are incommensurable. Now up to a point it *is* possible to compare competing objectives and establish orders of priority between them. Models can be constructed in which the costs and benefits of alternative lines of action are standardised and the behaviour of agents is analysed by the technique of constrained maximisation. Provided that care is used in specifying costs, benefits and constraints, within certain limits goal selection can be explained in terms of choice theoretic principles.

Let us first ignore the problems arising from the divergence between the logics of individual and collective action. Imagine a cohesive group of workers who face a choice between the goal of higher wages and the goal of enhanced job control. This latter objective could be more tightly defined. For example, greater job control might take the form of less demanding work schedules permitting slower average work speeds; or greater discretion over the pacing of work and the timing and frequency of rest breaks; or more autonomy in the selection of work methods and the assignment of tasks among the workforce; or simply more freedom from overbearing supervisors even if the material aspects of the labour process are unchanged. However, as explained below, the precise specification of job control can, and indeed must, be left open if the case at hand is to be made amenable to a standard choice theoretic treatment.

Assume that the workers have a utility function $U = U(\Delta w, \Delta c, s)$, where Δw represents wage increases, Δc enhanced job control, and s the costs incurred in pursuing either objective. Their behaviour can then be analysed by assuming that U is to be maximised subject to certain specified constraints in the relevant environment. This procedure presupposes that the arguments of the utility function are well defined and quantifiable. There is no problem in devising an appropriate measure of Δw. Similarly, s might be measured by the length of strike which the workers anticipate they would need to sustain in order to achieve any given wage or control claim. They reason that their employer will not volunteer concessions on either front unless he calculates that the cost of resisting their demands exceeds the cost of conceding them. In general, they can galvanise this perception only be deploying or threatening industrial sanctions, of which the strike may be taken as the archetype. Higher concessions will be forthcoming only if they strike or threaten to strike for longer, thereby causing the employer's resistance costs to rise by more than the value of the additional concession.

The variable Δc, on the other hand, is problematic. 'Job control' is a multi-dimensional concept; the valuation which workers attach to any particular state of its various elements may well depend on their overall configuration rather than on each one considered separately; and even if it is thought appropriate to analyse the concept into its constituent components, there will often be no satisfactory technical units in which these can be measured. There are, therefore, several difficulties in constructing suitable social and physical indicators of Δc. These difficulties can be sidestepped by adopting a univalent monetary compensation standard of measurement. Suppose the workers specify the various possible changes in work organisation and practice which they would regard as constituting enhanced job control. Suppose further that for each such formulation of Δc, there is some sum of money which the workers would be prepared to accept as compensation for foregoing it. The Δc argument in their utility function can then be replaced by this hypothetical list of compensation prices.

The list is, of course, based on arbitrary, normative criteria: there is no presumption that the token money values which are taken to represent each version of Δc have any objective significance. They are simply a convenient way of accommodating an otherwise refractory variable. Moreover, it is always possible to use a given compensation scale, once fixed, as a base-line for investigating the consequences of alternative evaluations. This is, indeed, one of the main purposes of the analysis which follows. The proposed method of measuring Δc also has the incidental advantage of enabling us to represent both wage and control claims along a single, continuous scale. Thus, in Figure 6.1 below, any distance along the vertical axis above the origin can be interpreted interchangeably as the money value of a wage claim, given the state of job control; *or* as the token

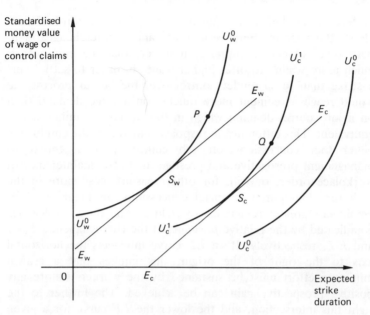

Figure 6.1

money value of a control claim, given the level of wages. It is convenient to describe wage and control claims as 'equivalent' if they have the same money value and would be equally costly to achieve. This does not imply that workers derive the same utility from claims which are equivalent in this sense. They may, as discussed below, hold non-monetary reasons for preferring, say, a control claim to an otherwise equivalent wage claim.

Imagine, then, that the workers have evolved a well-defined preference ordering over the various possible strike costs and gains. The curves labelled *UU* in the diagram trace out cost–benefit combinations between which the workers are indifferent. The shape of these indifference curves reflects the standard assumption that the benefit increments, which workers regard as offsetting a marginal increase in strike duration, grow larger the longer the strike envisaged. Furthermore, any given combination such as *P* will be preferred to any other combination such as *Q*, if *Q* lies on an indifference curve to the south-east of the curve passing through *P*.

To help fix ideas, suppose initially that workers have no

preference as between equivalent wage and control claims. Hence the same indifference mapping applies interchangeably to both types of claim. Suppose, however, that the employer is much more willing to offer higher wages in order to settle/avert a strike than to surrender control over the labour process: he would reach agreement more quickly on a wage demand than on a job control demand which in the workers' estimation was equivalent. This difference in response may reflect the employer's belief that concessions on job control pose a threat to management prerogative and prestige, or to the maintenance of workplace order, or will, for other reasons, cost more in the long run than purely financial concessions. In Figure 6.1 the employer's greater reluctance to yield ground on control issues is indicated by the relative *positions* of the curves labelled $E_w E_w$ and $E_c E_c$ respectively. If an EE curve intersects the horizontal axis to the right of the origin, this implies that a critical minimum effort must be sustained by the workers before any positive prospective gain can be achieved. The further to the right this intersection, and the lower the EE curve for a given issue, the poorer the prospects of a successful strike outcome. (The *slope* of each EE curve indicates the employer's rate of concession over time, as anticipated by the workers. For convenience, this is taken to be constant and equal for both kinds of demands.)

For the wage demand a settlement is available along $U_w^0 U_w^0$ at S_w. For the job control demand a settlement is available along $U_c^1 U_c^1$ at S_c. But $U_c^1 U_c^1$ lies everywhere below $U_w^0 U_w^0$. The wage demand is therefore the preferred objective. Given the workers' preferences, and given the structure of enterprise power – reflected in the relative positions of the two EE curves – which constrains their field of action, the workers maximise the return on effort expended to win concessions, by prioritising the wage demand and eschewing any challenge to management control over the labour process. Job control is definitely part of the workers' interest field. But, if the distance $0E_c$ is large, then for practical purposes it is excluded from their decision field. The workers' observed silence on this issue belongs to the second dimension of power. Let us call this Case 1.

As Crouch (1982) notes, the result just obtained depends critically on workers' evaluations of the two types of demand.

Suppose that workers were to attach some intrinsic non-monetary value to the job control demand. They may, for example, regard the high intensity of labour and loss of autonomy entailed by supine acquiescence in their employer's control over their workplace activity, as an affront to their humanity, dignity and self-esteem. They resent being made to work like galley-slaves, even if the pay is good. In this case the indifference maps for the two types of demand will no longer coincide. In evaluating the control demand workers will rate points along a curve such as $U_c^0 U_c^0$ as equivalent to points along the curve $U_w^0 U_w^0$ associated with the wage demand. This implies that workers are prepared to fight harder for a demand with a given financial value when it centres round a control issue than when it involves remuneration issues. Assuming that the employer's concession curves $E_w E_w$ and $E_c E_c$ remain as before, the workers will now select the control demand. The expected settlement point S_c represents a superior outcome to S_w since indifference curve $U_c^1 U_c^1$ is preferred to $U_c^0 U_c^0$ which, by assumption, is equivalent to $U_w^0 U_w^0$. Given this alternative scale of values the workers will pursue the objectively more arduous goal. Let us call this case 2.

It remains possible that the employer is so adamantly opposed to making any concessions on control that the anticipated concession curve $E_c E_c$ lies wholly to the south-east of $U_c^0 U_c^0$. In this case the wage objective will still be preferred. Although the workers hold a strong interest in winning greater job control, the strength of their preference for this goal over the wage goal – measured by the horizontal distance between $U_w^0 U_w^0$ and $U_c^0 U_c^0$ – is not sufficiently great to outweigh the employer's greater resistance to losing control over the labour process than to granting a pay rise – measured by the horizontal distance between $E_w E_w$ and $E_c E_c$. Let us call this case 3.

The model neatly illustrates the general point that workers have unequal access to different goals. Consequently, as Crouch (1982, p. 139) puts it: 'a choice of strategy is not just a choice between goals, but a choice of goals set in the context of the means needed to secure them. It may often happen that a union pursues a less desired goal because the means available to secure it are less hazardous than those needed for a more desired goal'. Nevertheless the model yields a determinate solution to the problem of goal selection only as of a *given* preference ordering. Granted that the structure of enterprise authority and power makes different goals objectively more or less costly to reach: the model does not allow us to predict *which* goal will be pursued by rational agents unless we already know their scale of values. Situations of the first type – where workers' selection of goals runs along the line of least resistance – may seem more probable on general grounds. But we cannot rule out *a priori* situations of the second type – where action follows the line of greater resistance. The model can only be closed by investigating the determinants of workers' 'tastes and preferences'. Otherwise either its predictions must be considered culturally relative, or the model becomes merely a framework for interpreting and rationalising behaviour after the event, when agents have already made their choices and revealed their preferences by their deeds.

The need to take the question of cultural formation seriously becomes all the more compelling when it is realised that the foregoing analysis is not intended to represent any actual historical episode of industrial life, but rather to convey a *typical* configuration of opportunities and desires in the enterprise (see Crouch, 1982, pp. 145–6). It is not pretended that workers really perform the nice calculations depicted above. What happens is that *over a period of time* workers learn to adjust their actions to the structure of power. They do not waste time on fruitless pursuits, but set themselves targets which they have some chance of achieving at a 'reasonable' cost. The resulting pattern of behaviour then persists at least unless some decisive shift either in the balance of one- and two-dimensional power, or in their underlying values, stimulates workers to reassess their objectives.

Thus the choice-theoretic model of goal selection is intended to condense a social learning process which extends over a succession of encounters and experiences. But on this interpretation it becomes implausible to treat workers' preferences as exogenous data. The issues around which workers order their interests and priorities may become *endogenous* to a particular enduring framework of action. Suppose that workers initially experience great difficulty in making headway on some contested issue, or find that some feature of their environment is so inaccessible to any influence they might bring to bear that they do not seriously contemplate making it an 'issue'. Then it is not just their outward conduct which is liable to adapt to the unfavourable constellation of one- and two-dimensional power: their inner values, attitudes and feelings may also be affected.

Someone who prudently submits without a fight to *force majeure* (dimension 2), lives to fight another day. By the *manner* of their submission (e.g. feigning stupidity or showing excessive literalness and zeal in executing orders), they may even contrive small moral victories over their dominators.[2] When the goals which people choose to pursue are constrained *only* by what they can realistically hope to get, the implication is that if the constraints on their action were relaxed, then previously submerged goals would resurface with undiminished vigour.

Consider case 3 above. Workers are strongly attached to the *principle* of job control. But they decide not to press the issue because the cost of attempting to overcome management's resistance is too high. Now suppose that management's stance on job control eases slightly: the concession curve E_cE_c shifts to the left. Assuming that workers' preferences are unchanged, this alteration in the structure of opportunity would precipitate a swift reversal of workers' objectives. The situation would switch from case 3 to case 2.

But imagine that the situation portrayed in case 3 persists over a long period of time. Even if the workers once engaged in debates and struggles over the job control objective, as time goes by and the composition of the labour force changes, the proportion who can recall the old days will steadily fall. Those veterans in whom the memory lingers on will have difficulty in perceiving the *relevance* of their history to present realities; for new cohorts of workers this history will be a closed book. In these conditions it would be misleading to depict the workers as continuing to nurse secret dreams of wresting control of the labour process from an autocratic management. In some very long-term perspective the idea may not have been totally extinguished: but it will certainly have become overlaid by new levels of consciousness.

Protracted experience of constraints on choice will modify not just the outward show of action, but its internal conscious springs. In this case, even if at some later stage the structure of opportunity were to change, as we supposed before, the force of desire required to convert opportunity into results would be lacking. What began as case 3 would by slow degrees have been transmuted into a situation resembling case 1. Indeed, if workers cease to regard job control as a possible 'issue', or never imagined that it could be, even to subsume the situation under case 1 would be misleading: the issue simply does not figure on any meaningful agenda of choice.

There is still a further twist to the story. So far we have faithfully adhered to the standard choice-theoretic assumption that agents treat the specified constraints in their environment as literally binding. But this assumption is often questionable. A great deal of behaviour in all spheres of life is directed towards loosening constraints on action. In case 3 workers who feel strongly about the job control issue, but are frustrated in finding any *immediate* outlet for their concern, are likely to search for ways of improving their terrain of struggle. Examples of what this might involve are taken up in the next section. On the other hand, workers whose culture has been shaped (or reshaped) in the ways described above, will not only neglect job control as an immediate issue, but also ignore the possibility of working to create the conditions in which it could become an issue. Three-dimensional power conjugates in both the indicative and the subjunctive moods.

This section has dwelt on the particular conflict between job control and wages merely in order to flesh out the analysis of the choice-theoretic model and its limitations. Other illustrative goals would have served the purpose equally well. A different example is developed in the next section. The requirements of formal analysis may give the discussion in this section a somewhat artificial air. This impression can be corrected by considering a historical transformation which broadly matches the hypothetical case outlined above.

When Taylorist principles of scientific management and Fordist techniques of assembly-line machinofacture were first introduced in the United States during the first two decades of the twentieth century, they received considerable adverse publicity (see Rose, 1978, chs 3 and 4). The employers who pioneered these innovations encountered high voluntary quit rates among the workers they recruited. Their employees were accustomed to less exacting and demeaning methods of work organisation. After experiencing the shock of the novel methods, and despite the wage differential they could earn, they were inclined to quit their jobs and seek their fortunes with some other 'old fashioned' employer. (Since trade unions had secured few footholds in the industries concerned, collective resistance to 'rationalisation' was only sporadic.)

But this escape route lay open only so long as alternative sources of employment continued to offer labour processes organised along traditional lines. Public hostility to Taylorism and Fordism abated as practitioners overcame their teething problems and refined the more blatant psychological and sociological crudities of the early prototypes. Above all, the new methods proved to be so effective in raising labour productivity that even allowing for the high wage premium required to avert voluntary turnover, employers who clung to the old ways were seriously handicapped in the competitive struggle. The innovations spread steadily across most areas of industrial employment.

Like the North American Indians at an earlier period in the country's history, workers discovered that running away from the power which had confiscated their territory was no longer an option. Equally it was now too late to make a successful stand against the invader. The only practical alternatives were either to settle for a reduced and stagnant existence on the marginal reservations, or to undergo assimilation into the dominant culture.

The process of assimilation was never absolute and unqualified. Just as remnants of Indian culture survived as reference points for future claims of restoration against the white man, so echoes of bygone industrial freedoms returned to sound discordant notes in the new industrial order. But overall, once the new order was entrenched there could be no going back to the system which had preceded it. And with the disappearance of any practical model of workplace autonomy, the very *idea* that industrial labour processes can and should be designed to accommodate the human interests of those who operate them, fell into decay. In a similar way the principle of harmony between human society and its natural environment, which had characterised the 'primitive' culture of the indigenous peoples of the New World, became lost to popular sensibilities in a mode of production which compulsively ransacked nature's bounty and traumatised her eco-systems.

3   Systemic Goal Containment and Countervailing Pressure

I now wish to develop further the idea that workers' goals may become imprisoned within a particular frame of reference which is reproduced by prevailing industrial practice, and to examine the conditions in which these cultural bonds might be broken. For this purpose it will be helpful to change the example use in the last section, whilst still for the time being retaining the choice-theoretic framework.

Suppose that a group of workers, knowing that their firm's product market is in decline, anticipates that their employer will shortly take steps to reduce the size of the labour force. Assume that there are two broad alternative strategies for job- and income-protection. One is a defensive, damage-limitation campaign to minimise the number of compulsory redundancies, to secure generous terms of redundancy compensation and to win the right of co-decision with management in determining how the impact of job losses will be divided between reduced recruitment, natural wastage, voluntary severance and compulsory redundancies; and how agreed overall levels of redundancy are to be distributed across the various categories of the labour force. For the sake of the argument we may take it that the workers evaluate the programmatic demands associated with this campaign in purely financial terms. Jobs retained might be valued at existing wage levels; jobs destined to disappear at the discounted value of redundancy compensation plus prospective income from alternative sources such as unemployment benefit; the practical accounting details need not detain us. The workers' union may also attach some positive non-pecuniary value to the right of participation.

Alternatively the workers may go on to the offensive and decide to devise and campaign for their own independent corporate plan. This would consist of a programme indicating how jobs could be saved through product diversification and development. The plan would need to specify in detail how the company's existing plant and equipment and the workforce's existing skills could be redeployed to produce an alternative pattern of output. Its proposals would have to be demonstrated to be both technically feasible and commercially viable.

There is no reason in principle why the idea of constructive alternatives to redundancy need entail any departure from standard business practice. But the most impressive of the workers' plans which emerged in Britain in the 1970s – that developed by the Lucas Aerospace Shop Stewards' Combine Committee – contained a novel and powerful radical thrust. Indeed it seems probable that without the social vision which inspired it, the Lucas Plan would never have aroused the enthusiasm, dedication, energy and patience which, as we shall see, are needed to resist the temptation to adopt a purely defensive approach to job protection. In order therefore to understand the significance of the workers' plan concept a brief outline of the Lucas case is required.[3]

The Lucas Plan was born out of the unease felt by some of the shop stewards at the contradiction between their interests as wage earners and their interests as citizens and political activists. On the one hand they knew that in a period of rationalisation and technological labour-displacement, their jobs depended on maintaining the flow of government defence contracts which provided the staple market for the company's aerospace division. On the other hand, it was the national policy of almost all the unions represented on the Combine Committee that there should be cuts in defence expenditure. The Combine proposed to set about resolving this contradiction by systematically investigating how the division's human and material resources might be switched to 'socially useful' production. Three criteria of social usefulness were employed: (1) products should cater for important collective needs which were left unsatisfied under the existing market-determined allocation of resources; (2) product design and applications should be environmentally wholesome; (3) products should incorporate technologies which were carefully adapted to the context and needs of their users – for example, high tech was appropriate in designing remote handling gear for undersea oil-rig maintenance, whereas intermediate technology was applied in the proposal for a lightweight, rubber-wheeled, road-rail vehicle which would cope with difficult terrain in remote regions of Third World countries. In addition the Plan contained radical ideas for new modes of work organisation and control. Advanced computer systems were to be used to preserve and enhance rather than fragment the skills of engineers and designers; and integrated production teams were to link the experience of shop-floor and office with the scientific knowledge of the technical staff. The complete Plan consisted of five 200-page documents outlining some 150 new products together with related proposals for reorganising production.

There were clearly many special features of the Lucas case. The aerospace division combined a highly skilled workforce with a versatile technology designed for one-off items, or small batches, rather than standardised mass production. The fact that government or government-owned enterprises were major customers made it possible to envisage public sector support for product diversification. At the same time the Lucas management may have grown slack inside the cocoon of soft, cost-plus defence contracts. This may have helped to convince the workers facing impending redundancy that they could make a better job of running the organisation. The very fact that the shop stewards had succeeded in sustaining a cross-plant, multi-union Combine Committee representing 13 000 workers dispersed over seventeen sites was itself remarkable. Combine organisation is frequently stymied or wrecked by conflicts of interest (real or imagined) between shop-floor and staff; by endemic plant parochialism; by hostility from the trade union establishment; or by management's refusal to confer recognition, and their preference for keeping negotiations at a decentralised, plant-level, whilst retaining for themselves the advantage of centralised corporate coordination and control.[4]

Notwithstanding the special circumstances of the Lucas Plan, the 1970s witnessed numerous cases in which workers went beyond merely describing their grievances and set out to prescribe their own remedies by bidding for democratic control over production. At least for a period before the onset of deep recession in 1979 the type of offensive strategy we are considering here was a real option in a variety of industrial settings (see Coates, 1978).

It would be unrealistic to adhere to the assumption of the previous section that the strike is the only method of bringing pressure to bear on management. The workers may also envisage publicity campaigns and efforts to mobilise external support for their cause. Assume that the costs of pursuing either a defensive or offensive strategy can be roughly measured by the time workers expect to elapse before management concessions are forthcoming. The EE curves can now be taken to represent the anticipated return to any given campaign duration.

Little reflection is needed to see that the concession curve associated with the campaign for the workers' plan (corresponding to the E_cE_c line in our previous example) will lie well to the right of the concession curve associated with the defensive strategy (corresponding to the E_wE_w line). This need not imply that *quick* concessions can be expected along E_wE_w. As strikes in nationalised industries in the depressed economic conditions of the 1980s have shown, defensive resistance to closures and redundancies may need to be sustained over many months, and even then may yield meagre results. The point is that the returns from elaborating and promulgating a workers' plan are likely to be even more remote and uncertain.

A long chain of obstacles will have to be overcome even *before* the plan reaches any agenda of joint decision-making. The authors of the plan must first assemble the information, expertise and imagination needed to formulate their own ideas for alternative products, and must show that these ideas are technically sound and marketable. They may be able to draw on outside assistance at this stage, though the Lucas workers' appeal for help from academic institutions and from the environmental and alternative technology movements initially elicited very few hard suggestions. At the same time the supporters of the plan will have to convince their fellow workers that they are offering a worthwhile and practicable strategy for safeguarding their interests. Considerable powers of persuasion and organisational skills will be needed to transcend the cautious and defensive mentality engendered by the practice of passively reacting to the employer's initiatives rather than bidding openly to encroach on management prerogatives. Many shop-floor and office workers in their hearts legitimise the established management hierarchy. Jocular scepticism about management competence does not necessarily outweigh the belief that relative place in a hierarchy is a reward for relative merit, and that subordinate workers cannot and should not presume to take over managerial functions.

Workers' responses will also be coloured by political attitudes. 'Right wingers' will argue that it is not the responsibility of trade unions to choose new products, and will find unholy allies on the left ready to denounce a line of action which leads down the road to cooption and 'class collaboration'. The plan's advocates may also have to cope with hostility from other levels of trade union organisation. Union officials may fear that combine organisation will disrupt the established routines of industrial relations, detract from their own standing and create a rival power base within the union.

If all these problems are surmounted the next stage in the campaign will be to bring the company to concede that product development is a negotiable issue. Top management will be reluctant to recognise any combine organisation and even more reluctant to negotiate over product choice. To grant the right of workers to participate in an area of company policy of such strategic importance would be to concede the case for industrial democracy across the board and to open the way to a total reconstruction of the system of enterprise government. It might also be interpreted as an admission that management could have omitted to exploit all the potentially viable alternatives to redundancy within its sphere of competence. The loss of moral authority on both counts would be considerable. At best it would complicate the task of governing the enterprise in the future, and would corrode the prestige and self-confidence of professional managerial personnel.

Finally, even if the workers were to succeed in extending the range of joint decision-making to include product choice and job design, there can be no guarantee that their proposals will actually be adopted as company policy. Managerial resistance is unlikely to have exhausted itself in the preceding battle to bar the entrance to the negotiating chamber. Conceivably the formal right of co-decision might be conceded as a ploy to teach the upstart workers that there is infinitely more to the job of running a large and complex business than they had bargained for.[5] Alternatively the management might seek to draw off the money-spinners from the Plan and dilute its radical overtones. Moreover, even if the company's negotiating stance were entirely untainted by professional élitism or diplomatic guile, unless the managers really had been complacent or incompetent in the past, there are unlikely to be many unexploited market opportunities, given the existing level and composition of market demand.

The Lucas Plan sought to counter this last kind of difficulty by linking the bulk of its proposals to a shift in government expenditure from military hardware to socially useful civilian projects in the health, energy and transport sectors. The argument that alternative products *would be* viable under a different composition of demand, is certainly useful for propagandist and agitational purposes. But it also reveals another set of pitfalls between the conception of the Plan and its implementation. The proposed reallocation of government spending raised difficult and controversial questions of national defence and foreign policy. In the absence of extensive public support for a redefinition of military programmes and priorities, the Plan risked being smeared as 'politically motivated' subversion rather than any 'genuine' attempt to protect jobs and develop workers' participation in management. The point here is not that the existing pattern of output is somehow politically neutral; nor that concern about the ethical and political implications of product choice is an illicit, irrelevant or trivial consideration compared with the economic issue of job security. It is simply that defenders of the status quo normally possess a built-in advantage in resisting radical change. They can rely on the sheer inertial force of habit and familiarity with the existing order to give weight to the charge that the proponents of radical change are politically motivated in a way which conservatives are not. The magnitude of this political bias is thus a further factor to be reckoned with in appraising the prospects of a campaign around a workers' plan.

Now it may seem from the preceding discussion that the disparity between the return/cost ratios associated with the two types of strategy is so gross that the outcome is almost certain to correspond to cases 1 or 3 distinguished earlier. The workers would have to place an extraordinarily high non-pecuniary value on the workers' plan option to compensate for its exiguous prospects of success and yield an outcome corresponding to case 2. Yet before this conclusion is accepted two further deficiencies in the choice-theoretic model need to be pointed out.

The first is that the analysis conducted in Section 2 is a partial equilibrium exercise. It offers a microeconomic view of the workers' environment which takes the balance of political forces both within the enterprise and in the wider society outside as given. It is this balance which largely determines the relative position of the two employer concession curves. It is, however, not difficult to imagine political configurations which would cause the 'tough stance' curve, E_cE_c, to shift to the left. Top company management would become more isolated and vulnerable the greater the successes of the workers' plan campaign on each of the following four battlefronts: (1) in winning allies among the ranks of junior management; (2) in gaining the sympathy of the general public and the mass media; (3) in linking forces with other similar campaigns by workers in other firms and industries; and (4) above all in receiving the active support of the state so that pressure mobilised from below could be complemented by incentives and sanctions deployed from above.[6]

It is perfectly true that at any particular moment without prior advances on the fourth and most critical of these fronts, the room for manoeuvre on the others will be limited. Failing the election of a government which was committed to extending democracy in industry and had already completed the legal, institutional and political preparations required to make this commitment effective, there could be little hope for suddenly accelerating the progress of a grass-roots workers' plan by government intervention. In that sense the disposition of forces at any given time has to be taken as given. On the other hand, even in the very short run the dynamics of political power struggles make a difference to agents' perceptions of their possibilities. At a critical juncture events such as a Parliamentary vote, a judicial decision or a conference resolution may tip the balance one way or the other, even if the *main* lines of battle have already been predetermined. But leaving aside the immediate contingencies of political engagement, the general point remains that over a longer span of time the parameters of one- and two-dimensional power may shift and be shiftable. Rational agents who are aware of this will frame their plans accordingly even in a narrow calculus of goal selection.

It is not only strategy and movement in the political sphere that introduce fluidity into the choice-theoretic model. There is also the possibility that workers' preference patterns may alter as a result of contestation in the ideological theatre of conflict. This is the site of a slow-moving and largely unseen struggle between rival principles of social thought and organisation. Since the characteristics of this struggle are very different from the open and more volatile conflicts of the economic and political theatres, some explanation is called for.

As we have seen, underlying the economists' datum, 'tastes and preferences', are more basic values and attitudes. These are the intellectual and emotional building blocks out of which people construct their definitions of social reality. They are shaped and reshaped in the course of ideological contention. Vast armies of mostly unwitting combatants at all levels of the social formation, from palaces and boardrooms to public houses and shopping precincts, daily renew the struggle to make sense of changing social experience. Two factors are at work to conceal the significance of cultural polemics. If these factors are not borne in mind it might be assumed that the ideological arena is irrelevant to the issue of goal selection. The first is that apart from a minority of self-conscious standard bearers of social apology or criticism, most of us for most of the time are unaware of the ulterior meanings of the surface flow of comment, opinion, conversation, jest, anecdote, etc. which interpolate our social intercourse.[7] But this continual interchange of ideas is the process through which we orient ourselves towards the world around us, and seek to explain and justify our stance. And, though we may not recognise it, these engagements enlist us as partisans on one side or the other of a series of undeclared cultural wars.

The second factor is that the time scale of significant cultural change is normally long and its tempo slow. Ideological warfare is a warfare of position. The opposing trench systems and strongholds created to defend cherished values and principles are resistant to sudden incursion. And even if they are temporarily overrun by the enemy, they cannot easily be obliterated. Provided that a counter-attack is not delayed indefinitely, ground lost can always be recovered later.[8] Consequently the fronts in this theatre may give the appearance of frozen immobility for years on end.

Nevertheless the balance of cultural forces does change over time. The greater part of the transformations that occur cannot be said to correspond to any grand strategic conception: they are the resultant of various intersecting vectors of force, 'of human creation, but not of human design'. This is because of the nature of the projects in which people are engaged as they acquire and adapt their ideological dispositions. As Anderson (1980, p. 19) puts it:

> Throughout history to date the overwhelming majority of people for the overwhelmingly major part of their lives have pursued 'private' goals: (cultivation of a plot, choice of a marriage, exercise of a skill, maintenance of a home, bestowal of a name). These personal projects are inscribed within existing social relations, and typically reproduce them. . . . There have also, of course, been collective or individual projects whose goals were 'public' in character: quantitatively far fewer, involving lesser numbers in more fitful endeavours. . . . Will and action here acquire an independent historical significance as causal sequences in their own right, rather than as molecular samples of social relations. . . . However, these too in their overwhelming majority have not aimed to transform social relations as such – to create new societies or to master old ones: for the most part [their goals have been] inserted within a known structural framework, taken for granted by the actors. . . . Finally, there are those collective projects . . . [involving] . . . a conscious programme aimed at creating or remodelling whole social structures.

Anderson suggests that the very notion of this third type of self-conscious historical project scarcely predated the Enlightenment. The American and French Revolutions were the first major historical movements deliberately aiming at social reconstruction and even their premeditated programmes were limited to the politico-juridical level of society: they did not intentionally aim to recast the whole mode of collective existence.

The goals which workers pursue belong predominantly to the first two of Anderson's three types of project. But the novel and ambitious objectives of a Lucas-style workers' plan begin to approximate to the third, *transformatory* type. And it is precisely one of the aims of a transformatory project to refashion the consciousness of its agents so that they choose to pursue goals which are objectively arduous and distant, *despite* the costs and sacrifices this will entail. The authors of the project knowingly work to gain ideological ground over a long period in order to overcome the forces ranged against them. It is almost inevitable that the first steps in any 'long march' will be taken by visionary pioneers who are prepared to pit themselves against overwhelming odds. But each small subsequent advance may not only strengthen their determination to continue, but also win new adherents to the values and principles they are fighting for. Thus the situation of the majority of workers may initially resemble our cases 1 or 3. But a dedicated minority can always hope to shift hearts and minds in the direction of case 2 – not, of course, all at once, but by slow degrees. And at least sometimes such efforts succeed.

To see this, project the choice-theoretic framework backwards in historical time. It is not difficult to adapt it so as to 'explain' why objectives which now seem commonplace, but once appeared no less heroic than the goal of the workers' plan, would have been rejected on the basis of a rational comparison of returns and costs. Consider, for example, an age when trade unions organised few members, disposed of slender resources, enjoyed negligible employer recognition and operated on the margins of legality and public respectability. Imagine an individual worker in these conditions having to choose between individual and collective remedies for industrial discontents. The prospective material benefit/cost ratio of a long-term commitment to building up trade union organisation would have compared unfavourably with the various forms of individual self-help – job-market search, migration, personal thrift and sobriety, investment in marketable skills, birth control, and so on.

As in our contemporary example, it is possible to postulate certain parametric shifts in the average worker's environment which would offset the relative disadvantage of trade unionism – changes in the legal status of trade unions, movements in public opinion, government pressure on employers to award recognition, etc. But as I argued above, such exercises in comparative statics tell us nothing about the historical process through which such developments came to pass. *A fortiori* they neglect the role of workers and their organisations as active participants in that process. To this general point it can now be added that the relevant history consists of more than successive rearrangements in the balance of political forces (i.e. *political* history). It also includes mutations in working class and popular consciousness and the dialectic between opposing tendencies of social thought.[9,10,11]

If, as was suggested earlier, the model of goal selection is intended to encapsulate stylised history, then *all* its elements stand in need of explanation: both the location and trajectory of the concession curves depicting the 'objective' distribution of one- and two-dimensional power; and the position of the indifference curves which display workers' 'subjective' preferences. If these elements are simply taken as given, the model offers no more than a static taxonomy of completed historical results without reference to the historical processes underlying these results. It can *describe* two-dimensional power relations; but it cannot *explain* the interplay of forces between the agents involved which either reproduces a stable and enduring pattern of behaviour, or, alternatively, restructures their relationship into a new pattern. This neglected interplay proceeds on two levels: one consists of those actions by means of which agents may affect the balance of political forces. The other, for which the choice model has no language, consists of the systemic suppression or distortion of choice and the countervailing pressure of transformatory action.

4 The Transformatory Project

The utilitarian caculus of choice theory is inappropriate for understanding cases where labour's goals are informed by an articulate vision of an alternative political economy. As we have seen, action along the line of greater resistance will be undertaken when its goal is highly regarded for non-pecuniary reasons. Such action is intelligible only if we widen the motivational basis of analysis beyond that of immediate material interest. The degree of commitment and self-sacrifice needed to sustain a struggle for a distant, transformatory goal will be forthcoming only if workers are strongly convinced that it is both possible and desirable to reconstruct the social relations of employment.

At one historical stage 'reconstruction' might mean no more – but for the historical actors themselves no less – than the establishment of a viable and legitimate trade union movement. The immediate aim here is simply to build a counterweight against unbridled employer power. The project acquires transformatory significance to the extent that trade unionism's challenge to enterprise despotism and market anarchy is seen as the harbinger of a new collectivist system of social organisation. It was in this sense, for example, that Marx hailed the enactment of the Ten-Hour Bill as a 'victory for the political economy of the working class'. What he meant was more than that the legal limitation of the working day would, if effectively enforced, prevent gross overwork and lighten the burden of toil in factories and mines. The very fact of statutory intervention to regulate the terms of exchange between capital and labour inscribed an alien principle of social policy into the design of *laissez-faire* capitalism.

At a later stage the reconstruction envisaged by the Lucas Plan meant assuming the outlook and capacity needed to exercise managerial responsibilities and control. Again the immediate purpose was to protect workers' interests as wage earners. But the project was clearly also intended to prefigure an economic system based on democratic self-management and suffused by a caring attitude towards the natural and human consequences of social production.

Now workers may perceive such alternative futures with greater or lesser clarity; and their hopes and expectations may turn out to be more or less well founded in the light of subsequent events. There is nearly always scope for disagreement in assessing whether any given collective human endeavour is 'realistic' or 'Utopian'. In general it is easy to criticise the sentiment expressed by Robert Browning's lines: 'Ah, that a man's reach should exceed his grasp/Or what's a heaven for?' Robinson and Mayhew's (1983, p. 12) comment that 'these lines . . . are hardly the basis for practical policy-making' is well taken. But there is another side to the matter. That people's dreams should outrun the realistic chances of achieving them may well be a necessary psychological condition for conceiving and embarking on any substantial enterprise.[12] Without some admixture of Utopianism many human projects would remain stillborn. Aspiring social innovators may need to aim at heaven even if they intend to retain close contact with the earth. In any case, what concerns us here is not the conditions in which a transformatory project may succeed or fail, but the nature of the project as such.

This question can best be approached by analysing what exactly has happened when a formerly subaltern group declares itself to be enslaved, oppressed or degraded by existing social conditions, and proposes some new model of social organisation. Clearly such a group has ceased to be mutely submissive. But more than this:

it has also advanced beyond a state of direct, spontaneous and unreflective rebellion. Indeed, it is characteristic of a subordinate class or group mentality to alternate between submission and rebellion. This pattern is exemplified by the history of peasant uprisings in the Middle Ages. The selfsame serfs who at one time were capable of erupting into violent unrest would later revert to a 'normal' state of servile docility. Now if we accept the premise that no ruling or exploiting class can *permanently* hold down a discontented populace by sheer force of arms and terror, whatever short-term subjugation can be achieved by a policy of repression, such cyclical behaviour can only be explained on the supposition that peasant revolts did not in fact aim to recast the feudal order. Rather the rebels fundamentally accepted and approved the principles binding state, church, land and labour in a hierarchical, organic society. Their discontent was directed *within* not *against* this system. Typically their grievances stemmed from some failure by one or the other section of their social superiors to abide by the terms of the unwritten social contract governing the mutual rights and obligations of the respective feudal classes. Their demands sought to recall errant princes, nobles or clergy to their true and rightful duties.

In our own day a great deal of trade union militancy, particularly with regard to wage issues, displays a similar syndrome. It expresses not the strivings of an ascendant class for social regeneration, but the demands of a truculent, but none the less subordinate, stratum for a portion of capitalism's bounty. More often than not, militant wage bargaining simply internalises prevailing notions of what are to count as 'goods', what values and standards are worthy of aspiration. Admittedly *collective* wage determination represents an advance in social control by comparison with a purely atomistic labour market. But as long as collective bargaining continues to be conducted on a decentralised and uncoordinated basis, it remains trapped within the amoralism and anarchy of market allocation. As a *method* of settling wages it is perfectly consonant with the essential principle of a free market system: that all agents are free, and properly so, to use whatever resources, luck and muscle they possess to press their claims for a share in the spoils of affluence.

A group embarked on a transformatory enterprise has broken out of this circle. It has begun to detach itself from the social bases of obedience and to resist the systemic influence of social power. Implicitly at least, the group's members have recognised that no new society can ever emerge simply out of the negative energy contained within the contradictions of the old; social transitions need also a positive pole of attraction. This higher order goal rises above immediate material concerns. It motivates its followers to act on the basis of some long-term conception of their interests, even if this may go against their immediate, sectional interests. The transformatory project takes the world not just as it is, but as it ought to be, and as it can be made to become through correctly judged action. In short, it is a project informed by an active, ethical ideal.

The word 'active' in this context signifies two things. First, it marks a contrast with a purely contemplative stance. The ideal which guides the project commits its adherents to work actively for its realisation. Its spirit is that of James Connolly's dictum: 'The only true prophets are those who carve out the future they announce'. Second, the word 'active' is intended to convey the sense in which a strong, ethical ideal vitalises and uplifts those who espouse it. Commitment to an ethical strategy engages both the reasoning and the feeling faculties of the mind. This is apt to provoke suspicion among non-partisans. Unduly animated minds can easily become fanatical. But in so far as labels such as 'fanatical' or 'extremist' are more than mere terms of derogation and abuse, they imply some imbalance between intellect and passion – the domination of heart over head, or vice versa. Now it is undoubtedly true that idealists sometimes allow the canons of logic and scientific integrity to be overruled by the promptings of sentiment. (Moral insensibility and cold detachment from the subjective, inner world of sentience indicate equal distortions in the opposite direction, whether practised by scientific researchers, military strategists or desperate terrorists.) But the *risk* of falling into these pathological deviations by no means implies that those who feel passionate about the objects of their thought are *ipso facto* deranged. According to Aristotle *every* voluntary action is the conclusion of a practical syllogism whose major premise expresses some morally evaluative proposition (see MacIntyre, 1967, ch. 7). What distinguishes transformatory action is that this premise is explicit and active in the agent's mind. Habitual, unreflective or narrowly instrumental actions, take for granted their environment and ask no questions about ulterior goals: their moral antecendents lie dormant. It is this inert, inattentive or uncritical state of mind which lowers the individual's resistance to infection by the influence of systemic power.

There are therefore no grounds for regarding transformatory action as irrational. It clearly belongs to the general category of social action which Poole (1984, ch. 8), following Weber (1968), labels 'value-rational (*Wertrational*). This he defines as action 'determined by a conscious belief in the value for its own sake of some ethical, aesthetic, religious or other form of behaviour independently of its prospects of success'. The other three categories he distinguishes are: '*instrumental-rational*' (*Zweck-rational*), referring to the calculated use of means to utilitarian ends which serve material interests; '*affectual*' behaviour, determined by the actor's affective intentions and emotional states; and '*traditional*' behaviour, determined by ingrained habituation.

Not all value-rational action carries transformatory significance. Consider a government which seeks to preserve the status quo by an incorporationist strategy aimed at promoting harmony and avoiding crisis in the national industrial relations system. Its programme might stem not from any concern with system performance, but from a belief in the organic unity of all social classes and groups in the higher reality of 'the nation'. On the other hand, transformatory action does have special significance as a form of value-rationality. The hallmarks of human rationality are ingenuity, inventiveness, clear-sightedness, imaginative empathy, and a respect for justice. These capacities – capable of only limited development in each individual – have almost unlimited possibilities of growth in the species as a whole. It is through the intermittent, but recurring exertion of these capacities that the species has in the course of its evolution managed to loosen the material and cultural constraints on individual and social action. When people become aware of the ways in which social roles and relationships contract the realm of human possibility and deform social values, and when they deliberately set out to transcend these conditions, they align themselves with this larger theme of human history. They reaffirm the indispensability of autonomy, creativity and control in overcoming the crises, agonies and injustices of human existence.

A further characteristic of transformatory social practice is its broadly, inclusive, comprehensive scope. In the process of throwing off old habits of thought and synthesising a new conception of social organisation, formerly oppressed groups begin to discover hitherto unsuspected connections between the diverse facets of their collective experience. This in turn generates new ways of handling that experience, leading to fresh insights and opportunities for action. For example, the second wave of the feminist movement which emerged in North America and Europe in the second half of the 1960s went much further than its fore-sisters in the first two decades of this century in constructing a transformatory ideology and practice. Contemporary feminism strives not so much for the ending of male privilege and the admission of women into society as it has been made by men; but more for the reconstruction of social relations around distinctively feminine values and attributes. Feminists approach social analysis and policy from a standpoint which is caring, compassionate, nurturing, cooperative, non-hierarchical, non-violent, pragmatic and life respecting.

Thus the authors of a transformatory project adopt a holistic view of social maladies and a correspondingly system-based, as opposed to piecemeal, remedial programme. Holistic outlooks and programmes are necessarily multiplex and cannot be reduced to any single aspect of social organisation. Of course, the tactical exigencies of politics often compel radical movements to assign overriding priority to certain partial, proximate objectives. If this scaling down process is misunderstood, or misrepresented, the movement may lose its way and become conservative and ossified.[13] But, in principle, social transformation aims at systemic alternatives to existing patterns of social organisation, consisting of interrelated and mutually reinforcing elements. It is no accident that radical movements typically describe the future they aspire to as 'a new order'.

These features of the transformatory project have an important analytical implication: ethically-derived composite goals cannot sensibly be reduced to any unitary and representative value – least of all the kind of one-dimensional, monetary measure which, as we have seen, is used to compare alternatives in the choice-theoretic model of goal selection. Thus, to revert to our earlier examples, the pioneers of trade unionism may, as a matter of fact, have believed that workers' material living standards would be better served with trade union organisation than without it. But, as the banners, symbols and language of the trade union movement testify, this was scarcely the whole of what they were fighting for; and they would almost certainly have persisted in their efforts even if they had had reason to doubt this belief. There could, for example, be a trade-off between the starting *level* of real wages and their future rate of growth. If so, a non-unionised labour force which was forced to acquiesce in an initial combination of low wages, high profits and a rapid rate of capital accumulation, would eventually enjoy a permanently higher wage level than a unionised labour force which used its strength to shift the initial distribution of income in favour of wages. But only on a very crude view of class interest would it follow that trade unions actually damaged workers' interests.

The fundamental objectives behind the formation of trade unions were normative and complex in character. They are probably best summarised by Flanders (1970, pp. 38–47) as the creation of a social order in industry. The rules of this order were to be framed through procedures in which workers participated through union representation; and they were to embody a code of industrial rights protecting not only workers' material living standards, but also their security, status and dignity. Similarly with the Lucas Plan: the immediate occasion for the development of the Plan was the imminent threat of redundancies; but the vision which inspired the workers' response went well beyond any purely instrumental purpose: it envisaged a new industrial constitution founded on democracy, ecological balance and social responsibility.

Thus a transformatory project offers an explicit answer to labour's existential problem: it is a self-conscious attempt to integrate workers' divergent interests into a unified conception of an alternative mode of collective life. The substantive content of this conception is of necessity historically and culturally relative. As our illustrations have shown, advances which represent the highest aspirations of one generation may become absorbed into the normal functioning of economy and society. They may well come to seem tame and commonplace to later generations. But if the substantive answers it receives are historically mutable, *the form* of labour's existential problem is abiding. If the problem is not resolved by an autonomous effort of strategic integration, it will, by default, become resolved in a heteronomous and piecemeal way. Unless each generation renews the struggle to devise its own transformatory project, there will be a strong tendency for workers' conception of their interests to be shaped by systemic pressures and to reproduce the prevailing pattern of social relations.

Notes to Chapter 6

1. Crouch's model is a good illustration of the point made in Chapter 1 that rational choice theory is not inherently tied to neo-classical economics: it can be retained as a central explanatory principle alongside a more realistic account of the inequalities within the labour market.
2. Cf. Jaroslav Hašek's famous folk-hero in *The Good Soldier Schweik* (Hašek, 1942).
3. The history of the Lucas Plan is recounted in Wainwright and Elliott (1982).
4. See John Purcell and Keith Sisson, 'Strategies and Practice in the Management of Industrial Relations', in Bain (1983) for an analysis of the factors determining management's choice of bargaining level. Plant bargaining effectively denies trade union organisation any role in determining broad company policy, and leaves corporate management free to develop policy without any need to *justify* decisions to trade unions, let alone bargain over them.
5. Watt (1973, p. 229) relates how in the heady revolutionary atmosphere in Germany during the days immediately prior to the Armistice which ended the First World War, the self-styled 'Executive Committee of the Supreme Headquarters Soldiers' Council' presented themselves at the headquarters of the German army's Supreme Command. The soldiers' delegates demanded a voice in the command of the army during its retreat, including the right to countersign orders and to ensure that the army in the field was not used for any counter-revolutionary purpose. They were courteously received by a certain Lieutenant-Colonel Wilhelm von Faupel, who assured them that the officer corps was not opposed to the government, and showed them into the Supreme Command's map room. 'Everything was laid out on a gigantic map which occupied one wall: the huge complex of roads, railway lines, bridges, switching points, pipelines, command posts and supply dumps – the whole an intricate lace of red, green, blue and black lines converging into narrow bottlenecks at the crucial Rhine bridges. Faupel pointed to and discussed the details of the map with calculated and easy familiarity. The seven soldiers were stupefied; they had never dreamed of such complexity. Faupel then turned to them. The Supreme Command had no objection to the soldiers' councils, he said, but did his hearers feel competent to direct

the general evacuation of the German Army along these lines of communication? . . . The disconcerted soldiers stared uneasily at the immense map. One of them allowed that this was not what they had really had in mind – 'This work can well be left to the officers'.

6. This is the concept underlying the vision of planning agreements which has figured prominently in most versions of the 'Alternative Economic Strategy' advocated by the British left since the mid-1970s. A *system* of planning agreements would involve permanent institutional arrangements whereby representatives of all the various stakeholders in the decisions of large companies – shareholders, professional management, employees, customers, suppliers and central and local government – would be brought together to negotiate over the major aspects of corporate policy, their decisions in turn being coordinated by parallel representative bodies at industrial, regional and national levels.

7. It has been above all the modern feminist movement which has sought to raise popular sensitivity to the significance of everyday words, deeds and gestures under the slogan 'the personal is political'. Hitherto this work of revelation has largely been the province of a few social commentators and novelists.

8. For a detailed illustration of this phenomenon on the intellectual front see Smith (1979). Smith dissects the 'Great Debate' of the inter-war years on planning and democracy, and follows up its practical political sequel in the rise and fall of the post-war collectivist consensus. The case developed by the anti-planners, spearheaded by von Mises and Hayek, in each of the disicplines of economic theory, political philosophy and political science, was that freedom and planning were irreconcilable. As a practical matter the case was lost: the post-war liberal democracies were dominated by a statist version of the collectivist paradigm. And, as Smith shows, virtually all the planning imitiatives undertaken by successive British governments in the 1960s and 1970s had originally been outlined by the pro-planning camp in the 'Great Debate'. Yet during the 1970s the anti-planning, neo-liberal paradigm regained its vitality, and by the end of the decade was clearly in the ascendant.

9. The argument of this paragraph should not be taken to imply that trade unions represented a novel cultural force in the nineteenth century. It was possessive individualism that was revolutionising social mores. Trade union organisation and consciousness can be viewed as a *re-active retrieval* of traditions going back to the craft guilds of the medieval towns.

10. For an overview of British politics since the Industrial Revolution in terms of the dialectic between the collectivist ethic of fraternity, social justice and public welfare and the individualist ideals of personal liberty, the rule of law and the limited state, see Greenleaf (1975).

11. For a study of British trade union history which stresses the long-term influence of divergent national cultures on trade union development, see Currie (1979). Currie argues that the conflict between social

collectivism and what he sees as the dominant values of British society – individualism materialism and utilitarianism – has not so much ranged the trade union and labour movement against the rest of society, as divided the movement against itself. The movement has taken up a social collectivist stance towards the control of the economy only to retreat from the logic of this stance as soon as it is seen to require any considerable sacrifice of immediate material interest and sectional autonomy.

12. 'Goal attainment scaling' is a well known technique used in psychotherapy. Clients are invited to imagine what their lives would be like and how they would feel if they had managed to overcome completely whatever problems afflict them, and conversely, what their situation would be if their problems got significantly worse. They are then asked to use their 'utopian' and 'dystopian' visions to locate intermediate situations, including their current state, along a scale of goals in order of feasibility. This is an interesting example of the way in which the achievement of a small improvement depends on imagining a total change.

13. For a discussion of this phenomenon in Marxist political practice see David Fernbach, 'Eurocommunism and the Ethical Ideal', in Prior (ed.) (1981).

collectivism, and what he sees as the 'continual' rivalry in British society – individualism abundant and 'altruistic' – has not only most ranged the modernized and labour power it against the rest of society, it divided the working class against itself. The movement has rallied up a socialistic (to its standpoint itself). The discovery of the power of being harness that the light of this stance is such as it welcome to regard any circumstances in the conditions than material interest and workers' enjoyment.

That statement without is a well-known technique used to combine the up ... Consumers intend to imagine why their first would realize and he will even said that it was interchanged between the employers, whether or professionalist theory, and otherwise with their situation realities that it employees will might only worse. They are then asked to receive these lines that ... said to happen within enthusiastic enterprise ... reckoning their current state at special scope of class in order of recruiting, this is an interesting culture of the way in which the adjustment of a small narrow circle, is provided a sweeping central limit.

(for a discussion of this phenomenon that is to political transformation, Harold Perkin, The Commercialization and the Cultural Conflict in the Perkin (1969).)

Part Two
The Future of the Labour Market

7
Capitalism, Gender and Toil

1 Introduction

The second part of this book consists of an extended application of the conceptual framework developed in Part One. Its underlying theme is the qualitative difference analysed in Chapter 6 between projects which are contained within the prevailing relations of social reproduction, and projects which set out to transform them. The focus is the activity of work – the overall amount of time which society devotes to various kinds of work, whether paid or unpaid; the distribution of this total between different sections of society, and especially between men and women; the alternative patterns of social life, along with the distribution of power and advantage associated with different social divisions of labour; and the subjective meaning and value attached to work by those who do it.

This chapter begins by noting that there are, in principle, two alternative ways of enjoying the fruits of the prodigious growth in labour productivity engendered by capitalism: one is to expand output and consumption; the other is to reduce the amount of human toil. Section 2 shows that the capitalist mode of production itself contains a built-in bias against the option of toil-reduction. Section 3 reviews the recent experience of the advanced capitalist countries, and concludes that there is no evidence that this structural bias is diminishing despite the recent growth of interest in 'reduced working time'.

In theory it would be possible for the workers' movement to resist capitalism's aversion to toil-reduction. Section 4 argues that this possibility is foreclosed by the gender system and the mutual relations between men, women and work. It follows that any serious countervailing pressure demands a perspective which sets its long-term sights on the abolition of gender division, and aims in the meantime to reset the gearing between waged work and domestic labour.

Detailed investigation of a transformatory approach to work is carried out in Chapters 9, 10 and 11. To prepare the way Section 5 of this chapter analyses the component parts of working time; distinguishes between work and toil; and briefly touches on some of the factors which determine how far human beings experience their work as toil.

2   Capitalism and Working Time

It is convenient to take as our starting point what Cohen (1978, ch. XI) calls 'a distinctive contradiction of advanced capitalism'. Cohen's argument is as follows: it is undeniable that the tendency of capitalist competition is to promote the growth of productivity. If enterprises are to survive and prosper in the multi-dimensional competition for sales, finance, materials, skills, etc., which characterises a capitalist economy in all its stages of development, they are compelled to raise the productivity of industrial and commercial processes. This ubiquitous pressure on enterprises to revolutionise their techniques of production may be reinforced by certain more specific factors. Thus the downward rigidity of real wages during periods when a slump in output depresses the rate of profit, is likely to induce capitalists to search out more creative and less disruptive ways of reducing production costs than forcing their workers to accept wage cuts. Moreover, whether productivity growth takes a labour- or capital-saving form, the result is to raise the ratio between the volume of output and the extent of labour input.

Now, in principle, from society's point of view, increased productivity is open to two uses. It may be devoted to reducing toil and extending leisure. (The meaning of 'toil' and 'leisure' will be considered in Section 5.) Alternatively, output may be increased whilst the input of labour time remains the same.

Cohen contends that the very same competitive imperatives which continually enhance productivity, also engender a structural bias in favour of the output – expansion option as against the reduction of toil. When firms become more efficient they do not take the opportunity which is theoretically available to reduce working time; or, more generally, to relieve their employees of burdensome toil, whilst producing the same output as before. Instead they produce more output – for the same product markets if sales there are expansible; or, if these markets have become saturated, they open up new lines of production. Firms select the output-increasing option because, in general, only by producing and selling more output can they expand the exchange value at their disposal. And this in turn they must do – at least on average and over the long run – if they are to match and, if possible, surpass the competitive challenge of their rivals.

Of course, at the aggregate level the point of effective demand sets a short-term limit to the profitable expansion of output.[1] During slumps, when firms' expectations concerning the monetary demand for output are depressed, capitalism's tendency to expand output will not be realised. But slumps are capitalism's internal mechanism for clearing away obstacles to renewed accumulation. Over the long run capitalism is an inherently expansive system. Nor do output recessions normally provide greater relief from toil for the labour force as a whole. When firms are under pressure to restore profitability, the drive to raise productivity through a radical reorganisation of production is at its most intense. Yet there is no similar pressure to reduce average hours of work for workers who remain in employment. The characteristic concomitant of an output recession is not an across-the-board cut in working time and an egalitarian share-out of the reduced hours of employment on offer. Rather the majority of the labour force continues in 'full time' employment. The burden of adjustment is loaded on to those workers who are thrown into the enforced idleness of unemployment.

Output expansion does not *necessarily* require or induce rising levels of consumption per head. Demographic trends, income distribution, savings propensities, taxation and various other factors intervene to loosen the ties between the growth of output and the growth of personal consumption. Nevertheless it is reasonable to suppose that an economy geared to a boundless expansion of output will also be geared to a boundless expansion of individual consumption.

Now, in general, people benefit both from increased consumption and from reduced toil. It can be presumed that from a starting point of material scarcity the social benefit of capitalism's output – expanding bias continued for a long period of time to outweigh the cost incurred in toil. Cohen's argument is that for some value of 'high' and some value of 'substantial', the benefit/cost balance of these alternative uses of productivity growth reverses itself when consumption becomes 'high' and toil remains 'substantial'. Unfortunately, when this crossover point is reached (and Cohen suggests that it *has* now been reached, at least in the USA), it becomes impossible to adjust capitalism's distinctive priorities. Like the Sorcerer's Apprentice, the system lacks any means of countermanding the formula of its initial success. As Cohen puts it:

> The productive technology of advanced capitalism begets an unparalleled opportunity for lifting the curse of Adam and liberating men [*sic*] from toil; but the productive relations of capitalist economic organisation prevent the opportunity from being seized. The economic form most able to relieve toil is least disposed to do so. (Cohen (1978), p. 306)

This inherent bias towards output and consumption expansion meets a certain cultural and political resistance. But the Green movement's efforts to protect the environment, slow down the exhaustion of finite natural resources and restructure patterns of employment and work, are relatively weak brakes on the galloping consumption of the dominant culture.

Cohen's argument is cogent and is certainly consistent with broad trends over the past century. This period has witnessed both a rise in real wages and a decline in total hours worked per employee per year. But the disparity between the relative magnitudes of these changes is striking. Maddison (1977), surveying the performance of sixteen advanced capitalist countries from 1870 to 1976, estimates that their total output multiplied by a factor of 19 and output per head of population by a factor of 6. Even in Britain, the sluggard of the group, the coefficients of multiplication were 7 and 4 respectively. Average real wages in Britain are now between four and five times as high as in the mid-1870s (see Phelps-Brown and Browne (1968), p. 344).

Maddison suggests that this historically unprecedented growth[2] was accompanied by a decline in average hours of work per year from 3200 to 1800 or 44 per cent. This figure is almost certainly an overestimate. Allowing for two weeks' holiday per year, and assuming no interruption of work through unemployment and sickness, average weekly working hours would have had to be 64 to clock up an annual total as high as 3200 in 1870. The Department of Employment and productivity (1971, Tables 1–5) records that in those selected industries and occupations for which the available data are comparable, normal weekly hours of work varied between 55 and 60 in 1870. There are no data on overtime working at this date. But subsequent experience suggests that an inordinately large fraction of the labour force would have to have worked an exceptional additional proportion of overtime to bring the annual total up to 3200. At the same time Maddison's estimate of contemporary annual hours of work is probably too low. Townsend's monumental national survey of household resources and standards of living carried out in 1968–9 yields a weighted average of 2050 hours worked by employed men in the previous 12 months (Townsend (1979), Table A39, p. 1024). (The corresponding figure for women employees was 1580.) This estimate applies to both manual and non-manual workers combined, and does take account of absence from work because of sickness, unemployment or other reasons.

The uncertainties in these estimates preclude anything stronger than order of magnitude calculations. But it seems safe to conclude that annual working hours over the century after 1870 declined by between 30 and 40 per cent. Moreover, it is arguable that this comparatively modest fall did little more than eliminate the overwork imposed during the forced march of the Industrial Revolution. Wilensky (1961) shows that total hours worked per year, though much lower in 1950 than in 1800, had merely recovered towards the levels experienced by medieval peasants, many of whose days were made idle by the weather and by observance of the Christian calendar.

3   'Part-time' Work and Reduced Working Time

Nothing that has happened since the onset of a low-growth, high-unemployment phase of capitalist development in the mid-1970s provides any reason to modify this conclusion. Two phenomena in particular deserve attention since they might be thought to signify the beginnings of a shift in capitalism's system dynamics. One is the recent expansion in 'part-time' employment, predominantly among women workers, and especially among married women. The other is the increased salience of 'reduced working time' in public debate about unemployment policy.

Part-time employment, as I argue later, certainly meshes with the gendered 'needs' of women. But its increased incidence does not reflect any *economic* realignment in favour of the objective of toil reduction, though it could form the basis for a new *cultural* disposition towards working time. The creation or extension of part-time work is one of a number of ways in which employers, struggling to improve profitability in a hard market environment, have sought to offset or circumvent the power of organised labour. Other methods include the growth of subcontracting to small non-union firms which enjoy wage flexibility and are exempt from, or able to disregard, protective labour legislation; the use, particularly in the construction industry, of 'labour only' subcontracting; the reintroduction of 'outwork' undertaken by individuals and family groups in their own homes; and increased reliance on the hiring of temporary staff.

What all these cases have in common is that the workers involved lack effective organisation. Indeed, as Goldthorpe (1984) argues, because their commitment to work and their expectations from it tend to be strictly limited, they may also lack any strong motivation towards or interest in trade unionism.[3] Hence both their forms of employment and their location within the wider social structure tend to inhibit any challenge to managerial prerogatives. The use of non-standard forms of production and employment enables employers to increase the degree to which labour is commodified. The wages, conditions, work tasks, job security, etc. of non-standard workers are exposed to the direct and unmediated effects of market forces and managerial authority. They lack the protection afforded by statutory rights, work rules embodied in collective agreements, custom and practice, or simply the capacity for organised action.

The broader, societal consequences of these developments are unlikely to dignify the status of 'part-time' work or stimulate any revision of the view that it is an inferior form of employment. The expanded flexible and commodified zone of the labour market surrounds a reduced, but still vigorous, 'core' of more rigidly structured and privileged employment. This combination closely resembles the traditional Japanese pattern: a fluctuating periphery of satellite employment provides a buffer which enables major firms to offer 'core' workers 'lifelong' jobs, meritocratic career progression and a modicum of group-participation in workplace decision-making. Goldthorpe (1984) speculates that, if unchecked, the tendency towards the 'Japanisation' of Western economies will fragment and depoliticise the working class. 'Core' workers, enjoying high wages, advanced working conditions and relative job security, are likely to lack either the will or the means to apply their collective strength for any purpose other than the defence of their own sectional interests. They have increasingly little in common with the underclass of workers in the unorganised 'periphery'; they may, indeed, come to regard the growth in the size of this class as a threat to their own privilege.

Within the organised sector of employment 'reduced working time' has reappeared on public platforms and bargaining agendas since the end of the long post-war boom and the passing of the full employment era. In principle reduced working time could take any of the following forms: (1) reductions in standard weekly hours; (2) reductions in the incidence of overtime; (3) longer holidays (and therefore, other things remaining the same, fewer annual working hours); (4) earlier retirement or delayed labour force entry; (5) the introduction or extension of sabbatical leave; and (6) job-sharing, or the institution of 'part-time' employment as a permanent career with no loss of rights relative to 'full-time' employees. Both employers and unions have evolved characteristic policies towards reduced working time. An analysis of their respective positions points to a definite ordering of these six issues in terms of eligibility for joint negotiation and decision.

Employers and their organisations tend to be suspicious of

any proposal for reduced working time unless offset by reductions in pay or improvements in productivity (see CBI, 1981). They are particularly hostile to the shorter working week. Their main objections are that this would raise unit costs by increasing hourly rates of pay; and would impair international competitiveness unless uniformly introduced and effectively policed in all the major capitalist states simultaneously. Curbs on systematic overtime tend to be acceptable to employers only in the context of comprehensive productivity agreements linking increases in basic hourly rates of pay with changes in working practices and staffing levels. Skill shortages and the practical difficulties of recomposing work tasks into 'half-time' jobs are regarded as major obstacles to any widespread introduction of job-splitting, though employers are not opposed to such schemes in principle. However, since neither job-sharing nor sabbatical leave has attracted much interest from trade unions, employers have rarely been called upon to define operational policies on these issues.[4]

Longer holidays have received qualified support from employers. Indeed there is a marked contrast between the larger number of firms agreeing to extra holidays, even when this demand is not strongly pressed by trade unions, and the much smaller number consenting to reduce the normal working week (White, 1980). Additional holidays with pay add to overall labour costs, but have the advantage over uncompensated cuts in the working week that they do not raise hourly rates of pay. Moreover staggered holiday arrangements, which have long been replacing the traditional local shut down, hold out the possibility of offsetting higher labour costs through rescheduling work rotas and duties. Given these attractions longer holidays may be offered as a sweetener to soften the impact of the employers' rejection of anything more than gestural cuts in weekly hours.

Finally, earlier retirement and reduced hiring rates to permit labour force contraction *via* natural wastage, are almost invariably the first and least contentious options to be considered by negotiators when market conditions dictate a policy of labour shedding. If, after the easy options have been used up, redundancies prove unavoidable, age may consciously or unconsciously be used as a crude index of productive value to decide which workers are to lose their jobs. The use of age as a selection criterion is also likely to affect redundant workers' chances of subsequent re-employment. Moreover, as argued below, these considerations tend to be reinforced by the attitudes of workers and trade unions to labour displacement and job scarcity. The combined effect of these factors is to promote that form of reduced working time which squeezes both the youngest and oldest workers out of employment.

Trade union interest in reduced working time has grown over the past decade (see European Trade Union Institute, 1980; TUC, 1980–1983; Hughes, 1980). In Britain the TUC has been committed to the target of the 35-hour week since 1972. Progress towards this target has, however, been slow and painful. The period 1979–83 witnessed a flurry of agreements on reduced working hours involving over 9 million employees. The majority of these agreements covered manual workers and provided for the shortening of the working week by one hour to 39 hours, though some groups managed to reach 38 or 37 hours. After 1983 the movement towards reduced working time lost momentum; both wage earners and employers became increasingly averse to any further cuts in weekly hours.

The most celebrated and sustained attempt to obtain the 35-hour target occurred in West Germany. Following a call to action by the 1982 Congress of the German Trade Union Confederation (DGB), in the 1983–4 bargaining round the engineering and metal workers' union, I. G. Metall, supported by the SPD, launched a campaign for the 35-hour week with full pay. The employers responded to the initiation of strike action in May 1984 with a lock-out. The strike lasted 7 weeks and at its peak directly involved 190 000 workers with a further 260 000 indirectly involved. After conciliation the union settled for a reduction of the normal working week to 38.5 hours from 1 April 1985 with no loss of earnings and with approved ceilings on the amount of permissible overtime. This experience suggests that employer resistance combined with the insistence of workers and unions on the maintenance of weekly earnings severely limit the scope for progress towards the shorter working week.

Trade unions (as distinct from their members) have traditionally been opposed to systematic overtime both as a device which depresses basic hourly rates of pay and as an affront to worker solidarity in periods of high unemployment. Nevertheless it is still the case that approximately half of all male full-time workers regularly or periodically work overtime, with average overtime for these men amounting to about 10 hours a week. It is also likely that the slight diminution in overtime work in the early 1980s owed more to the effects of recession than to union policy.

The lack of union interest in job sharing and sabbatical leave has already been noted. Given the configuration of the unions' inclinations and opportunities, it is hardly surprising that the main forms of reduced working time to have been realised in practice are longer holidays and earlier retirement/delayed labour force entry. Additional holidays offer some male workers more amenable prospects of moonlighting than cuts in weekly hours. And even if holidays are devoted to leisure pursuits, these are not generally activities which pose awkward questions about the allocation of roles, responsibilities and time within the family. Domestic conventions and preferences also skew employment opportunities in a context of job scarcity. The male role as primary breadwinner establishes a presumption that prime age male workers have the strongest claims over a shrinking supply of jobs in view of their financial responsibilities towards dependants. Hence the priorities of employers, workers and their organisations converge to compress the age distribution of employees from both sides.

On balance then the characteristic bias of capitalism has emerged unscathed from the labour market upheavals of the past decade. In terms of the analysis of Chapter 6 this structural bias means that workers enjoy unequal access to the goal of toil reduction compared with the goal of higher wages and consumption. Wage bargaining may provoke conflicts and trials of strength between workers and their employers; but, in a capitalist economy, employers can be more easily persuaded to make concessions on pay than on reducing hours of work or redesigning jobs so as to lighten the burden of toil.

Now, as we saw in Chapter 6, the mere fact of unequal access to different goals does not in itself exclude the possibility that workers could nevertheless decide to press for toil-reducing demands. But the cultural formation of workers and the distribution of power within the working class, particularly between men and women, prevents this possibility from materialising. This is not just a matter of high-pressure advertising and the prevalence of consumerist images in the media. The whole social organisation of employment, consumption and domestic life disposes workers towards conceptions of their interests which cut with, rather than against the grain of the structural bias. The key feature of this pattern of social life is that it is structured by the gender system. This argument is developed in the next section.

4 Gender and the Sexual Division of Labour

In order to appreciate the role of gender division in forestalling any serious movement to countervail capitalism's tilted priorities, a brief digression is required concerning the distinction between gender and sex. Human beings are sexually differentiated by their biological constitution. This is one of the material properties of human society (see Cohen, 1978, ch. 4). In our own world, apart from a minority of sexually indeterminate persons, human individuals are either permanently male or permanently female. It is not excluded that some distant future generation may apply the techniques of genetic engineering to the biological material of the species in order to phase out the sexual distinction altogether. One science fiction writer has imagined a world in which recognisably human beings have evolved a hermaphrodite nature: each individual is equally capable of assuming either a male or female role in love-making and procreation (see Le Guin, 1981). This extension of the sway of culture over nature would be no more than a continuation of developments such as extra-uterine gestation which are already well within the horizon of possibility. But, however we may eventually decide to control our biological destiny, sexual differentiation belongs very definitely to the *natural* base of human society.

Gender, on the other hand, refers to a *cultural* division. It is a division which follows the line of sexual demarcation; but it is not determined by the mere fact of sexual demarcation. Gender differentiation involves the development of male and female individuals into distinct masculine and feminine personalities, and their assignment to different functions and positions in society. The emergence of gender division was a product of historical, not of natural evolution. It seems probable that the female role in procreation together with the greater average physical size and musculature of the male sex, laid down a predisposition towards a certain line of cultural adaptation. The primitive sexual division of labour within the hunter-gatherer band was functional to survival in an environment which human beings had not yet learned to manipulate. But it was precisely as our species enlarged and diversified a distinctive sphere of human culture, based on its success in pushing back the constraints of nature, that a gender *system* came into being. This system places women in a subordinate position to men – not because of men's arbitrary action, but as a structural element in an overall pattern of social organisation.[5]

The gender system of domination/subordination permeates society. In the contemporary labour market it manifests itself in an ensemble of institutions, practices and beliefs which systematically disadvantage women both in employment and in the home. First, despite the twentieth-century revolution in women's labour force 'activity rates', women's participation in paid employment remains restricted compared with men's. The counterpart of their unequal presence within the public world of waged labour, is the unequal division of private, domestic labour between men and women. Second, women employees are largely, though not exclusively segregated into a narrow range of industries and occupations. Third, and partly as a consequence of occupational apartheid, women's average earnings are significantly lower than those of men. Fourth, women are less willing than men to seek, and less able to gain access to jobs at the higher levels of skill, grading and seniority through training, education, mobility and promotion.

One particular aspect of women's inferior power, status and rewards in the labour market is especially germane to the argument of this chapter: this is the conventional definition of a 'proper' job and the lifestyle of a 'real' worker. Anna Coote and Bea Campbell (1982, p. 64) provide the following description:

> A 'proper' job begins after school and continues without a break until retirement age. It lasts for at least eight hours a day; it might spill over into evenings and weekends; and its most demanding phase tends to be the first twenty years, as training is acquired and vital steps are taken towards a higher

earning capacity. This coincides with the period when children are young and most in need of parental time. However, a 'real' worker does not have distracting family commitments, and is available for overtime and night work if necessary. A 'real' worker is able to move from one part of the country to another if that is what the employer requires

Clearly, this model of 'full-time' waged work entails absenteeism from domestic responsibilities. 'Real' workers must be supported by others who do their domestic work for them. The labour of mature women has long since ceased to be *exclusively* devoted to reproduction, childcare, housework and the servicing of geriatric relatives. But the model of the 'proper' job implies that most women do not qualify as 'real' workers. They cannot (and may not wish to) qualify since the gender system assigns to them the major responsibility for home-based, caring work. Domestic labour has a prior claim on their time and energy: outside commitments, including paid employment, take second place. This is reflected in the 'secondary' characteristics of large numbers of 'women's' jobs: they are casual, peripheral and lack any established career and training structure. It is uneconomic for employers to hire, train and promote young women in 'real' jobs if they are expected to interrupt their employment when their children are young.

When women re-enter employment after the most time-consuming and exacting phase of procreation and childcare is over, they remain handicapped in the job market. A woman's work is never done: domestic responsibilities linger on. School timetables, childhood illnesses and the demands of other members of the family for a variety of services ranging from washing clothes and organising meals to homework consultancy and ego-nurturance, frequently restrict feasible job choices to 'part-time' work. And 'part-time' jobs stand at the bottom of the employment hierarchy. They generally carry lower status, less protection, fewer benefits and lower pay than 'full-time' jobs. Even women who make their labour-power available on a 'full-time' basis continue to be disadvantaged by the discontinuity in their employment record. Having temporarily withdrawn from the labour market they are considered to have missed (rather than gained) valuable experience. Their job-related skills and self-confidence usually need refurbishing. They never catch up with men in the seniority stakes. They accumulate inferior entitlements under contributory pension schemes. And as aged parents or siblings lose the capacity to lead independent lives, they may again be called upon to give up employment and re-enrol as unpaid nurses.

These profiles represent archetypes. Not all women fail to qualify as 'real' workers. Some engage in 'full-time' employment without interruption throughout their working lives. A proportion of the most able, talented and determined of these women manage to reach the summit of their chosen career paths. But success has its costs. Career women have to contend with the multitude of hidden discriminatory practices by which men protect their job territories. It is proverbial that top women must out-perform their male counterparts in order to attain any given rung on the ladder of advancement. And discrimination by gender is all the more galling for women who have consciously chosen to deviate from the standard of femininity.

But even if relationships and practices *within* employment were to re-align with a norm of gender impartiality, so that women could compete for 'proper' jobs on equal terms with men, the underlying sexual division of labour would still impose unequal costs on women competitors. One way of avoiding patriarchal subjection and the double shift of domestic and public labour is to remain single. Single women (in contrast to bachelors) can expect to extend their actuarial longevity. They also escape the traumas and conflicts of the marital state. At the same time, if they live alone, they lose the economies of scale enjoyed by joint households; and they forfeit the potential of conjugality for love, security and companionship. Spinsterhood still carries a residual social stigma, whilst the spectacle of lesbian cohabitation arouses even greater public disapproval. Communal living arrangements, though possibly less disreputable, also afford less intimate and stable sources of personal support, and are impeded by legal, financial and architectural conservatism.

Married women who decide to remain childless miss out on the joys as well as the burdens of childrearing. Whether productive success compensates for reproductive barrenness is a quandary which is ended – though perhaps not resolved – only by the menopause. And despite the greater ease and frequency of divorce in secular societies, parental ties to children still tend to strengthen the bonding between spouses, in the devotional/affiliative, as much as in the constrictive, sense of this word. Working mothers whose earnings are ample enough to allow the purchase of substitute mothercare, are prone to similar feelings of loss, perhaps compounded by guilt about neglecting their maternal role.

In each of these cases the difficulty of balancing gain against loss springs from the tension between gender roles. The woman who trespasses into the male preserve of 'real' work makes real (or imagined) sacrifices on the female side of the sexual division of labour. Individual women may evade these dilemmas by settling down so thoroughly into the male domain and deserting domesticity that they become, and are accepted as honorary men. But this kind of cultural transvestism merely defers to the conventions surrounding the nature and distribution of public and domestic labour; the aping of dominant males celebrates gender stereotypes and in no way anticipates a new social dispensation.

As in all relationships of domination/subordination it is not only the dominated who lose – there are debits as well as profits in the life accounting of the dominators too. The prevailing model of 'real' work lowers men's participation rates in domestic labour. By the same token it reduces their share of the intrinsic satisfactions of nurturing and socialising new human infants; and, more generally, it rigidly standardises men's lifestyles and career patterns, suppressing individual eccentricity and frustrating secret dreams.

To summarise: the sexual division of labour determined by the gender system places men and women respectively in completely different relationships to waged labour and the disposition of time. The pre-eminence of public labour in the overall process of social reproduction ensures that it is men's experience and values which are decisive in shaping the attitudes of employees towards the theoretical choice between the goals of toil-reduction and higher consumption. It is not inevitable that this should be so – it is at least conceivable that workers could decide to pursue a different set of priorities despite the greater resistance this would meet from their employers. But a serious commitment to the goal of toil-reduction could emerge only as part of a wider project of social transformation. A generalised and sustained drive to reduce the average proportion of the labour force's weekly, annual and life-long time budgets devoted to paid employment would demand radically new ways of organising the world's work. It would need a programme for redistributing time and activities between men and women, and, more generally between the privileged and disadvantaged sections of society.

5   The Components of Toil

To help fix ideas and in keeping with the overall structure of the argument presented in this chapter, it is useful to maintain a conceptual separation between the demand and supply sides of the labour market. Let us assume therefore that the demand for labour inputs originating in the decisions of capitalist firms, confronts workers as a binding constraint. At any given time the level and composition of output and the techniques used to produce it are determined by enterprises subject to the competitive imperatives described earlier. Firms' production decisions generate a derived demand both for a total quantum of labour input and for a labour force with a particular occupational structure. It is convenient to treat the aggregate level and disaggregated composition of firms' labour requirements separately. The division of a given labour force into specific occupations and activities within the labour process is considered in Chapter 10. This section focuses on the total quantity person-hours of labour time which firms require in order to implement their production decisions.

The demand for hours of work may be specified at various levels of aggregation – economy-wide, industry, enterprise, plant, department or some other subdivision of an operational unit. From time to time I shall borrow a term from Marx and refer to the combined workforce of human beings who supply their labour power for some specified aggregate of time as 'the collective labourer'. It is not a condition of this loan that the borrower accepts Marx's theory of value. It is simply sometimes illuminating and suggestive to think of the unit of labour supply in collective rather than individual terms.

Labour time requirements may be calculated for various periods of calendar time – daily, weekly, monthly, annually or even over a span of years. Which time period is appropriate depends on the form of reduced working time being considered. Overtime ceilings, for example, would normally be specified on a weekly or monthly basis; longer holidays on an annual basis; sabbatical leave over a longer cycle. Much of the discussion which follows is independent of any particular time base. I shall, however, be particularly concerned in the next chapter with sabbatical leave, job-sharing and reductions in standard weekly hours. As we saw in Section 3, the first two of these three have remained minority interests, whilst the shorter working week has been the form of reduced working time which is most resistant to change. The analysis of Section 4 suggests that a progressive narrowing of the gap between 'full-time' and 'part-time' hours of work would also have the greatest impact in undermining the gender system.

At this point we need to take cognisance of the fact that 'toil' is not coextensive with time spent in paid employment. On the one hand, there are certain ancillary activities which are undertaken outside working hours, not for their own sake, but either as necessary preconditions of effective job performance or in order to remove the unwanted consequences of work. Examples are time spent travelling between work and home, the preparation of materials that will be required at work, or after-work reparations such as washing and cleaning. Not infrequently the boundary of 'job-time' is itself disputed, as in the conflict over washing time at BL's Cowley plant in 1983. Another case in point is the withdrawal by schoolteachers from certain quasi-voluntary, out of hours activities such as school meal supervision and parents' evenings. To the extent that workers find these ancillary activities unappealing, and would not undertake them unless they had to, whatever toil is associated with job-time extends beyond formal working hours.[6]

On the other hand, not all job-time activities count as toil. Some time may be spent on prescribed tasks which are intrinsically rewarding, and which workers would wish to continue to perform even if their livelihoods were otherwise provided for. Other less intrinsically gratifying prescribed tasks may still confer side benefits such as the opportunity for informal conversation and the cultivation of friendships. Finally, workers at all levels invariably contrive to divert greater or smaller packets of job-time away from the duties formally prescribed by their employer, by indulging in a variety of unofficial, and more or less clandestine, activities. These range from illicit cigarette breaks and sabotaging equipment to private sidelines and extended lunches, according to the workers' location along the curve of the 'time span of discretion'. To the extent that 'soldiering' affects either planned or realised levels of labour productivity its influence is subsumed under a later discussion of the intensity of labour. Here the significance of systematic time pilfering is that it may affect workers' subjective assessments of the arduousness of their work.

To simplify the discussion all the factors which determine how far a given quantum of collective job-time is to count as toil are for the moment swept together into a single numerical measure. Let us define θ as the 'aggregate toil rating'. θ is a factor of proportionality which, when multiplied by aggregate job-time, indicates the amount of toil associated with it. From the previous discussion it is clear that the value of θ may be greater or less than one depending on whether intrinsically unrewarding ancillary time outweighs intrinsically rewarding job-time. It follows that the general goal of toil reduction comprises not only reduced working time as conventionally understood, but also reductions in the value of θ. This is simply a formal way of registering the concerns of those who cleave to the time-honoured tradition of the dignity of labour; or wish to challenge the ancient division between mental and manual labour; or seek improvements in the quality of working life; or simply regard with deep misgiving the distant future prospect of a fully robotised economy from which all human labour has been expelled. For the time being the value of θ is taken as parametrically given. The possibility of reducing this value is taken up again in Chapter 10.

Let H denote the total quantity of person-hours of labour time required at some specified level of economic organisation over some relevant unit of time. Making use of the distinction between job-time and toil, the amount of toil, T, associated with H can be defined as:

$$T \equiv \theta H \equiv \theta h[1 + (i - \bar{i})]n$$

where *h* is the average number of hours worked per worker; *n* is the number of employees; and *i* is an index of the intensity of an hour's labour time relative to some arbitrarily chosen base line of intensity denoted by $\bar{\imath}$.

Only the variable '*i*' in this expression calls for any comment. The 'intensity' factor is intended to capture the undoubted fact that even with given equipment and techniques, the rate of output producible by a given number of workers in a given time period is immensely variable (see Hodgson, 1982). Ignoring downtime due to mechanical breakdown, shortages of material inputs, accidents, retooling, etc., productivity varies within quite wide limits according to how 'hard' people work. What counts as 'working hard' varies with the material aspects of the labour process and with the opportunity for discretion over work tasks. Sustained concentration on the visual display unit of an office computer calls for a kind of effort which is qualitatively different from the speed and dexterity demanded of the employees who assembled the computer's hardware, or the problem-solving skills of those who designed its software. And since the computer can be programmed to monitor the work of its own keyboard operator, she will enjoy fewer opportunities for stretching out or varying the pace of her work than the traditional, personally supervised secretary. Strictly speaking, therefore, *i* is a vector concept defined on all the various dimensions of effort. Nothing is lost, however, if we treat *i* as a scalar and speak as if working more or less hard involved variation within a single dimension.

The inclusion of an intensity variable in the formula for *T* emphasises that it is management's job to ensure that in the labour process $i \geqslant \bar{\imath}$. If $i < \bar{\imath}$, either output falls short of planned production schedules; or, alternatively, production targets may be fulfilled, but only by employing a greater than planned complement of labour, whether in the form of unanticipated overtime – a rise in *h* – or by hiring extra workers – a rise in *n*. A rise in *i* above its base value, for given values of *h* and *n*, entails a rise in measured labour productivity. Such intensified labour is formally equivalent to an extension of working hours. The toil performed by the collective labourer increases if workers are persuaded to or coerced into 'working harder' than 'normal' over a given span of time, in just the same way as if they worked at the 'normal' standard of effort for a longer period of time. The former case corresponds to what Marx (1976, chs 16 and 17) called a 'rise in relative surplus value' – due, say, to speed up or a successful management drive to eliminate customary, informal breaks; the latter to a 'rise in absolute surplus value' – due to a lengthening of the working day/week/year.

The forces bearing on the determination of the 'normal' level of labour intensity itself are complex. Any satisfactory account would have to encompass the extent to which industrial relations actors hold shared or conflicting conceptions of their interests; their long-term (instrumental- or value-rational) strategies; and the constraints on strategic choice rooted in the macro-social environment, organisational structures and institutional processes.[7] For our purposes it is unnecessary to investigate these forces; this would in any case need a whole book to itself.

It is, however, worth noting that any tendency for standards of intensity to fall over time opens up another route to the general goal of toil reduction. Difficult conceptual and judgemental problems are involved in comparing average 'effort' levels across long stretches of history when labour processes are revolutionised. There is, for example, an obvious sense in which a higher level of exertion is required to extract coal from an underground seam with picks and shovels than with a mechanised coal cutter; or to do the weekly laundry with washboard, mangle and clothes-line than with an automatic washing machine and spin drier. At the same time great care is needed in interpreting the consequences of technical change for the experience of human toil. Work which becomes demonstrably less physically strenuous may simultaneously become less agreeable depending on the social and psychological consequences of different technical systems and the methods by which work is coordinated and supervised.

Trist and Bamforth (1951) make precisely this point in their classic study of the replacement of 'hand-getting' by the longwall method of coal-mining. The longwall layout was introduced into British mines from about 1900 onwards in order to exploit the new moving conveyor belt. The new system greatly reduced the physical effort involved in transporting coal from coal face to surface. Its introduction was accompanied by the destruction of the six-man 'marrow' group of all-round, composite craftsmen.

These close-knit, independent groups were replaced by task forces of specialised workers each tied to particular operations on a particular shift. This system violated the miner's belief in general equality by creating a new status system linked to job gradings and specialised tasks. It also eliminated his traditional source of esteem based on all-round skills. Colliery managers faced continual problems of coordination and inter-worker disputes, whilst the miners resented increased supervision and 'outside' interference.

The longwall method raised output per man-shift by comparison with hand-getting. But tonnage produced was invariably well below theoretical potential, and absenteeism and sickness rates mounted. Rose (1978) suggests that these features of the new system were obscured by the Depression and the bitter strife between mineowners and union during the inter-war years; they emerged into prominence only after post-war nationalisation and the drive to maximise coal output.

To adapt this case to the framework presented here: there may be a tendency for technical change to reduce standards of required effort at the same time as raising output per measured unit of labour input. But it is entirely possible for a fall in i to be counter-balanced by a rise in θ. Hence whether technical change brings about a net reduction of human toil depends on which of these effects predominates. This illustrates yet again the point made in Chapter 4 (pp. 77–9) that in judgements about standards of life and work there is ultimately no way of evading 'subjective' and normative questions. The great virtue of a transformatory perspective is that it confronts these questions openly and with measured passion.

Notes to Chapter 7

1. Strictly speaking, the point of effective demand is determined by the intersection between the aggregate supply schedule, showing the monetary sales revenue firms in the aggregate would require to induce them to offer any given level of employment, and the schedule of aggregate monetary demand as actually expected by firms at a given moment in time. For a lucid exposition of the concept of effective demand and the semantic confusion surrounding it see Chick (1983), ch. 4.

2. To quote Maddison (1977), 'Until the eighteenth century most of the world was caught in a Malthusian trap. Population rose by about 0.04 per cent a year over the two millennia preceding 1700, and world income no faster'.
3. J. H. Goldthorpe, 'The End of Convergence: Corporatist and Dualist Tendencies in Modern Western Societies', in Goldthorpe (ed.) (1984).
4. Job-sharing tends to be overwhelmingly employee-initiated. An EOC (1981) survey shows that the bulk of shared jobs fall into the professional category and are initiated by employees with high levels of secondary education attainment and post-school training. Of employees approaching their employers with job-sharing proposals 75 per cent were women of whom half had children. Of the remaining 25 per cent only half were men with families.
5. For an elaboration of this highly condensed account of the sex/gender distinction see Fernbach (1981).
6. It follows that the improvement of local transport services or the introduction of workplace canteens are some of the ways in which the toil associated with paid employment can be diminished. As Minister of Labour in Britain's wartime coalition government, Ernest Bevin paid close attention to reforming these details of working life. This was no doubt one of the reasons for Bevin's huge popularity with ordinary working people in contrast to the Treasury's disdainful reference to him as 'an unskilled labourer'. Bevin's reforms went some way to alleviating the burden of long hours necessitated by the drive to maximise the output of the war economy. See Bullock (1967).
7. Poole (1986) develops a conceptual framework along these lines which he recommends for use in all comparative and historical studies of industrial relations.

8

Reduced Working Time and the Redivision of Labour

1 Introduction

The formula for collective toil presented in the final section of the previous chapter implies that the demand for labour inputs could, in principle, be accommodated by a variety of combinations of numbers employed – n; average hours of work – h; and labour intensity – i. This chapter examines two of the ways in which reduced working time could be achieved:

(1) a reduction in h, given n, could be compensated by a rise in i as of a given base value $\bar{\imath}$;
(2) a reduction in h, given i and $\bar{\imath}$, could be compensated by a rise in n.

The purpose of this exercise is to explore in detail the obstacles which inhibit any serious challenge to capitalism's structural bias. This in turn will reveal the principal tasks and themes of a transformatory approach to toil reduction.

Section 2 looks at the first of these two ways of recomposing the collective labourer's working time. It is argued that the establishment of a right to periodic leave of absence from work would have some suprisingly radical implications. Section 3 turns to the second case and investigates the difficulties which are conventionally invoked to dismiss as impractical anything more than token cuts in the standard working week. All but one of these could be relatively easily overcome given the political will and appropriate supportive action by the state. The one really recalcitrant problem is the opposition likely to be encountered if any substantial shortening of the working week were accompanied by a pro rata fall in weekly wages, or, equivalently, by unchanged hourly rates of pay.

In order to explore the sources of this opposition Section 4 analyses in detail the different kinds of households which would regard themselves as worse off if hourly wages were held constant whilst working hours were cut. The resulting taxonomy of losers determines the agenda of issues to be resolved by any strategy which aims to reduce toil, re-divide society's labour and improve the quality of life and work for everyone. The particulars of a winning strategy are outlined in the next three chapters.

2   A Modest Proposal for Reducing Working Time: Sabbatical and Caring Leave

In the introduction two methods were identified for reducing hours of work whilst continuing to meet a given demand for aggregate labour input. On a superficial view the first of these involves a comparatively minor adjustment of working patterns. Taking as given the number of employees enrolled within the collective labourer, each one could enjoy more off-job time, at no additional cost to the employer, if his/her colleagues were prepared to cover for periodic leave of absence by accepting a larger workload and a higher intensity of labour. The leading example of such arrangements are the provisions for study leave found in institutions of higher education. Practice varies between institutions and departments; but, subject to differing degrees of conditionality, rights to one term's leave for every two to three years of service are widely recognised. The administration of study leave arrangements rests with departmental heads or worker-elected committees depending on the extent of workplace democracy.

Academics are, however, rather exceptional (in this respect at least!). The rationale and benefit of study leave are obvious: lecturers can complete research, update their knowledge, explore new fields of study, and thereby advance their careers and enjoy themselves at the same time. For academics and most higher professionals the boundaries between job time and free time scarcely exist; work autonomy is high, effort standards elastic, and toil ratings correspondingly low.

In other contexts provisions for periodic leave might be thought an unattractive option. Any such scheme would have to be endorsed by the employer since there would need to be some arrangement for continuing to pay the wages of those on leave; an unofficial, worker-controlled system of income maintenance would be difficult to organise, and would probably run foul of company rules. Moreover, quite apart from the burden of providing cover, employees might reasonably fear that their employer would exploit any indication on their part of willingness to accept more exacting effort standards. In stepping up their work rates they might attract unwanted attention to the countless ways in which workers contain the intensity of their labour below its theoretical maximum, or reappropriate job time from the employer's to their own uses. The employer might then be galvanised into a full-scale assault on workers' customary job controls across a broad front.

Anxiety about unhinging the customary wage-effort ratio might be compounded by fear that a leave of absence scheme would imperil the workers' future job security. The prospect of being able to produce the same output with a smaller work team might tempt the employer, looking for easy cost savings in a tight market, to use his power as paymaster to cancel the leave arrangement and cut back his labour force. Alternatively, even if the scheme survived, normal employment contraction during an output recession would present the workers with a difficult choice: they would either have to abandon their previous gain in reduced working time, or accept further increments of labour intensification. Since the leave scheme would have raised the base-line of intensity, the marginal disutility of any additional intensification would be greater than if it had never been adopted in the first place.

In view of these risks it would appear understandable if workers refused to trade concessions along the internal frontier of job control for what amounts to a reduction in *average* hours of work. There are, however, three objections to this defensive response. First, it would be surprising if all the practices on the workers' side of the frontier embodied well-judged and rationally defensible interpretations of workers' interests as producers. For example, restrictive practices intended to maintain employment in the face of labour-displacing technical change and mass unemployment, are frequently admitted by the workers who resort to them to be absurd and demoralising, justified only on the principle that in a jungle one must defend oneself as best one can.[1] The workers know that they are fighting a losing battle. But they are determined to extract whatever advantage remains in the declining assets still under their control. Yet jungle warfare under the looming prospect of defeat and surrender embitters and coarsens the combatants. It neither secures a line of retreat to a fall-back position, nor establishes a bridgehead to a broader and strategically more promising terrain.

Second, however, suppose that on mature reflection the practices workers wish to protect are judged to serve highly valued objectives. Now, as we have seen, a leave of absence scheme would have to be formally negotiated with the employer. It should therefore require no more than normal trade union vigilance to obviate the risks of abuse outlined above. *Negotiated* adjustments to the frontier of control need not be the prelude to wholesale incursions. It could also be insisted as a *sine qua non* of the scheme that, once under way, it could not subsequently be terminated without the workers' consent. This condition would in itself give the workers a potentially tradeable asset with which to ward off unwelcome future pressure on labour intensity. The granting of consent to the cancellation of a long established right could plausibly be represented as a concession of such magnitude that it would be monstrously unreasonable of the employer to demand more. This bargaining stance would, in effect, transmute worker-held assets from one form, reflecting one version of workers' interests, into another, reflecting a different version. Effort controls are often treated as securities held for precautionary or fraudulent motives depending on the observer's interests and sympathies. Either way they are potentially convertible, if the price is right, into cash. An alternative, more profitable rearrangement of workers' human wealth might be to exchange some of these holdings for reduced working time.

This last point connects with the third and most important argument against refusing to contemplate a leave of absence scheme. The balance between prospective gain and risk begins to appear in a different light if the demand for reduced average hours of work is presented in the concrete form of a claimed right to periodic sabbatical leave; or the right of working parents with young children – or anyone with responsibilities for the elderly or infirm – to readjust their personal time allocations between their jobs and domestic, caring work. What might be termed 'caring leave' could be taken in a single lump sum or in a succession of smaller instalments depending on individual needs and circumstances.

In one sense the institution of sabbatical and caring leave paid for by the acceptance of collective responsibility for the consequential increase in workloads, would simply regularise matters which, as things stand, are settled surreptitiously by informal management–worker interaction. It would impose an element of conscious joint regulation on dubiously legitimate absenteeism and management's pragmatic responses to it. Prudent managers and supervisors will allow for some 'normal' anticipated rate of absenteeism in setting staff quotas and targets for labour intensity. It is also standard practice to administer the rules governing workplace attendance with a certain flexibility and generosity, depending on the trust which exists between the various parties involved.[2] The formal legitimation of time off for certain recognised purposes would, as suggested above, be the working hours equivalent of self-financing wage rises based on productivity deals.

But productivity agreements signify no new principle of work organisation beyond the narrowly rationalist aim of reducing inefficiency in the labour process by integrating the wage and effort bargains into a single set of negotiations. By contrast, to claim the right to time off in order to acquire new skills, sample new experiences, promote one's personal development, look after dependants, or simply enjoy a long rest, has a deeper symbolic and transformatory significance. First, it affirms that the private, unwaged sphere of social reproduction is as important to social well-being as currently prestigious activities in the public, waged sphere. Second, it asserts that caring work is the collective responsibility of society – not necessarily in the sense that everyone should be directly involved in it; but certainly in the sense that all able-bodied persons should make a contribution to ensuring that caring work is less disadvantageous for those who do it than it is under our current social arrangements. Third, worker-initiated leave arrangements would establish a novel form of collective self-help and welfare provision. There would be a direct and visible linkage between benefits created and the labour tax exacted to pay for them. This would avoid the disconnection between beneficiaries and taxpayers which is characteristic of state welfare systems; it would also avoid the institutionalised divorce and mutual antagonism between the agencies which dispense welfare benefits and the clients under their control.

Finally, caring and sabbatical leave arrangements would focus attention on people's personal time budgets. We all make constant adjustments to our timetables at the margins. But few of us in 'full time' employment ever pause to take stock of the overall balance of our lives between paid employment; domestic labour; unpaid voluntary work; education, training and personal growth; and the residual category of hobbies, pastimes and recreation. Regularised sabbatical and caring leave would invite 'full time' workers to reconsider their personal time profiles from a standpoint which was not so much anti-work as pro-life. Waged work in the public domain is likely to remain an important part of any rounded human experience – so important that the grotesquely unequal distribution of access to it in the advanced capitalist countries today is a standing affront to any concept of social justice.

At the same time there is the potential for significantly reducing working time. The tendency of a scheme for sabbatical and caring leave would be to encourage workers to welcome this prospect as a source of liberation rather than a cause for alarm. This would help to straighten out the kink in human psycho-social development bequeathed by a work ethic which has now outlived its useful social purpose. Someone who embraced this perspective would warm to the appeal of the simple, but startlingly subversive, idea that 'This is my life; and it is the only one I am going to get'.

Thus even this comparatively modest project contains a powerful transformatory charge. The release of its ideological energy would set up a counter-force against the tilted priorities of capitalist accumulation. This would not in itself abolish the competitive rivalry which underlies capital's restless expansionism. There would remain objective constraints on the practical scope for redressing the balance between waged work and unwaged activities.[3] But the capitalist principle and its concomitant mentality would have to contend with a rising competitor; over the long run these overgrown life forms would be checked by the retrieval or discovery of fertile patches of cultural soil in which the seeds of social transformation can be planted and tended.

3   The Obstacles to a Shorter Working Week

Consider now the second of the two alternative ways of accommodating a given demand for collective labour time identified earlier: a reduction in h, holding i constant, compensated by a rise in n. This case corresponds to two of the forms of reduced working time discussed in Chapter 7: job-sharing and the shorter working week. The analysis of this section applies to both these forms. However, prospective job-share partners would not initiate a proposal to split their existing 'full-time' jobs, thereby creating a new job opening, unless they were already content to exchange lower employment income for more free time. This means that the most intractable difficulty standing in the way of any generalised cut in standard working hours does not arise with job sharing. For this reason the discussion concentrates on the shorter working week.

The demand for a shorter working week tends to be raised during periods of high unemployment. It elicits two conventional responses: from the Keynesian left and the realist right. The former object to the use of supply-side remedies for demand-side problems; this attitude is considered in Chapters 9–11. The latter dismiss as wholly impractical the suggestion that a shorter working week would expand the number of job openings and promote a less unequal distribution of waged work. These alleged practical obstacles are dealt with in this section. Obstacles can be viewed as challenges as well as impediments. The search for ways of circumventing, weakening or redirecting their force is part of the long haul to a new type of political economy.

The first hurdle to be surmounted is the adjustment costs

which employers would incur if they cut h and increased the number of employees on their books. These costs would consist of the expenses of attracting suitable candidates for new job vacancies – placing advertisements, screening applicants, etc.; the incremental book-keeping costs of maintaining a larger labour force; additional employer contributions to social insurance funds and any other payroll taxes; and any consequential costs due to the need to reorganise the labour process in order to accommodate a larger workforce and/or a change in the pattern of hours worked per day or per week.[4] Within a single enterprise these adjustment costs could be offset if incumbent employees were willing to entertain an increase in labour intensity. But this would be expecting the 'ins' to display an uncommon degree of altruism towards the 'outs'. It would also be counter-productive: an increase in average output per worker would diminish the number of new job openings created by the initial reduction in h. A more effective way of tackling the adjustment problem would be for the state to offer the incentive of lower corporate or payroll taxes and/or employment subsidies to any employer who implemented a package of lower h and higher n.[5] Fiscal inducements to employment expansion would signal public commitment to the objective of reduced working time and help shift the balance of popular attitudes towards work and the redistribution of waged and unwaged labour. Whilst such measures could be introduced independently of other policies, they would fit comfortably into a framework of planning agreements sponsored by the state in partnership with the employers and the other principal interest groups holding a stake in enterprise decisions (see Chapter 6, note 6). The impact of fiscal incentives could also be enhanced by macroeconomic stimuli to job creation of a more conventional kind. By their nature *conditional* tax/subsidy rewards could not *guarantee* that firms and workers would actually choose to negotiate the desired kinds of package deals. But if the idea had no great popular resonance in the first place, it would be unwise to rely overmuch on state compulsion, especially in such a sensitive area of social policy: the road to freedom is littered with the wrecks of enlightened attempts to force the people to be free.

Even if the adjustment problem were resolved, employers would still have two further worries about the effect of a shorter working week on their costs. A fall in *h* could be accompanied by a rise in *n* at no additional cost to the employer only if: (1) additional employees were no less productive than the employer's existing labour force; and (2) the wage per hour remained the same. The first of these two conditions becomes harder to satisfy: (a) the longer the preceding period new recruits have remained outside employment, whether counted as unemployed or as non-participants in the labour force; (b) the longer the period of on-the-job training required before new workers can be expected to attain average standards of performance; and (c) the poorer the standard of their general education, training and work experience.

Again these problems point to the need for the transition to a shorter working week to be guided and facilitated by appropriate state action. Problems (a) and (c) fall within the brief of state agencies concerned with training, retraining and work experience initiatives. Problem (b) could be tackled by means of a temporary subsidiary to defray part of the wages paid to the new recruits during their induction period. As the number of persons in employment rose the state would gain from a fall in its social security outgoings and a rise in its tax revenues. These budgetary savings could be redeployed as a temporary training subsidy paid to employers who hire and train new workers. Ironically the term of the subsidy need not exceed two or three months at the outside for the vast majority of unskilled and semi-skilled jobs. One of the consequences of the detailed division of labour within the modern industrial enterprises is that the technical tricks of a great many trades can be picked up very quickly.[6]

New employment and training subsidies might provoke complaints from employers about the administrative burden of establishing their qualifications to receive benefit and processing the resultant financial flows. From a social standpoint, however, this bureaucratic cost would be offset by the lower cost to the state of handling reduced numbers in receipt of social security benefits. Employment creation represents a more valuable use of the social resources tied up in bureaucracy than maintaining the incomes and policing the lives of the unemployed.

In practice it is the second of the two conditions listed above which looms largest in the widespread belief that any substantial shortening of the working week would impose an intolerable cost burden on employers. If established employees insisted on the same weekly wage for fewer hours worked, the hourly wage rate would automatically rise. Only if productivity per worker-hour rose by the same proportion would firms' labour costs per unit of output remain unchanged. But in this case no extra employment would be created, and only established employees would benefit from the reduction in hours of work. Alternatively, if productivity remained the same, employers would be able to meet their previous output targets only by hiring additional workers; hence unit costs would rise.

But why should incumbent employees insist on receiving the same weekly wage for fewer hours of work? A pragmatist might argue that the reasons are irrelevant: what matters is that this is what happens in practice. As we saw in Chapter 7, trade union claims for cuts in weekly hours are invariably accompanied by the demand for 'full pay'. On the other hand, it is hardly satisfactory to treat the response to a shortening of the working week as a matter of brute economic or natural law. Nor will it suffice to invoke the phenomenon of downward wage rigidity. 'Real wage resistance' is normally taken to refer to opposition to any implied reduction in wages per hour when hours of work are held constant. It cannot be assumed without further argument that a symmetrical response will be forthcoming when the matter at issue is a fall in weekly earnings as a result of lower hours of work with a constant wage per hour. The ratchet mechanism which locks the weekly real wage at the highest notch it has previously attained is stripped down and inspected in the next section.

4   The Shorter Working Week: a Taxonomy of Losers and the Agenda for a Winning Strategy

The sources of upward pressure on *hourly* wages when working hours are cut can best be analysed by focusing on the household context of labour supply. This will enable us to identify the different kinds of households which can be expected to suffer a loss – in their own eyes at least – when the working week is shortened. This exercise in turn will uncover the social roots of the cost-inflationary side effects of a programme combining reduced working time with job expansion and a redistribution of employment opportunities.

For convenience the analysis of the text is summarised in Table 8.1 below. Three preliminary points need to be noted in interpreting this table. First, the analysis is not restricted to households consisting of a standard heterosexual couple with or without dependants: both one- and multi-person units are included; their sexual persuasion is irrelevant. Both one- and multi-person households would be exposed to all but two of the types of loss identified below: the two exceptions are indicated in the table. It is, however, worth drawing attention to the special problems of one-parent families of whom there are just under a million in Britain today. This group are handicapped in adjusting their supply of hours of work. On the one hand unemployed single parents with young children are poorly placed to take advantage of new employment opportunities. On the other hand those already in full-time work would be hard hit by an uncompensated cut in working hours. The plight of this particular 'misfit' type of household anticipates one of the main conclusions of the analysis which follows: that a sustainable programme for reducing working time would need to unravel the threads which weave gender division into the pattern of work organisation.

Second, to avoid overuse of the conditional tense, I shall speak as if an economy-wide cut in h and expansion of n has already taken place. 'Losers' are identified by comparing their situation before and after this adjustment. It is also linguistically convenient to refer to persons who are already in employment before the change as 'primary' employees; and to those who may gain employment as a result of it as 'secondary' employees. This nomenclature deviates from customary usage. It goes without saying that the terms 'primary' and 'secondary' carry no normative significance.

Finally, it should be borne in mind that the categories listed in the table are analytically based 'ideal-types', not mutually exclusive, empirical classes. If real households were to be grouped according to these categories, the groupings would almost certainly overlap: many households would qualify as losers – in their own estimation – on more than count.

178

Table 8.1 Categories of household liable to lose from the introduction of a shorter working week with unchanged hourly rates of pay

Employment status of household before shortening of working week	Effect of shorter working week on combined household income from all sources	Characteristic source of loss	Type of household
No primary employee	1. (a) Employment status and income unchanged	Possible increase in relative deprivation	Both
	(b) Potential employment gain, but income unchanged, reduced or only slightly increased	Unemployment trap	
At least one primary employee	2. Income reduced to a level: (a) at or below subsistence	Poverty trap due to low hourly wage of primary employee	Both
	(b) above subsistence but modest	Low hourly wage available to secondary workers	Multi-person only
	(c) substantially above subsistence	Preference for higher consumption/ saving over lower primary employee hours of work	Both
	3. Income unchanged or increased	Possible conflict over division of domestic labour income, status and power	Multi-person only
	4. Income increased, reduced or unchanged	Primary worker deprived of intrinsically gratifying work and/or positional privilege	Both

(i) The unemployed

Four principal types of loser can be distinguished. Consider first those households with no primary employee. Some of these gain as those of their members available for employment obtain jobs. For this to happen, however, these secondary workers' earnings must raise the household's total income-from-all-sources by a sufficient margin. In many cases this proviso is not satisfied: such households find themselves stuck in the unemployment trap. On the one hand, their potential wage earners are confined by a variety of social disabilities to jobs which offer low hourly rates of pay; and, *ex hypothesi*, they cannot boost their weekly earnings by working long hours. On the other hand, they are penalised by the perversity of the social security system. Many of the means-tested benefits in cash or kind to which they were previously entitled (and which, let us suppose, they actually claimed), would be withdrawn as the household's income from employment rises above zero. As is well known, the loss of conditional social security benefits can in some cases impose on earned income over a certain range an effective marginal rate of taxation in excess of 100 per cent.[7] And even effective marginal tax rates below 100 per cent are still a strong disincentive to households squeezed between poor earnings prospects and the rules governing eligibility for state income support. A small net gain in income-from-all-sources might fail to compensate for the loss of free time and the toil associated with menial, hazardous and incommodious forms of wage labour. The only potential gain for this group of households, labelled 1(b) in Table 8.1, would be escape from any social stigma attached to being unemployed and financially dependent on the welfare state.

The other potential losers in the first category, labelled 1(a) in the table, would be those households whose members would on balance wish to enter employment, but are unable to capture one of the newly created job openings. The hindrances to these potential secondary workers include age, disability, ethnic identity, educational background, personal history or plain fecklessness. Other things being equal, the employment status and incomes of this group remain unchanged. They might, nevertheless, still judge themselves worse off than before. This is because whatever stigma and sense of relative deprivation are experienced by an unemployed person might actually increase in intensity when the ranks of the jobless are being thinned. According to the theory of relative deprivation a disadvantage which someone endures without complaint as long as its incidence within that person's peer group remains widespread, becomes less bearable/more unbearable when the proportion of the peer group sharing the disadvantage falls (see Runciman, 1972).

There is another sub-group of potential losers among the unemployed, not listed in Table 8.1, but mentioned here for the sake of completeness. Unlike those who experience unemployment as a source of relative deprivation, this group, consisting mostly of young and single people, do not feel downtrodden, outcast or ashamed of their condition. They have rejected the work ethic and any sense of obligation to a society which has rejected them. Far from wanting to find regular employment they have adapted to a life of subsistence leisure, supported by social security giros and, perhaps, the occasional foray into the black economy and the sub-criminal underground. In some ways a return to fuller employment is likely to disturb their preferred non-conformist lifestyle. They might experience a diffuse social disapproval and pressure to enter the job market. After all, anyone who believes, with Beveridge, that 'the first condition of human happiness is the opportunity of useful service' (see Beveridge, 1944, p. 122), can easily (though not very logically) be roused to animus against work dodgers, drones, the idle poor and those engaged in socially useless activities. On the other hand, an expansion of employment accompanied by a shorter working week might avoid the climate of puritanical zeal which surrounded the efforts of the post-war Labour Government to maximise production and maintain employment at the high levels achieved during the war.[8] A programme intended to reduce and redistribute working time would, so to speak, go halfway to meet those whose personal aspirations are to be maximally unemployed.

(ii) The low paid and the not so low paid

Consider next those households with at least one primary employee. The second category in Table 8.1 consists of those with a combined employment income lower after the introduction of a shorter working week than before. Single primary workers living alone automatically fall into this category, unless they obtain promotion to better paying jobs (see (iv) below). Multi-person households are included if the loss of their primary worker's earnings is not compensated by the earnings of secondary workers – mostly wives and young adults.

There are three distinct sub-groups within this category corresponding to three levels of household income. Group 2(a) are the working poor: their primary employee is in a job with a very low hourly rate of pay. If s/he is prevented from exceeding the new lower standard of weekly working hours, the household's combined income falls below some socially defined subsistence level. This poverty trap clearly overlaps with the unemployment trap in which Group 1(b) is caught.

The primary workers in Group 2(b) enjoy an hourly rate of pay sufficiently high to yield an income above subsistence even at reduced hours of work. Nevertheless these households are unable to maintain their previous modest level of income because the jobs available to their secondary workers carry much lower rates of pay than those earned by their primary workers. Under the prevailing structure of male and female employment and the associated inequality between male and female earnings, male workers enjoy a comparative advantage in earning power. The substitution of secondary for primary hours of waged labour would be an inefficient allocation of joint time budgets.

These two cases draw attention to the general problem of low pay and the related difficulty that women's hourly earnings are much lower than men's. In Britain since the Equal Pay Act came into effect in 1975 the average gross hourly earnings of full-time women employees aged 18 or over, whose pay was not affected by absence, have fluctuated between 72 and 75 per cent of the corresponding figure for men.[9] This in turn is due to the low relative pay in the industries and occupations into which women workers are concentrated (see Hakim, 1979); and to the tendency within any industry or occupation employing both women and men for proportionately more women to occupy the lower levels of skill, grading and seniority than men. It is for this reason that any general attempt to improve the relative position of low paid workers would predominantly work to the advantage of women, though it would also benefit a minority of low paid men.[10]

Group 2(c) consists of comparatively affluent households. Their primary workers' rates of pay are so high that, although the household's income is reduced, it remains substantial even at lower hours of work and even without additional supplementation by secondary earnings. The loss experienced by this group arises from their preference for the extra consumption (or saving) they would enjoy if the primary worker's hours of work exceeded the new shorter working week. They prefer this pattern of consumption and waged work to the release of the primary worker's time either for leisure or for redistribution to other household members with lower earning capacity. In adjudging Group 2(c) as losers the assumption made is that this particular preference ordering is shared by all household members.

This assumption is questionable. It is arguable that relative valuations of consumption and free time reflect the interaction between work and gender. As we have seen, women are busy: the attempt to combine even a 'part-time' job with looking after homes, children and husbands can easily stretch a working woman's hours of labour up to 12–16 a day. What most women need is more time. By contrast, most men manage to avoid juggling with the competing demands of work and home: their domestic lives and their working lives exist in separate compartments. Home-based, caring work receives little priority in their scale of preferences. In consequence male dominated trade union policy and practice come to be narrowly focused on the workplace. The duties (or pleasures) of extra-workplace life are a private matter outside the concern and legitimate remit of public policy. Patterns of job-time and the theoretical choice between consumption and free time are distorted by the equation of 'full time' work with men's work. How genuinely autonomous individual men and women would strike a balance between hours of work and free time in the absence of this distortion is unknown.

(iii)   Domestic labourers

The third category of households is defined by exclusion from the first two, though its characteristic loss could occur in any type of household. The members of Group 3 stand outside the unemployment trap afflicting Goup 1, and, unlike Group 2, suffer no fall in household income. Since primary workers in this group are supplying fewer hours of waged labour, and other household members have gained employment at rates of pay sufficient to compensate for reduced primary earnings, the group would appear to have made an unambiguous gain. But this is to omit domestic labour from the balance sheet. Assume for simplicity that the total time devoted to domestic labour remains constant. Then this third category contains two kinds of 'losers' If domestic labour is redistributed between household members – presumably for the most part from women to men – those who find themselves doing more of it might object.[11] Alternatively no redistribution occurs and many working women face the familiar problems of the 'double shift'.

The question of responsibility for domestic labour confronts all households. In Group 3, however, the issue arises in a 'pure' form, free from other complicating factors. The assumption that aggregate domestic labour time remains unchanged is unrealistic. When married women increase their hours of waged labour – whether from zero to some 'part-time' figure, or from 'part-time' to 'full-time' levels – the amount of time devoted to domestic labour is likely to fall. Neither the duration nor the intensity of housework and childcare are fixed: both are determined by custom and intra-familial negotiation. On the other hand, only a handful of very rich families can nowadays afford to hire servants, nannies, etc. For the vast majority of households the lower limit to which domestic labour time can be compressed is a binding constraint. The problems identified in Group 3 are serious.

(iv) Workaholics, husbands and bosses

Conflict over domestic labour is not a straightforward matter of bargaining over time allocations. Social and psychological tensions can be expected if readjustments in the employment status of different household members and in their relative contributions to household income disturb the family's internal authority and status orders. By further exploring this interface between the material and social aspects of labour, first in the home and then in the workplace, we shall discover the fourth and final category of losers. The households in the previous three categories conform to the standard assumption of the theory of labour supply: that income and free time are both positive goods: they evaluate waged work negatively as detracting from free time and positively as a source of income. For the fourth group this assumption is inappropriate:

primary workers in this group find their work intrinsically gratifying; they resent having to do less of it regardless of the net effect
of shorter working hours on total household income.

This need not entail that Category 4 primary workers are wholly
indifferent to monetary incentives. Their unfamiliar preference
patterns can be clarified by the simple device of reversing the
direction of measurement on the time axis of the standard
diagram used to model the individual's supply of hours of work.
Traditionally economists measure the individual worker's free time
from the origin of the time axis rightwards: hours of waged labour
are depicted as a subtraction from free time; hence they are
measured leftwards from the point at which the worker's budget
constraint intersects the horizontal time axis. In the case of primary
workers in Category 4 job time is measured from the origin
rightwards; their preferences as between income and job time can
then be represented by the usual indifference map.

For reasons that will become apparent I shall assume that the
worker whose preferences are shown in Figure 8.1 below is male.
His off-job time consists of whatever portion of God's hours are
left over after he has worked up to the maximum limit permitted
by legal rules or collective agreements, the natural demands of
human physiology and whatever minimum amount of domestic
duty and off-job social life he can get away with. This maximum
limit is indicated by the point labelled h_0 in Figure 8.1. Given an
hourly wage rate of w_0, his feasible choice set is bounded by $0Ph_0$.
He optimises by selecting a corner solution at P, supplying h_0
hours of work for an income of y_0. It is assumed that initially he is
the household's only source of income.

Now suppose that the shorter working week reduces his potential
maximum working hours to h_1. At the same time let the combined
income of his household be maintained at y_0 as other members of
the household enter gainful employment and bring in earnings of
s_1. His feasible choice set is now bounded by the figure $0s_1Qh_1$,
and his constrained optimum lies at Q, which he regards as
unambiguously inferior to his original position at P. There is,
however, some level of income-replacement which would just
compensate for the diminished opportunity to indulge his appetite
for job-time. If secondary earnings were as high as s_2, the worker
would be restored to his original indifference curve I_0 at R.
Alternatively – and the significance of this point is taken up below –

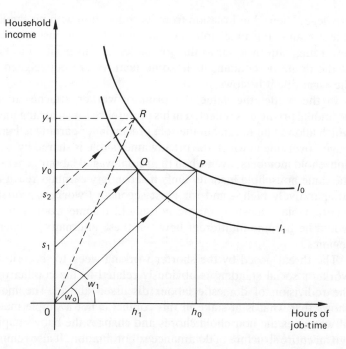

Figure 8.1

he could remain the household's exclusive source of financial support and still attain point R provided that his hourly wage rate were increased from w_0 to w_1.

It might be thought that this curious model applies only to pathological workaholics and to that minority of highly specialised workers such as creative writers and artists whose work has become their life. But the model is capable of a much broader interpretation which captures an important and neglected aspect of the redivision of labour entailed by reduced working time. Consider first the domestic economy. Suppose that some men to a high degree and most men to some degree value the power and status they derive as heads of households and family breadwinners. They will then be aggrieved at any measure which threatens to erode this gender privilege. Viewed in isolation from its connection with his familial role a man's 'full time' job may not in fact be intrinsically very rewarding. But in so far as this job underpins his position as king of the domestic domain, its irksome features are outweighed by the regal title it bestows.

In the model the value the primary worker attaches to his positional privilege is reflected in his preference for an arrangement which allows him to remain the sole breadwinner earning a 'family wage,' over one in which the breadwinner's role is shared by other household members, even when their joint waged labour generates the same household income. Only if secondary earnings reach the comparatively high – and for most secondary workers probably unattainable – level s_2, raising household income from y_0 to y_1, would he become indifferent between these alternative domestic regimes.

The threat posed by the shorter working week to the primary worker's social standing is obviously related to the conflict over the redivision of domestic labour discussed above. The model shows that what is at stake in this conflict is not a simple matter of who does the household chores and changes the baby's nappy, but an entire structure of dominance/subordination. It also reminds us that one of the facets of a transformatory approach to reduced working time is the education of desire. The transition to a shorter working week would be eased if men were prepared to shoulder a larger share of domestic labour; it would be positively accelerated if their evaluation of job time and free time were reversed. The 'loss' suffered by primary workers in Category 4 arises entirely because of their masculine devotion to 'full time' work.

The case of the *paterfamilias* can be generalised to other hierarchical structures within the workplace. To appreciate this it is necessary to abandon the conceptual separation so far maintained between the aggregative and compositional aspects of the demand for labour. The concept of the collective labourer has served as a useful fiction for discussing the effects of reduced working time. But it has to be borne in mind that the parts of the collective labourer are not all equal: the job slots within any operational unit carry different degrees of responsibility; and in all organisations above a certain minimum size responsibility is closely associated with the hierarchy of authority and status. If those who occupy the higher reaches of this hierarchy value their jobs as positional goods, they too will lose from any measure which they perceive as downgrading their privilege.

The precise content of job responsibility obviously depends on the material features of the labour process. But in general it can be said that responsibility varies positively with the degree to which the employer's interests are affected by the employee's actions, especially where negligence or error would damage these interests, or where the employer's public reputation depends on the employee's willing maintenance of high standards of work intensity. Responsibility varies negatively with the degree to which the employee's actions are subject to external control and supervision. Wood (1978) points out that responsibility and authority may be divorced: some employees such as skilled maintenance workers, research scientists and other expert professionals score high on both measures of responsibility, but generally come low on the scale of executive authority. Nevertheless, with some exceptions, positions of responsibility are also positions of command.

It is often argued – especially by top job-holders themselves – that responsibility involves anxiety and stress. If this were the sole or main determinant of social attitudes towards responsibility, then it would be appropriate to treat top jobs as if they exacted a toilsome sacrifice comparable to, though obviously different from, the physical and psychic hardships undergone by workers in menial jobs. (It would, of course, still be possible to argue about the *weights* to be attached to these different kinds of sacrifice; but a casual perusal of the Registrar General's Occupational Mortality Tables does not suggest any very strong moral case for assigning a greater weight to the former kind.) Every sort of responsibility involves some stress; but there is abundant evidence that most people also place a high value on the opportunity to exercise authority and on the independence, power and esteem which are its normal concomitants (see Wood 1978, pp. 30–1, 189–95).

Now the positional value of jobs arranged in a hierarchy is double-edged: for all except the highest and lowest levels of the hierarchy the positive attractions of controlling the work of subordinates have to be balanced against the disagreeableness of being in turn subordinate to those at higher levels. No doubt different individuals will form different assessments of the combined effect of these three determinants of the responsibility value of any given job – the stress factor, positional advantage and positional disadvantage respectively. Nevertheless some plausible generalisations can be advanced about the relationship between these factors at different levels in the hierarchy. Recall the image of an upright pyramid or cone which has become the standard metaphor in our culture for describing organisational hierarchies. Imagine the organisational cone divided into horizontal sections at equal intervals along its vertical axis. The jobs included in any given truncated section will all possess approximately the same positional value. It is plausible to suppose that positional values will vary: (1) directly with the number of employees in lower sections holding positional inferiority – n_1 (this corresponds to the number of employees directly or indirectly subordinate to someone occupying the rank in question, and is commonly used in organisations as a measure of responsibility); (2) inversely with the number of employees at the same level with whom positional rank is shared – n_2; and (3) inversely with the number of employees in higher sections holding positional superiority – n_3. The geometry of a cone dictates that as one ascends from base to apex, n_1 rises, whilst n_2 and n_3 fall, and that the rate of rise or fall continuously increases.

It may be concluded therefore, that the positional value attached to the various jobs in an organisational hierarchy will become increasingly positive as one approaches the top. Admittedly the stress factor also rises with rank in the authority and status orders. Nevertheless, it is reasonable to infer from the large surplus of willing candidates for top job vacancies that this negative component of overall job valuation is steadily overcompensated by the accretion of positive positional value.

Now the more the positive elements inhering in positions of responsibility predominate over their negative elements, the more closely such jobs approximate to our previous model. It follows that top job-holders will be reluctant to acquiesce in any substantial shortening of working hours. A shorter working week for everyone would entail a redistribution of responsibilities all the way down the line of command from top executives to foremen and supervisors. (Recall that we are notionally holding standards of work intensity constant.) Excess workloads at each level in the hierarchy would have to be absorbed by some combination of new recruitment, upwards promotion or downward delegation of responsibility. The feasibility of such a general redivision of collective labour is considered in Chapter 10 along with its implications for occupational pay differentials. The point to be noted here is that a reallocation of job responsibility devalues and dilutes occupational privilege in the enterprise in much the same way as it undermines gender privilege in the family. Bosses ally with husbands as opponents of the shorter working week.

(v) The agenda for a winning strategy

The starting point of the analysis of this section was the claim that a shorter working week could not be combined with unchanged hourly rates of pay. The conclusion emerging from our long taxonomy of losers is that there are indeed formidable obstacles to any attempt to reduce hours of work whilst holding hourly pay constant. Cases 1 and 2(a) draw attention to the connections between the objective of toil reduction and the problems of unemployment, the unemployment trap and of low pay and poverty. Case 2(b) points to the partially overlapping issue of the inequalities between men and women in job opportunities and earning power. A successful strategy for dealing with this nest of problems would have to bring about three related kinds of redistribution:

(a) Between persons already holding full-time jobs and those who seek, but are denied access to employment, or can obtain it only on inferior terms;
(b) Between low paid and more highly paid workers;
(c) Between the privileged job territories occupied by male workers and the underprivileged zones allotted to women.

The first two of these redistributive issues place the question of a policy for incomes firmly on the strategic agenda. Item (a) poses the familiar macroeconomic conundrum: how to ensure that an expansion of employment is not frustrated or cut short by a renewed upsurge of wage and price inflation. Under a decentralised and uncoordinated system of wage negotiation and price setting the money wage bargains struck by unions and employers are liable to generate sharp and unwanted jumps in the overall level of money wages and prices as the balance between job seekers and job vacancies swings in favour of the former. Item (b) runs up against entrenched popular attitudes towards the appropriate differentials between low paid and well paid jobs. The problem that bedevils all schemes for hoisting the relative level of the lowest rates of pay and compressing the structure of wages from below, is the danger that popular attachment to the customary pattern of inter-occupational pay differentials will simply ignite a chain-reaction of restorative wage demands throughout the upper levels of the structure. This danger clearly exacerbates the overall stabilisation problem. In both cases the central strategic question is whether workers and unions can be persuaded to under-utilise their potential power to force up money wages in their own particular bargaining units in order to create space for the requisite redistributions.

Item (c) above also appears on another section of the agenda. The losses experienced by households in Categories 2(c) and 3 together with the sub-group of 'husbands' in Category 4, are rooted in the basic contemporary form of the sexual division of labour. As long as men's primary responsibilities lie in the public sphere of waged labour and their responsibilities as husbands and parents remain strictly secondary, male resistance to any significant redistribution of time and activities stands in the way of any generalised reduction in job time. The sub-group of 'bosses' in Category 4 also shows that privileged access to the opportunity to exercise responsibility under the prevailing hierarchical division of labour interposes a similar barrier.

What must be emphasised, however, is that none of these sources of resistance to reduced working time needs to be seen as part of the natural order of society. From a transformatory perspective the boundary between the 'natural' and the 'artificial' realms of social practice is a movable object. At any given moment what is called 'natural' – the working out of economic processes and social institutions – constrains the scope for argument and negotiation over the apportionment of social resources and roles. But, on a longer view these processes are malleable: they can be redesigned and redirected. The task of a transformatory project to demonstrate that the 'natural-artificial' boundary is, in principle, shiftable; and to indicate a sequence of steps for bringing about the requisite shift.

Chapter 7 opened with the unequal contest in a capitalist economy between toil-reduction and output-expansion. The subsequent argument has shown that any serious programme for redressing this imbalance must at the same time deal with the problems of unemployment, poverty, low pay, wage inflation, consumerism, gender division and occupational hierarchy. The next three chapters outline a strategy for overcoming each of these problems and appropriating the historic legacy of capitalist development as a base for cultural rejuvenation.

Notes to Chapter 8

1. See Robert Doyle, 'The Print Jungle', in Fraser (ed.) (1968).
2. See Terry (1977) on the inevitability of informality in workplace negotiation and administration.
3. It is for this reason that I have been careful to respect capital's demand for aggregate hours of work as a constraint throughout the analysis of Chapters 7 and 8. Some particularly intractable practical problems would arise if cuts in working hours were followed by labour shortages, reduced productivity or, as argued in Section 3, increases in unit costs. For one thing any country which took unilateral steps to channel the fruits of productivity growth into toil-reduction rather than output-expansion would place its own nationally based enterprises under a competitive handicap. This in turn would jeopardise the success of any purely national initiatives in this area as domestic capital came under pressure to evade or subvert the policy. This kind of problem which recurs in many other areas of policy – arms control, pollution abatement and tariff reductions are the main examples – is ultimately due to the primordial and feeble character of the agencies for international regulation compared with the highly developed, but nationally limited, state. Nevertheless, it is not stretching the imagination too far to envisage coordinated and graduated reductions in working hours under the auspices of the EEC or the OECD along the lines of the lowering of trade barriers negotiated under the GATT in the 1950s and 1960s. Moreover, not all domestic industries are exposed to international competition. There would still be room for innovation in the sheltered sector.
4. In continuous process production, which by its nature requires shift work, the need to avoid awkward shift patterns would probably constrain the form of shorter weekly hours per employee to extra days off in lieu of shorter shifts. More generally, the malleability of job-time patterns is limited by a variety of socio-technical factors. The optimal design of the size and staging of the discrete blocks of time into which a working week of given length can be divided up, will depend on variables such as travel to work times; how long is

required to set up and finish off prescribed tasks within a single block; the time needed to build up an efficient working rhythm; and so on. Such questions make up the standard agenda of flexitime schemes.

5. For a demonstration that employment subsidies offer a greater increase in employment for a given outlay than either increases in public expenditure or cuts in personal income tax, see Metcalf (1982).

6. The knowledge required for effective job performance also includes familiarity with idiosyncratic enterprise routines and custom, and adjustment to the peculiarities and interpersonal dynamics of the established workforce. Learning the ropes in this wider sense may take longer.

7. See, for example, Dilnot *et al.* (1984), ch. 2.

8. See for example the discussion of the early post-war period in Alan Deacon, 'Unemployment and Politics in Britain since 1945', in Showler and Sinfield (eds) (1981).

9. See *Employment Gazette*, October 1981.

10. As Anna Coote and Bea Campbell (1982, p. 59) point out, this much neglected fact was recognised in a backhanded way by the Prices and Incomes Board Report on *General Problems of Low Pay* (NBPI, 1971). The Board agreed that it was 'necessary to consider the problem of men and women separately; otherwise the problem of low pay could become practically synonymous with that of low pay amongst women, and this could ignore the social significance of the fact that men's earnings are normally the main source of family income . . .'

11. To the objection that men and women ought to specialise according to their respective comparative advantages, the feminist reply is: 'Any ruler can cook!'

9
Basic Income, Social Security and the Labour Market

1 Introduction

The key to dismantling the interlocking barriers which stand in the way of a strategy for reducing collective toil and redividing social labour, lies in the idea of an unconditionally guaranteed basic income (BI) allocated to every man, woman and child in society. Precisely what this idea involves is explained in Section 2. Section 3 argues that BI connects an old theme of enlightened social thought with certain desirable shifts in the parameters of social organisation which the evolution of advanced capitalism has now brought within the horizon of possibility. This account of the secular preconditions for basic income is followed in Section 4 by a critique of the assumptions underlying the post-war Keynes–Beveridge regime of full employment and social insurance. It is the crisis arising from the breakdown of this regime which establishes BI as an idea whose time has come. The ways in which BI answers some of the most urgent needs of our age and simultaneously opens up new prospects of social transformation are elaborated in Chapters 10 and 11.

2 The Meaning of Basic Income

'Basic income' is a new name for an old idea. Other names include 'universal grant', 'social dividend' and such less felicitous titles as 'citizen's wage' or 'social wage'.[1] Whatever the nomenclature the idea is to consolidate all existing direct cash transfers payable under social security programmes – whether tied to individual insurance contributions or non-contributory, whether universal or selective; all indirect financial benefits in the form of various personal tax allowances; and all other state grants to persons such as student maintenance allowances and self-employment or small business subsidies. BI replaces this patchwork of personal income support by an unconditionally guaranteed minimum income allocated regularly to every single member of the entire population permanently resident within the jurisdiction of the nation state. BI allocations would be graduated according to *age* – children receiving less, older people more; and according to *degree of disability* – supplementary incomes would be available to cover the contingencies of maternity, bereavement, invalidity, and handicap. The level of the universal BI allocation would be set at some consensually determined standard of subsistence. For practical purposes this standard would almost certainly have to correspond initially to existing supplementary benefit scales. Illustrative BI scales devised on this basis together with their approximate annual cost for the UK in 1985 are set out in Appendix 1 to this chapter. It is worth noting at the outset that these scales are far from generous.

BI is unconditional in the sense that the right to receive it is independent of any of the characteristics commonly used to determine benefit eligibility under the existing social security system or under proposed alternatives such as negative income tax. Specifically, BI is independent of:

(1) *Current employment status*: BI is received alike by employees with jobs, full-time or part-time, by unemployed workers and by persons inactive in the labour market;
(2) *Willingness to enter paid employment*: there is no test of 'availability for work';
(3) *Past work performance*: in contrast to contributory national insurance benefits, entitlement is not affected by the length and continuity of a person's employment record;
(4) *Income from other sources*: BI is paid to rich and poor alike: there is no means test;

(5) *Majority/minority or marital/parental status*: children receive the appropriate rate of BI as well as adults; and adults' entitlement remains the same whether they are single or paired, married or unmarried, heterosexual or homosexual, childless or parents;

(6) *Size and composition of household*: BI is paid to everyone whether they live in single- or multi-person households, nuclear or extended families, communes or institutions;

(7) *Sex, race and citizenship*: there is no discrimination on any of these grounds: the only qualifying conditions are permanent residence within the national territory and the periodic filing of an income tax return.

Certain presuppositions are made in what follows about the operation of the BI system. These concern, respectively, work obligations, the treatment of housing costs, the financing of BI payments and the definition of the tax/benefit unit.

First, not all advocates of BI agree on unconditionality in sense (3) above. Some insist that the right to a minimum guaranteed income must be linked to a reciprocal obligation on all able-bodied adults to perform some publicly acknowledged and specified minimum contribution to total social labour at some time in the course of their working lives. Any such *generalised* requirement would raise immense problems of monitoring and enforcement. It might be administratively feasible, and perhaps culturally desirable, to impose a degree of *age-specific* labour compulsion on young persons graduating from full-time education. Suppose, for example, a transitional form of BI were initially introduced for children and young persons before the system was extended to the rest of the population. This would, after all, be no more than a rationalisation of current arrangements for child benefits, youth supplementary benefit, student maintenance grants and payments made to young people under Special Employment Measures. There would be certain precedents for imposing a labour service obligation on all young persons receiving BI. Many states continue to require their young men (and, less often, their young women) to undertake a period of national military service. There is also a degree of compulsion in the youth training and work experience schemes. Beyond this kind of limited conditionality, however, the administrative and political difficulties of linking BI entitlement to an individual's work record multiply. The general issue whether labour performance can be left as a moral obligation only, or ought to be legally required and sanctioned, is discussed further in Chapter 11.

Second, it is notorious that housing costs vary enormously from one individual to another according to where they live and according to the size and composition of their household, even leaving aside variations due to the standard of accommodation. Both for this reason and in order to contain the initial costs of financing BI payments, it would almost certainly be necessary, at least at first, to exclude housing costs from the calculation of subsistence. This in turn entails the retention of separate arrangements for income support to cover housing costs on a means-tested basis similar to the current housing benefit system administered by local authorities in Britain. The scales and costings presented in Appendix 1 exclude housing costs. Following Hermione Parker (1985), on whose work this illustrative exercise is based, this version of BI might be referred to as *modified* or *partial* BI. Inevitably the retention of a limited element of means testing implies that householders who qualify for housing benefit are subjected to high marginal tax rates as their income from other sources rises. Some ways of ameliorating the impact of this problem are indicated in Section 2 of Chapter 10.

Third, in principle BI allocations could be financed from a variety of sources of tax revenue – income- or wealth-based, direct or indirect, personal or corporate. There are, however, powerful reasons for preferring a method of finance which *integrates* BI with the system of personal income taxation. In what follows it is assumed that BI payments are financed by a progressive tax on the other – earned or unearned – income of each individual. A single personal tax schedule replaces the present dual system of personal income taxation and national insurance, each administered by separate departments of state. Since it is not the intention of BI to discourage personal saving, tax reliefs for contributions to occupational pensions schemes and life assurance premiums are retained. All other personal tax allowances are abolished.

Even within an integrated tax benefit system it still has to be decided how far the system should be *self-contained* and *functionally separated* from other elements of taxation and public expenditure. Suppose that BI payments are the only public expenditure programme financed from the proceeds of personal income tax, all other state spending being defrayed from other sources of taxation or borrowing. This *functional* as distinct from merely *conceptual*, self-containment has the important, and in my view decisive, political advantage of transparency. People know exactly what the taxes deducted from their other income are used for. Moreover, because everyone receives BI, including those whose high incomes attract correspondingly high tax liabilities, they are also regularly reminded of what those with no other sources of financial support have to make do with. The potentially far-reaching implications of maintaining a fully self-contained tax and benefit system are further pursued in Chapter 11.

The drawback with the proposal that personal income tax revenue should be fully hypothecated to basic income is that at present this revenue contributes to *other* public expenditure besides social security benefits. If advocates of BI insist on self-containment, they have to contend with the conventional requirement that proposals for fiscal reform be evaluated on a revenue-neutral basis. In order to keep the state's total tax revenue unchanged they are obliged to propose some addition to other tax levies, or some new type of tax altogether. But this complicates the assessment of the effects of BI and might damage its political credibility. For purposes of comparison Appendix 2 below presents two alternative calculations of the standard rate of personal income tax which would be required to finance the BI scales laid out in Appendix 1: first on the assumption of revenue-neutrality; second on the assumption of full hypothecation.

The fourth point of contrast between BI and all existing or proposed alternative tax/benefit systems is that BI is *individualised*: the tax/benefit unit is the individual person, not any group, un/married couple, nuclear family, household or any other community. For practical purposes children's BI would probably have to be paid to the child's designated primary carer up to the point – assumed in Appendix 1 to be the child's 15th birthday – when the child graduates to financial adulthood. Legal entitlement would, however, reside with the child not his or her carer. The financial rights of adults in need of full-time care would be similarly upheld. Individualisation enshrines two principles central to any non-discriminatory and non-paternalistic conception of individual rights: first, no adult should expect or be expected to be financially dependent on or responsible for any other adult; second, no individual's tax liability or benefit entitlement should be dependent on another person's circumstances.[2]

3 The Secular Preconditions for Basic Income

The intellectual lineage of basic income can be traced back at least as far as the French Revolution. Thomas Paine (1792; 1796) enunciated the principles that the provision of a minimum level of subsistence for all should be the first charge on society's resources; that the removal of poverty was a matter for public policy not private charity; and that in order to avoid invidious distinctions payments from an earmarked communal fund should be made equally to rich and poor alike. Throughout the nineteenth and early twentieth centuries the idea of a universal guaranteed minimum income continued to find exponents among social thinkers of a visionary cast of mind.[3] However, without certain material preconditions this idea could never have made the transition from Utopian dream to practical political programme. The broad, secular aspects of these preconditions are elaborated below. The specific historical conjuncture which gives basic income its contemporary relevance and leverage is dealt with in Section 4.

Some 10 000–12 000 years ago in the crucial 'Fertile Crescent' the hunter-gatherer mode of production gave way to settled agriculture. Paying the penalty for its failure to conserve the delicate balance between human population and natural resources on which hunting and gathering depend, humanity was condemned to quit the Garden of Eden and gain its collective living by the sweat of its collective brow. Since then every mainstream human society has had to produce a net output large enough to meet three principal claims: (1) the provision of a (culturally appropriate) subsistence standard of private consumption for all its members, including non-productive dependants; (2) whatever range and level of public consumption its rulers decided on and could persuade/coerce their subjects to pay for; and (3) whatever investment in facilities for augmenting productive capacity the dominant economic groups were able and willing to undertake. There have usually also been various forms of luxury consumption by privileged groups, and other 'wasteful' uses of social resources such as warfare. But even when all due allowance is made for 'unproductive' consumption, it is evident that the production of a net output sufficient to satisfy all three primary claims has necessitated a lot of work, particularly if the labour of human reproduction and care is included.

Certain historically and culturally variable groups, defined as 'dependants', were exempt from this labour – the very young, a few of the small numbers in each generation who survived into old age, the chronically sick and disabled. In addition the minority leisured classes enjoyed the privilege of full-time absorption in refinement, salvation, politics or debauchery according to their tastes, talents and opportunities. But the overwhelming majority of able-bodied, prime-age, non-privileged, non-dependants were compelled on pain of starvation or punishment to devote upwards of 50 per cent of their discretionary time to the various forms of social labour, whether in the public or domestic domains.

The precise combination of direct coercion, material incentives, non-material rewards and internalised moral imperatives on which societies have relied to elicit labour performance, has varied with the mode of production. The development of capitalism perfected the labour market and the wages system as highly effective and efficient methods of harnessing individual effort, skill and self-interest to the public realm of social production, though primary childcare and housework remained matters for private, familial responsibility. Both labour markets and the sexual division of labour persisted in those societies which expropriated their capitalists (or never had many in the first place) and opted for the state collectivist road to industrialisation and modernity.

The primacy of waged labour had several consequences. Material incentives were elevated as the pre-eminent inducement to supply labour to the public realm of social reproduction. Paid work became the dominant source of money income for the non-propertied majority of society. As the economy became more completely monetised, the acquisition and disposal of money became the proximate motivation in most economic decisions, for individuals no less than for enterprises. Social power and prestige came to depend on access to employment and position within its hierarchies. Excluded groups – the unemployed, the marginally employed, houseworkers, the sick and disabled, children, youths and old people – have generally been poor, powerless and disparaged.

Moreover, once established, the wages system proved to be remarkably resilient and stable. One potential source of trouble was that employers perceived the use of labour power as a cost of production just like any other, and applied to it the same logic of efficiency and cost minimisation. Yet despite repeated dramatic and arresting conflicts springing from the tension between this logic and the human interests of workers, class warfare rarely escalated into an unrestrained fight to the death. In part this was because class relations were not wholly reducible to a zero-sum game: on certain issues the interests of employers and employees, though distinct, converged. Even when conflicts did arise both sides often preferred the path of conciliation and compromise to total intransigence. And much potential conflict simply never materialised because workers' definitions of their interests were continually under pressure to conform to the values of the dominant culture. Thus when prolonged mass unemployment challenged the rationality of the wages system as a source of personal income, fulfilment and purpose, 'common sense' continued to hold that the remedy lay in creating *more* employment through economic growth and/or greater labour market flexibility.

However, alongside the expansion of employment and the wages system, two other long-term evolutionary tendencies began to open up the prospect of gradual emancipation from the 'curse of Adam'. These were discussed at length in Chapter 7. The first is the prodigious growth of labour productivity. The second is the rapidly diminishing urgency of utilising higher labour productivity for the purpose of output expansion rather than toil reduction. Beyond a certain point the higher interests of the species as a whole demand that HE (hyperexpansionism) gives way to SHE (sane, humane and ecologically viable priorities).[4] This point is reached as: (a) average private and public consumption standards scale heights towering above the meagre base-line from which the process of economic growth took off some three centuries ago; (b) the continued pursuit of material growth inflicts increasing damage on the natural base of human activity; and (c) rising levels of private material consumption act more to compensate for social powerlessness, psychological deprivation and spiritual vacuity than to civilise and liberate the consumers.

The convergence of these trends in the advanced industrial countries makes it both feasible and desirable to pursue a new range of options: to relax the grip of the wages system as the organising framework for public labour; to transform the experience and human relations of waged work; to rebalance social priorities between output growth and reduced working time; and to attenuate the link between personal income and contribution to public labour. In this context basic income falls into place as part of a more comprehensive re-adjustment of the course of social development. Specifically basic income would help nudge society gently along four new evolutionary paths: (1) personal income would be progressively decoupled from employment; (2) the total amount of time the collective labourer devotes to waged work would be reduced and redivided; (3) the economy would be re-organised around the concept of ecological sustainability; and (4) dependent and alienated forms of production and consumption would be phased out in favour of independent and emancipated patterns of working and living. Detailed maps of these new high roads are laid out in Chapters 10 and 11.

4 The Dual Crisis of the Labour Market and Social Security System

The Second World War brought about decisive shifts in the balance of political and ideological forces within the advanced capitalist democracies. In the aftermath of the war one country after another instituted reforms establishing or consolidating some form of welfare state. With hindsight it is possible to see that the new Keynes–Beveridge regime embodied six basic assumptions:

(1) Society's work consists of two categories: unpaid and paid. Unpaid work consists of domestic labour performed overwhelmingly by married women who are and wish to be financially dependent on their husbands. Paid work is organised on the basis of formal, stable contracts of employment between employers and individuals – men plus unmarried women within the age range 15 to 60 or 65.

(2) Paid employment is effective in preventing financial poverty for employees and their dependants. It is so effective (a) in the sense that full-time employment earnings are sufficient to keep a man, a dependent wife and one child out of poverty; and(b) in the sense that when the primary wage earner's employment is interrupted or terminated for any reason, family income is sustained at an adequate level through access to a variety of contingent benefits financed from compulsory contributions to the national insurance fund.

(3) Within employment jobs are composed on a standard full-time model and performed by a labour force consisting of primary employees who remain permanently active in the labour market from leaving the education system until retirement.

(4) An average state of full employment for this primary labour force is both feasible and desirable.

(5) High rates of economic growth are both feasible and desirable.

(6) Those individuals unable to support themselves from their earnings or from contribution-based national insurance benefits will be a small minority. To prevent destitution among this minority a residual safety net of means-tested benefits continues to be needed, but can be expected to play only a minor role in the overall system of income-maintenance.

Of these assumptions only (2), (4) and (6) were really made explicit at the time when the Keynes–Beveridge regime was installed. Assumptions (1) and (3) were unstated and uncritically taken for granted. Assumption (5) was grafted on to the rest in the 1950s and 1960s as capitalist economies experienced the most spectacular and sustained phase of growth in their history, and their governments explicitly committed themselves to the policy objective of high and steady rates of growth. Every one of these six assumptions is now either false or dubious. Each is considered in turn below.

Assumption 1: the sexual division of labour, the reconceptualisation of work and the nature of employment contracts

This assumption has been undermined from three directions. First the sexual division of labour has been eroded, though it is far from having completely disintegrated. To mention only a few of the relevant social trends in Britain:

— The all-age labour force participation rate of married women rose from below 10 per cent in the first two decades of the twentieth century to 22 per cent in 1951 and had reached 62 per cent by 1981.
— 54 per cent of women with dependent children were 'economically active' in 1981.
— In the same year the DHSS estimated that there were some 900 000 one-parent families, of which 750 000 were headed by women.
— Only 5 per cent of households of all types now conform to Beveridge's 'standard' model of male breadwinner with a dependent wife and children.

Second, society's work can no longer be neatly dichotomised between informal, unpaid, home-based work and formal, paid work undertaken outside the home on the employer's premises or under the employer's supervision. Additional categories are needed. The most basic distinction runs between work performed in the monetised and non-monetised areas of the economy. Traditional wage labour still predominates in the monetised sector, but it is less preponderant than it was. New forms of financially remunerated work have grown up around it. Homeworking and outwork have revived; there has been a rising, though imperfectly quantified, trend in self-employment; and a growing army of workers is now enrolled in Special Employment Schemes such as YTS and the Community

Programme. All these activities are legitimate. In addition a great deal of work is carried on in the cash-based, underground economy, the scale of which is notoriously difficult to gauge. Whether black-economy work consists of moonlighting by otherwise respectable job-holders, or illicit income-supplementation by social security claimants, does not alter the fact that it deviates from the traditional standard.

Less is known for certain about the profile of work in the non-monetised sector. In an era of upheaval in social conventions the perceived proliferation of household and community activity may be due less to the growth of genuinely new forms of production than to the increased salience of self-provisioning, voluntary work, informal neighbourhood work barter and what may be called 'workplay' pursuits straddling the boundary between labour and leisure. The composition of household output and its techniques of production have, of course, been transformed. But for any given household type neither the average amount of time devoted to domestic labour, nor its allocation between men and women appears to have changed much in the recent past.[5] On the other hand, to complicate further an already tangled picture, there is mounting evidence testifying to the emergence of the alternative economy. This corresponds to what Robertson (1985) calls 'personal and local ownwork'. Some ownwork is straightforward commercial entrepreneurialism. But much of the labour performed by 'lifestyle' or 'social entrepreneurs', or in community businesses, common ownership and cooperative ventures, cuts across the division between the monetised and non-monetised sectors.

Third, as regards wage labour itself, Chapter 7 has already adverted to the variety of ways in which the scope of traditional regulated labour market activity has diminished. Outwork, sub-contracting, temporary hiring, flexitime contracts, part-time work and conversion to self-employed status have all abridged the reach of the formal, stable contract of employment between parties who envisage an indefinite continuation of their relationship barring voluntary turnover, dismissal or redundancy.

*Assumption 2: the adequacy of waged work and national
insurance benefits in preventing poverty*

The definition and therefore recorded incidence of poverty are
problematic and disputed. Of the four poverty standards debated
in the literature (see Atkinson, 1984), the one most suitable for
present purposes is the institutional poverty standard based on
the state's supplementary benefit scales defined in law and
administrative practice. This has absolutely no theoretical
rationale; but it is widely encountered in research and public
debate; it carries an official imprimatur; and it allows the
performance of the Keynes–Beveridge regime to be assessed in
its own terms.

Townsend's meticulous survey (Townsend, 1979), revealed
that 9.1 per cent of his sample (representing an estimated
4 950 000 people) belonged to income units living in poverty
according to the state's standard. A further 23.2 per cent
(representing an estimated 12 600 000 people) lived in income
units on the margin of poverty. 'Margin' here means having a
net disposable income in the previous year lying between 100
and 139 per cent of supplementary benefit scales plus housing
costs. So 32 per cent of a total population of about 55 million
were estimated to be living below, at or marginally above the
state's definition of the poverty line. The fieldwork for
Townsend's survey was conducted in 1968–9, after 25 years of
full employment. The growth of unemployment since then and
the partial deregulation of the labour market in the 1980s are
hardly likely to have produced any improvement on this showing.

It is evident that neither full-time employment nor the national
insurance system are sufficient prophylactics against poverty.
Consider first the incidence of low pay. Taking £85.00 a week as
a compendium benchmark figure based on various possible
definitions of low pay, Pond[6] reports that in April 1981 there
were 1.4 million adult men and 2.3 million adult women who
worked a full week plus overtime, but whose weekly earnings
fell below the benchmark. Exclusive of overtime the total
number of men and women classified as low paid rose to 4.4
million – about one-third of all full-time adult employees.
Admittedly the degree of overlap between low pay and family
poverty is slight. This can be gauged by considering the numbers

claiming and entitled to Family Income Supplement (FIS). This means-tested benefit was introduced in 1971 in belated recognition of the plight of low-income families with children whose principal breadwinner was employed full-time. In fiscal year 1984/5, for example, some 210 000 people claimed FIS, a number estimated to represent a take-up rate of about 50 per cent. On this basis perhaps one-tenth of the full-time low paid experience financial poverty. On the other hand, the very existence of FIS invalidates Beveridge's axiomatic assumption that anyone in full-time employment had adequate resources to support a non-earning wife and one child. Moreover, the number of families who would be eligible for FIS would be much higher – perhaps three or four times higher – without the additional income contributed by secondary family wage-earners, principally married women and typically working part-time at low rates of pay.

Finally, it is also clear that the availability of national insurance benefits to cover the contingencies of sickness, old age and unemployment fails to prevent large numbers of people from relying in whole or in part on means-tested income support. By fiscal year 1984/5 the total cost of the three principal income-related benefits – supplementary pensions, supplementary allowances and housing benefit – had risen to £10 654 million, or 28 per cent of all expenditure on social security benefits. Means-tested income supplementation on this scale scarcely constitutes a fringe phenomenon and indicates just how far the existing social security system acts to *relieve* rather than *prevent* poverty. The shortcomings of the system are considered more fully in connection with Assumption 6.

Assumption 3: 'full-time' jobs and 'full-time' workers

According to the 1983 EEC Labour Force Survey 19 per cent of all employees in the UK were in part-time jobs. This figure is predicted to rise to 25 per cent by the end of the 1980s. As was pointed out in Chapter 7, the growing importance of part-time work reflects a double coincidence between the needs of employers for maximum labour force flexibility, and the gendered needs of women. Some 90 per cent of all part-time workers are women: part-time employment among men is virtually unknown except at the two extremes of the age distribution.

If we add together the number of part-time employees and the number of people defining themselves as self-employed, then already 25 per cent of work in the legitimate part of the monetised economy fails to conform to the 'standard' pattern of full-time waged labour. If we also take account of the numbers wholly unemployed, the proportion of the working population currently deviating from the alleged norm lies anywhere between 35 and 40 per cent depending on what definition of unemployment is used. These figures are not yet high enough to dethrone full-time employment as the numerically dominant form of work activity. They are, however, sufficient to refute any assumption that full-time waged labour represents a near universal norm. They also underline the fragmentation of the contemporary labour market.

Even the hours of work undertaken by so-called 'standard workers' have fallen since 1970, at least on an annual and lifetime basis (see Williams, 1983). As we saw in Chapter 7, the *forms* assumed by reduced working time tend to be distorted: the gender system reinforces the bias of capitalism against significant reductions in *weekly* hours of work. Nevertheless patterns of job time experienced by prime-age, male employees have changed sufficiently in recent years to disturb the previously unchallenged assumption that waged labour is and will remain their central life activity.

Assumptions 4 and 5: the full employment, high growth economy

From a policy standpoint these two assumptions can be considered together. With the prominent exception of the Greens, at all points in the political spectrum the remedy for large scale unemployment is believed to lie in the achievement and maintenance of faster economic growth. Both the feasibility and desirability of this policy objective are highly questionable.

Mainstream macroeconomic debate has focused almost exclusively on the feasibility issue. Space prohibits any serious engagement with this issue here. I simply indicate the scale of the policy problem presented by current unemployment in the UK and offer some general comments.

Officially recorded unemployment figures understate the true size of the *labour surplus* – the difference between the aggregate supply of hours offered to labour market activity, taking existing terms of employment as given, and the aggregate hours of employment actually made available by employers. This understatement arises from definitional adjustments designed to shift the basis of measurement from a 'registration' to a 'claimant' footing; from the effects of Special Employment Measures in reducing the official 'claimant' total; and from the omission of 'discouraged' or passively unemployed workers who are not actively seeking jobs but would (re-)enter the labour market if job prospects improved. In addition it seems probable that many, though not all, part-time workers would prefer longer hours of work if these were available. If the unemployment rate were expressed on a full-time equivalent basis the figure would exceed that officially recorded because the proportion of the unemployed seeking part-time jobs is smaller than the proportion of part-timers in employment (see Standing (1986), p. 94).

At a conservative estimate the true labour surplus on a full-time equivalent basis as a percentage of the working population in the UK in 1986 was probably about 15 per cent – equivalent to about 4 million people. Suppose that a target level of unemployment is set at 1 million – equivalent to 4 per cent of the current working population – to be achieved by steady economic growth sustained over a period of ten years. The calculations showing the rate of output growth required for this target to be attained are set out below.

Employment growth required

Reduction in unemployment from 4 million
   to 1 million   3.0 million
Probable growth in working population over
   ten years (equivalent to an annual average
   percentage rate of growth of 0.5 per cent)   <u>1.5 million</u>
Total increase in employment required
   (equivalent to a growth rate of 1.7 per
cent per annum over a ten-year period)   4.5 million

*Output growth required to meet employment
   growth target*
Basic (equal to annual required growth in
   employment)   1.7%

Plus probable productivity growth along
historic trends   2.0%
Annual required output growth rate   3.7%

These calculations are obviously approximate. In particular
the economy-wide productivity growth rate depends on the
unpredictable pace of technical change and the changing relative
weights of sectors with different factor intensities. The assumption
that its future course will be the same as in the past is made for
want of anything better. Also the calculations make no allowance
for reduced working time: this is in order to focus on the issue
at hand – the feasibility of a return to full employment as
traditionally understood.

The actual rate of growth of the UK's GDP (using the CSO's
average GDP estimates based on output, expenditure and
income data) over the 30, 20 and 10 years up to 1985 was:

         1955–85   2.3% p.a.
         1965–85   2.0% p.a.
         1975–85   1.8% p.a.

The highest average growth rate over *any* ten consecutive years
since 1948 was 3.4 per cent recorded between 1958 and 1968. It
seems improbable that under any government and any plausible
policy regime the UK economy could accomplish the spectacular
improvement over its own past growth performance which is
implied by the perspective of a return to traditional full
employment, even when the transition is allowed to occur
gradually (though steadily) over as long a period as ten years.

But even if the road back to full employment through faster
output growth appeared less formidably arduous than it does, it
would still remain to consider whether the goal of the journey
justifies the effort of attempting it. The unstated assumption of
both neo-liberal and reconstructed Keynesian policy programmes
is that the social benefit of high and sustained rates of economic
growth would unambiguously outweigh any associated costs. It is
precisely this issue of the *desirability* of the full employment,
high growth economy which deserves even more searching
thought and criticism than has been lavished on the feasibility
issue.

The matter is not susceptible to any precise and easily

quantifiable cost–benefit test. Amongst the issues ultimately at stake are: (1) the interests of future generations of humans; (2) the interests of non-human animal and plant species; (3) the risk of irreversible ecological damage; and (4) ethically based conceptions of human needs and social well-being. What is crucial is the frame of reference within which the issue is judged. On a local and historically myopic view there is little doubt that compared with the indefinite continuation of a low growth, high unemployment economy, a prosperous and dynamic capitalist (or, for that matter, state collectivist) economy would be preferable. But on a global and secular scale this kind of comparison appears inconsequential and pusillanimous. Both the low growth and high growth scenarios need to be weighed against a third: the sustainable, conservationist, economy. This alternative option would follow a restrained growth path biased towards energy-saving and the protection of the biosphere. Its industrial strategy would promote hi-tech, sunrise sectors alongside labour-intensive development based on the 4Rs – repair, reconditioning, re-use and recycling. Qualitative improvements in living and working conditions would be linked with an employment policy designed to redistribute job opportunities, reduce the average time spent in conventional paid work, and encourage the alternative economy of personal and communal ownwork.[7]

Assumption 6: the British social security system

Britain's social security budget currently absorbs 30 per cent of total government spending – equivalent to 12 per cent of GDP. Yet even before permanent mass unemployment began to strain the system to its limits, Beveridge's social insurance scheme never operated as its founder envisaged.

The intention of the scheme was that the insured population (i.e. virtually everyone except the minority who contracted out) would be entitled to receive cash benefits geared to their previous contributions. Benefit rates were to be set at levels sufficient to protect against destitution in the event of most contingencies liable to cause it – sickness, unemployment, old age, disability, maternity, loss of spouse's financial support through injury or bereavement. Contribution rates were supposed to be actuarially determined. This insurance system was to be supplemented by a safety net of means-tested benefits to support the minority of the population who for whatever reason lacked benefit entitlement or whose insurance benefits failed to meet their needs.

From its inception the National Insurance Fund was beset by inherent cost problems, particularly in relation to retirement pensions, the largest single item of insurance benefit outgoings. As the authors of a recent study observe, the Fund was rapidly reduced to a 'piece of arcane book-keeping' (see Dilnot *et al.* (1984), p. 18). Insurance contributions were simply levied at whatever rate was necessary to finance the current outflow from the Fund after taking account of the Exchequer subsidy which had been capped at a fixed proportion of the Fund's current income. It had been intended (and continued to be pretended) that contributions would 'pay for' the *future* pensions of those employees from whose pay they were deducted. Instead National Insurance became simply an alternative (and, because flat rate, regressive) form of taxation.

Moreover, despite this financial chicanery, flat rate insurance benefits were never high enough to cover *all* the subsistence needs of *all* those who received them. As early as 1950 more than 20 per cent of insurance benefit recipients depended in whole or in part on means tested National Assistance. This proportion fluctuated thereafter. It fell, for example, in the 1970s because old age pensions were uprated faster than the cost of living; it rose from the late 1970s onwards because of the rise in general unemployment, the rise in the numbers of long-term unemployed, and the erosion of the real value of unemployment benefit. By 1982 one-third of all insurance beneficiaries *also* received supplementary benefit (Dilnot *et al.* (1984), p. 22). An estimated 14 million people received some sort of means-tested benefit.

The present social security system is costly to administer. Because of its piecemeal and unplanned development it is institutionally complex and involves much duplication of information gathering and other clerical and administrative labour. In effect Britain has two separate systems of direct taxation, one administered by the Inland Revenue, the other by the DHSS. Four different general types of benefit are dispensed:

contributory national insurance benefits; non-contributory, non-means tested, categorical benefits; means-tested benefits; and various 'passport' benefits in cash and kind.

Complexity in turn arises because an insurance-based contingency benefit system is inherently susceptible to the gradual incursion of means-testing. Problems of cost, equity and inflexibility have long been recognised as points of vulnerability. First, contingency benefits necessarily cost more than selectively targeted, means-tested benefits. The former, by definition, are delivered to everyone who satisfies the stipulated benefit qualification regardless of their other income. It follows that the tax rate required to support contingency benefits will exceed that needed to finance income-related benefits. In order to relieve cost pressures and the perceived burden on taxpayers, contingency benefit rates are liable to be held down. But restraint entails that the poorest beneficiaries then require additional, means-tested income support to bring them up to a predetermined subsistence level. In this way a contingency benefit system is subject to pressures which undermine the intention of minimising reliance on means testing and give rise to a dual system of income maintenance.

Second, contingency benefits may be inequitable as between beneficiaries and taxpayers. Even if the system is *broadly* redistributive from high income taxpayers to low income beneficiaries, there are liable to be anomalous cases. Some atypical beneficiaries will have higher pre-tax/benefit incomes than some relatively poor taxpayers. If all beneficiaries receive a uniform flat rate benefit, this pre-existing inequality will be widened. In this respect too the principle of universality is vulnerable to demands for greater selectivity. The savings made by withdrawing 'unnecessary' benefits can be used to help low-income taxpayers either by raising the tax-threshold to remove them from the tax net, or by devising some new income-related benefit aimed in their direction.

Third, the social insurance principle is too inflexible both in cross-section and over time. Cross-sectional rigidity arises from the inevitable failure of flat rate benefits to cope with the differing circumstances of different individuals and households. Suppose benefit rates are set so as to constitute an actuarially fair return on past contributions. Only by a fluke will this actuarially determined *average* entitlement correspond to the subsistence needs of any particular person or family. Average benefit levels may, for instance, over- or under-provide for actual housing expenses. As a result some people end up with more than they need, others with less. If it is desired to obtain a closer correspondence between benefits and housing costs, there is no alternative to a means-tested housing rebate scheme. Similarly over time the social insurance principle is too slow to adapt to changes in social conditions and/or to new perceptions of social deprivation. The classic case of the former is the emergence of one-parent families. The classic case of the latter is the recognition of the plight of families dependent on the earnings of a low-paid worker in full-time employment.

The proliferation of means-tested benefits outside the social insurance system strengthens the hand of those who oppose the principle of universality. If a considerable element of means-testing has already penetrated the arrangements for income maintenance, and appears to be unavoidable, it becomes that much more difficult to resist the case for reconstructing the entire system around the principle of selectivity. Advocates of a negative income tax and other wholesale reforms can lay claim to both realism and compassion in demanding that the finite revenues squeezed out of reluctant taxpayers be more effectively and efficiently deployed by targeting benefits on those whose needs are greatest.

Means testing in a dualistic social security system also generates familiar operational problems. Bureaucratically administered payments intended to make up inadequate incomes to guaranteed levels are difficult to understand, cumbersome to process and repose a high degree of discretion in the hands of state officials. Outcomes in individual cases may be uncertain, arbitrary, inconsistent and inequitable. Litigation procedures intended to safeguard claimants' rights may be slow and intimidating. At the same time the prevention of benefit fraud is always liable to degenerate into a repugnant, undignified and intrusive process, particularly in connection with cohabitation and availability for work rules. For these and other reasons there is invariably a gap between the estimated numbers entitled to various benefits and the actual number of claimants.

Even if take-up rates were complete, means-tested benefits

necessarily entail high marginal tax rates over the range of income to which they apply. Workers whose effective choice is confined to low-paid jobs are caught in the unemployment and poverty traps. They may have little incentive either to enter the labour market or to make greater efforts at self-improvement once they are in it. Moreover, the fact that unemployment and supplementary benefits payable to those below pension age are *conditional*, perversely encourages idleness and fraud. Able-bodied claimants must be 'available for work' and must not place 'unreasonable restrictions' on the kind of work accepted. Whatever the objective state of the local job market, unemployed benefit claimants are effectively prohibited from doing anything other than 'looking for work'. In theory unpaid voluntary activities or training for more than a minimum number of hours per week are ruled out. In practice this rule is widely evaded. An unknown number of claimants manage to supplement the dole through regular or intermittent participation in the 'black economy'. Meanwhile the state, anxious to appease popular hostility to 'scroungers', searches for ways to curtail the idleness trap, eliminate benefit fraud and engineer cuts in measured unemployment. New controls are devised to comb out the ranks of the long-term unemployed. Though largely cosmetic, initiatives such as the Restart scheme give the appearance of vigorous physiotherapy on the labour market's creaking joints.

To summarise: Britain's social security system never worked as Beveridge intended. In any case social insurance is inherently flawed as a method of preventing poverty. And the proliferation of secondary, means-tested remedies for these flaws subverts the principle of universality and begets a welter of waste, irrationality and injustice. The next two chapters develop the positive case for basic income both as a solution to the crisis caused by the breakdown of the Keynes–Beveridge regime, and as the centrepiece of a transformatory project.

Appendix 1   A Partial Basic Income Scheme*: Illustrative Scales and Annual Cost for the UK 1985

	Numbers involved (millions)	Weekly rate (£)	Annual cost (£ billion)
Universal basic incomes			
1. Each adult	44.0	22.45	51.36
2. Each child	12.3	14.35	9.18
Basic income supplements (*added* to universal BIs)			
3. Each expectant mother	0.7	14.35	0.26
4. Each widow/widower	0.3	22.45	0.17
5. Each person aged:			
65–84	7.8	27.55	11.17
85 and over	0.6	32.55	1.02
6. Each invalid/handicapped person below age 65	1.0	27.55	1.43
7. Disability costs allowance	?	variable	1.70
		Total annual cost	76.29

* BI scales exclude housing costs. Means-tested housing benefit is payable to householders on the scales applicable in 1985 to cover rent, local authority rates and water rates, but not mortgage interest payments. With no other income beyond the BI allocation a claimant is entitled to receive a £5.25 householder element plus £2.05 heating addition plus rent plus rates plus water rates. Housing benefit is withdrawn at a rate of 33 per cent for every £1.00 by which total *household* income rises above the BI level.

Notes

1. The weekly rate corresponds to the ordinary supplementary benefit rate payable to single non-householders aged 18 and over as at November 1984.
2. The weekly rate corresponds to the ordinary supplementary benefit rate payable for children aged 11–15 inclusive. This scale could be graduated according to age.
3. The weekly rate equals the child's BI rate payable for 26 weeks.
4. The weekly rate equals the adult BI rate payable for 26 weeks after bereavement.
5. At age 65 both men and women become entitled to an age supplement which brings the basic 'old age pension' up to £50.00 per week for a single person. Of this total £15.00 is assumed to cover housing costs. There is no earnings restriction. A further £5.00 is payable at age 85.
6. Cf. the age supplement. There is no earnings restriction. The benefit unit is the individual invalid/handicapped person not the carer.
7. These are discretionary payments additional to universal BI and BI supplements and individualised. For a further discussion of the scheme see Parker (1985).

Appendix 2　Standard Rate of Personal Income Tax Required to Sustain the Partial Basic Income Scheme Outlined in Appendix 1*

*These calculations are entirely static and take no account of any of the economic adjustments induced by the introduction of BI. They can, therefore, be regarded only as illustrative of the orders of magnitude involved.

1. *Definitions and magnitudes* (all figures refer to annual values in £ billion for the UK 1985)

$BI = 76.3$ annual cost of partial basic incomes at scales set out in Appendix 1.

$HB = 3.0$ 75 per cent of local authority expenditure on housing benefit in fiscal year 1984/85: outgoings are assumed to be reduced by the vertical redistribution of income under BI and the high benefit withdrawal rate.

$A = 1.0$ cost of administering the BI scheme; equals approximately two-thirds of the cost of administering social security benefits in 1985.

$IT = 42.0$ total UK taxes on household income.

$NIC = 24.0$ total contributions to the National Insurance Fund by employers, employees and self-employed.

$PRT = 12.1$ employers' national insurance contributions; now replaced by a 7 per cent payroll tax yielding the same total revenue; exemption could be granted as a selective marginal employment subsidy.

$S = 45.9$ total social security benefits and other current transfers to households from central government.

$HRT = 3.5$ proceeds of higher rate basic income tax; corresponds to estimates of annual amount by which tax liability of higher rate taxpayers was reduced between 1979 and 1985.

$ITB = 189.7$ income tax base = total household income from all sources less BI less HB less employee contributions to occupational pension schemes less individual premiums for life assurance policies; total household income = direct money income from work and property (wages and salaries, income from self-employment, rent, dividends and interest) plus income in kind plus life assurance and pension benefits, social security benefits and other current transfers.

t　standard rate of personal income tax.

2. *Tax rate formulae*

(a) *Assuming personal income tax revenues are fully hypothecated to BI:*

$$t = \frac{BI + HB + A - HRT}{ITB} = 40.5\%$$

(b) *Assuming the tax rate is set on a revenue-neutral basis:*

$$t = \frac{BI + HB + A + IT + (NIC - PRT) - S - HRT}{ITB}$$
$$= 44.7\%$$

For comparison the standard rate of personal income tax in the UK in 1985 was 29 per cent, in addition to which employees paid national insurance contributions at an average rate equivalent to 9 per cent of gross earnings. Thus, *ceteris paribus*, the financing of a partial BI scheme would have required a rise in the effective standard tax rate of either $2\frac{1}{2}$ or 7 percentage points depending on whether assumption (a) or assumption (b) is adopted.

Sources of data : CSO, *The United Kingdom National Accounts* 1986 edition, London, HMSO (1986); DHSS, *Reform of Social Security: Programme for Action*, Cmnd 9691, London, HMSO (1985).

Notes to Chapter 9

1. 'Universal grant' translates the French expression 'allocation universelle' introduced by the Collectif Charles Fourier (1984). 'Citizen's wage' and other variants containing the word 'wage' are best avoided. The implied similarity with employer–employee relations is misleading when, as proposed here, income entitlement is unconditional, non-contractual and non-reciprocal. The traditional term 'social dividend' has more to recommend it. The assertion that each individual has an inalienable right to a minimum income regardless of his or her contribution to social labour, can be justified as a claim on the collective social capital bequeathed to the present generation by the cumulative work and inventiveness of all our ancestors going back to time immemorial. However, 'basic income' has become the accepted term of art, popularised in Britain by the Bulletin of the Basic Income Research Group (1985–6). The first international conference on basic income held in 1986 at Louvain-la-Neuve in Belgium led to the formation of BIEN (Basic Income European Network) to foster informed discussion on this and related issues throughout Europe.

2. For a fuller discussion of these points see Miller (1983).
3. For an outline history of this idea see Morley-Fletcher (1980–1).
4. These acronyms are borrowed from Robertson (1985).
5. See the studies edited by Lewis and O'Brien (1987).
6. C. Pond, 'The Low Paid', in Bain (ed.) (1983).
7. The broad conclusions of such a three-way comparison of growth scenarios for the Netherlands over the period 1980–2000 are reported by Hueting, R. in Ekins (ed.) (1986).

10
Basic Income and the Transformation of Work

1 Introduction

The consequences of any proposal for large-scale social reform are fraught with uncertainty. Nevertheless the claims advanced in this chapter on behalf of basic income amount to more than a merely speculative prospectus. A start has already been made in charting the broad features and developmental tendencies of a BI society and in marking the boundaries of its *terra incognita*.[1] Undoubtedly much more intellectual exploration is needed to push back these boundaries. But it should be borne in mind that theory and empirical simulations can only improve our knowledge of this new world up to a point: on some crucial issues extrapolations or predictions based on *current* behavioural patterns will never be a reliable substitute for actual historical experience. A case in point is the response of labour supply once the unprecedented step has been taken to convert waged work into an activity which is genuinely optional for everyone, not just for those with independent means.

Uncertainty about what will happen if a BI system is introduced, can usefully be compared with the similar problem which attended the century-long shift from property to persons as the subject of Parliamentary representation in Britain. Neither the supporters nor the opponents of universal adult suffrage fully anticipated the ramifications of a properly democratic constitution; nor could they have. Their irreducible ignorance did not prevent passionate debate and agitation over the franchise; nor should it have.

The analogy between BI and universal suffrage is instructive in another respect too: neither institution is a panacea for society's ills; yet each represents a decisive benchmark in human development. Both facilitate, though do not guarantee, the amelioration of power imbalances and social inequalities; and both regulate, though do not remove, the instability and conflict which nearly always bedevil relations between dominator and dominated. This is a recurrent theme of the argument which follows and is taken up again in Chapter 11.

For analytical and stylistic convenience this chapter assumes that the political transition from welfare state capitalism to basic income capitalism has been completed.[2] The strictly political feasibility of this transition is considered in the next chapter. Here BI capitalism is assessed both retrospectively by comparison with the system it has replaced, and prospectively in terms of the new evolutionary possibilities it opens up. The order of treatment corresponds to a steady rotation in the direction of assessment from past to future. Section 2 shows how BI remedies the principal defects of the contemporary social security system summarised in Chapter 9. Section 3 focuses on BI as a solvent for the obstacles to reduced working time and the redivision of labour identified in Chapter 8. Section 4 appraises BI's potential for deconstructing the power and status divisions which rest on the historic primacy of paid employment within the overall process of social reproduction. Section 5 investigates the forces impinging on the pursuit of toil reduction in a BI society.

2 Overcoming the Defects of the Present Social Security System

BI offers four improvements on the existing system of income support: it is more effective, humane, equitable and cheaper to run. It is more effective in the sense that since BI is paid to everyone as of right, there is no problem of low take-up rates. A birth certificate activates entitlement to the child rate of BI for each new human infant; a death certificate extinguishes each individual's claim.[3] Between cradle and grave the only obligation imposed on individuals to maintain their right to BI is the periodic filing of a tax return, just as the submission of an electoral return is a precondition for enrolment on the register of electors.

BI is more humane than previous arrangements because it is unconditional. With one transitional exception discussed below, it dispenses altogether with means testing. It follows that the old unemployment and poverty traps are greatly curtailed. Apart from any extra costs incurred in taking up or changing jobs – notably on account of transportation and any bought-in childcare – anyone who performs any paid work at all, for however few hours and however little remuneration, is financially better off than otherwise, even after paying the standard rate of tax. By the same token BI satisfies the traditional principle of 'lesser eligibility': no one who remains 'unemployed' obtains a higher income than the poorest employed person, other things being equal. The unconditional nature of BI also removes the idleness trap and the benefit fraud associated with the old 'availability for work' test.

The only limitation on BI's trap-springing power arises in connection with a *partial* BI system. As explained in the previous chapter, at first BI would probably have to operate in tandem with means-tested housing benefits. In such a hybrid system the effective marginal tax rate on low income householders exceeds the standard rate of tax. It is possible to minimise any resulting disincentive effects by careful design of the taper applied to housing benefits as earnings rise. A low earnings tax relief would also ease this problem. Disincentives would in any case be less extensive and less severe than today: only householders, not all low-income wage earners, would be at risk; and only one benefit, not several, would remain income-dependent. These vestigial survivals of earlier arrangements would naturally disappear if *partial* BI scales were subsequently uprated to provide a comprehensive subsistence guarantee.

A low earnings tax exemption would incidentally be useful in offsetting those costs of entering or changing jobs which still gave rise to residual unemployment and poverty traps. This device might also be needed to avoid unintentionally reinforcing the sexual division of labour. Otherwise married women with heavy family responsibilities who used to earn a little from part-time work, would be too readily tempted to withdraw altogether from the labour market. On the one hand BI would act as a windfall replacement for their previous earnings; on the other hand the higher standard rate of tax would cut their *net* hourly wages. Some women may choose this option anyway and take out the benefits of BI in the form of relief from the double shift. The point is not to set up an incentive structure which predisposes women to opt for full-time domestic labour.

BI avoids the redistributive inequities thrown up by a contingency benefit system. Everyone's untaxed minimum income is the same (allowing for age and disability supplements). Everyone's other income is liable to taxation. The relationship between pre- and post-tax benefit incomes is displayed in Figure 10.1 below. Pre-tax/benefit incomes are distributed along the 45°

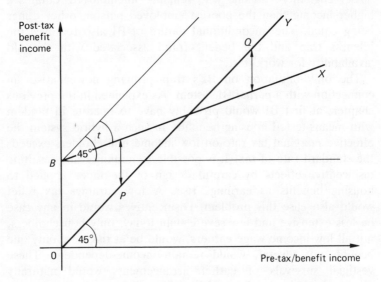

Figure 10.1

line *OY*; post-tax/benefit incomes along *BX*. The distance *OB* represents the level of universal basic income; the fraction *t* represents the standard rate of tax.

Consider any pair of individuals with pre-tax benefit incomes corresponding to points on *OY* such as *P* and *Q*. Basic income allocations and tax deductions between them shift these points upwards and downwards respectively on to the line *BX*. It is clear that the inequality in income between these two individuals cannot be *widened* by the operation of the BI system. Whether *overall* distributive justice is improved in the immediate aftermath of the changeover to BI is a separate issue which cannot be settled by *a priori* theorising. This question is in any case far less important than BI's *long-term* egalitarian dynamic, as explained in the next chapter.

The final advantage of BI over preceding systems is that once the transition is completed it is cheaper to run despite the much larger volume of income transfers entailed by true universality. The individualisation of the tax/benefit unit greatly increases the number of units to be processed. But this *scale* effect is more than offset by cost savings due to the *integration* and *simplification* of transfers. Redundant social security staff can be redeployed into the tax evasion branch of the Inland Revenue. More effective policing of tax returns increases the chance of detecting dishonesty. At the same time the abolition of the idleness trap diminishes the incentive to conceal 'black economy' earnings. On both counts the tax base is widened and a small virtuous circle builds up. The larger the tax base, the lower the tax rate needed to finance BI; the lower the tax rate, the less the gain from tax evasion; and the more the 'black economy' is regularised, the smaller the strain it imposes on social solidarity.

3   Reducing Working Time and Redistributing Employment

On plausible assumptions a BI system promotes the elusive double objective of reducing job time and redistributing waged labour. Consider the class of primary employees analysed in Chapter 8. Figure 10.2 below depicts their opportunities and preferences before and after the advent of BI. Assume that these workers belong to households with incomes above subsistence who do not, therefore, fall into sub-classes 1 and 2(a) of Chapter 8's taxonomy of losers. Assume further that their attitudes to job time are not distorted by the 'deviant' attachment to intrinsic or positional work rewards characteristic of sub-class 4. Two types of primary employee are distinguished in Figure 10.2 according to their relative valuations of free time and income. The first displays a traditional, 'masculine' set of priorities represented by the

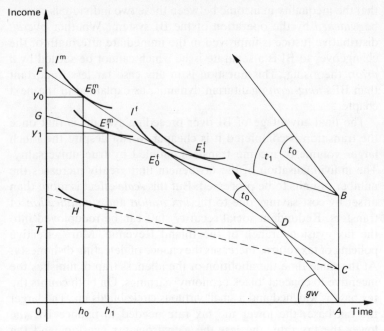

Figure 10.2

indifference map labelled I^m. The second goup's more 'feminine' preferences, represented by the indifference map labelled I^f, reveal a greater willingness to give up income in return for marginal gains of free time. The analysis focuses first on the 'masculine' group.

Prior to BI these workers face a budget constraint ADF determined as follows. Each worker's total time endowment is OA hours. The gross hourly wage is gw represented by the slope of AD. Personal tax allowances are such that the first tranche, $0T$, of income is exempt from tax. Above this threshold income tax is levied at a constant proportional rate t_0. Hence the budget constraint is kinked at D. A linearised equivalent budget constraint FDC is also shown. This 'as if' construction indicates that for workers who earn enough to attract tax liability, the tax rules are equivalent to a lump sum transfer of AC, after which every unit of earned income is taxed at the rate t_0.

Now suppose that the tax allowance is abolished and replaced by universal basic income at the rate AB. At the same time the tax rate on other income is raised to t_1. Assume provisionally that the gross hourly wage remains unchanged at *gw*. The workers' budget constraint now alters to *ABG*. Their previous standard working hours were Ah_0 corresponding to the equilibrium point E_0^m. BI restructures their feasible choice set. Assuming their preferences between free time and income remain the same, they now opt for shorter working hours of Ah_1 at the equilibrium point E_1^m.

The movement from E_0^m to E_1^m can be decomposed in the usual way into substitution and income effects. The relative price effect of the fall in the *net* hourly wage is shown by the movement from E_0^m to *H*. To avoid cluttering the diagram it is assumed that the price elasticity of labour supply is zero. (The prediction that primary workers will press for shorter working hours is, of course, strengthened if their labour supply curve displays a conventional, positive slope.) The income effect of BI is shown by the move from *H* to E_1^m. It is clear that provided the labour supply curve is not backward-bending, and provided income and free time are both normal goods, the workers are induced to negotiate a reduction in working hours.

The 'masculine' workers' post-BI equilibrium position, E_1^m, is less preferred than their original constrained optimum, E_0^m. In terms of the earlier taxonomy of losers these workers could belong to any of the sub-classes 2(b), 2(c) or 3, depending on what happened to their *household* income as a result of the transition to BI. It is not, of course, a necessary consequence of this transition that primary employees should perceive themselves as losing from it. The other group of workers shown in Figure 10.2 exhibit 'feminine' time priorities. Their equilibrium positions before and after the changeover to BI are E_0^f and E_1^f respectively. These workers were overemployed: they experience the gain from shorter working hours as outweighing the loss from reduced income. Thus even if labour supply preferences are taken as given, BI may still yield static welfare gains by loosening institutional constraints on possible patterns of job time and enabling some workers to achieve a more preferred balance of their time- and income-budgets.

It is also possible to doubt whether preference orderings would remain unaffected by the process of transition to basic income capitalism. As was argued in Chapter 6, the attitudes and values which underly preferences are continually being confirmed or revised in the course of political and ideological contestation. Before BI could be introduced major changes in society's political and ideological balances would have to occur, and these would be consolidated and perhaps augmented once the new system was in place. As the work ethic retreated, 'feminine' time values would gain ground over 'masculine' priorities.

Suppose, however, that primary workers fail to define their interests in this way and do not, therefore, experience what might be called a transformatory welfare gain. Even if significant groups continue to regard themselves as worse off after BI than before, from a distributional standpoint their perceived losses have to be weighed against others' gains. The employment consequences of the introduction of BI are depicted in Figure 10.3. Conventional assumptions are made about the aggregate hours of labour supplied and demanded in the labour market: *ceteris paribus*, the former

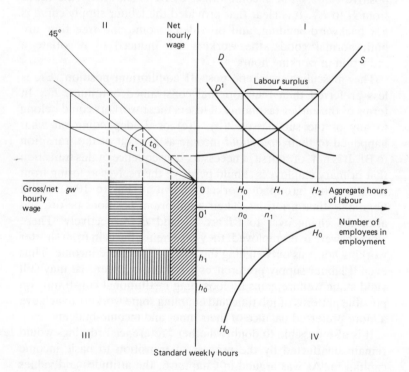

Figure 10.3

are an increasing function of the *net* hourly wage; the latter a decreasing function of the *gross* hourly wage.

The initial labour surplus is represented by the distance H_2H_0 in quadrant *I*. If the *gross* hourly wage, shown in quadrant II, remains at gw when the tax rate rises from t_0 to t_1, employers continue to demand H_0 hours of labour. Hence the labour demand curve drawn with respect to the *net* hourly wage is displaced vertically downwards from D to D^1. The fall in the *net* hourly wage causes aggregate hours offered to contract along the labour supply curve S and the labour surplus is reduced to H_1H_0.

In quadrant IV the unchanged quantity of employment hours is shown as the product of the rectangular hyperbola H_0H_0. When standard weekly hours fall from h_0 to h_1, there is an equiproportionate rise in the number of workers in employment from n_0 to n_1. There are thus two clear gains to be set against any loss experienced by primary workers: new workers obtain jobs, and society's labour surplus is reduced.

In practice these gains may be qualified. First, it is not certain that the position of the aggregate labour supply schedule will remain fixed as assumed in Figure 10.3. This depends on whether the effect of BI in improving incentives for workers previously excluded from the labour market balances its effect in prompting primary employees to opt for shorter working hours. The former pulls the supply curve out to the right, the latter to the left. The final size of the labour surplus may therefore be greater or smaller than shown in Figure 10.3.

Second, the relationship between standard weekly hours and numbers in employment may not be accurately represented by the rectangular hyperbola of quadrant III. As noted in Chapter 8, the productivity of primary employees may rise when hours of work are shortened; new employees may be of poorer quality than incumbents; and in any event employers will incur certain adjustment costs in moving from one level of employment to another. The post-BI number of workers in employment will lie below n_1 to the extent that productivity rises and/or the state fails to provide adequate tax concessions/subsidies to offset employers' adjustment costs and any costs of training inexperienced or unskilled workers.

Third, money-conscious primary employees may be prone to various forms of working hours recidivism. Some of the new jobs created may be taken up by moonlighters. Also negotiated cuts in the standard working hours may be followed by unscheduled overtime drift if incumbent workers attempt to stretch out work (reduce hourly productivity) in order to qualify for premium overtime pay. Temptations to claw back net weekly earnings by these routes could be diminished by a progressive tax regime which imposed higher tax rates on additional earnings above the standard rate band.

But the assumption which is really critical to the success of BI in promoting shorter job times and more jobs is that the gross hourly wage remains unchanged. Suppose that primary workers attempt to off-load the burden of higher taxes by pressing for higher gross wages, and that employers concede their claims. Several adverse consequences ensue. If individual labour supply curves are positively sloped, the incentive to negotiate shorter working hours declines. An increase in the gross wage reduces the employers' demand for labour hours below the level previously assumed, and the job-creation effect of any given cut in standard working hours is diminished. And if employers attempt to pass on higher unit labour costs in higher prices, the real value of BI is eroded. Quite apart from its undesirable consequences for the distribution of income, this erosion cancels out the income-effect of BI in encouraging primary workers to opt for shorter hours.

Three circumstances enhance the risk of unwanted upward pressure on gross wage rates. First organised labour's bargaining strength improves as the labour surplus falls and employment rises. Second, the wider impact of BI may disturb established pay relationships to the detriment of the higher paid. The forces acting to compress or stretch out the pay structure are discussed in Section 5 below. Third, it is inevitable that some workers, considered as individuals, will find that their net weekly income from all sources is lowered by the transition to BI. This is particularly likely to be the experience of higher paid, and in general better organised, workers.

Quadrant III of Figure 10.3 illustrates this last point. Suppose that BI is initially introduced at a weekly rate equal to the former social security benefit available to a single, long-term unemployed person. The pro rata hourly wage equivalent of this benefit level is indicated by the vertical intercept of the aggregate labour supply schedule in quadrant I: no one would have been willing to enter the labour market at a net hourly wage below this. Using the 45° line in quadrant II the *weekly* income contributed by BI can then be represented by the diagonally shaded area of quadrant III. The shorter working week reduces workers' net weekly earnings by an amount equivalent to the vertically shaded area. The higher rate of tax subtracts a further slice equal to the horizontally shaded area. Thus an individual worker's net income from all sources rises, falls or remains the same according as the first of these areas exceeds, falls short of or equals the sum of the other two. Evidently BI is less likely to compensate for the two deductions from pre-BI net weekly earnings, the higher is the worker's gross wage.

Whether the risk of wage inflation can be held at bay depends on the willingness of organised workers to under-utilise their bargaining power in the wider interests of society as a whole. A workable BI system cannot be introduced without the active support of organised labour. The conditions necessary to motivate and sustain the requisite social solidarity are considered in the next chapter.

4 Deconstructing Employment Status

In a fully operational BI system the conventional division of the population by employment status loses the significance it has today. Eventually the categories 'full-time employee', 'part-time employee', 'self-employed', 'unemployed' and 'economically in-active' would be discarded. For example, one effect of the progressive shortening of working hours discussed in the previous section would be to soften the current status division between 'full-time' and 'part-time' work. More generally the partial decoupling of income from employment diminishes the pre-eminence of waged labour compared with other types of work and other uses of time. This section examines the repercussions of this adjustment in four specific areas: domestic work and the sexual division of labour; lifecycle work patterns and the general division of labour; work in the alternative economy; and the measurement and recording of social reproduction.

Within families BI redistributes the balance of power and responsibility between men and women. The concepts of 'primary breadwinner' and 'the family wage' are fatally undermined. The proportion of average family income derived from employment declines relative to that derived from social transfers. The proportion of average family income accruing to women in their own right increases, especially if children's BI is paid to primary childcarers – in most cases their mothers. This in itself constitutes an important social advance. As recent studies of poverty *within* families have shown (see Brannen and Wilson (eds), 1987), material hardship and an abject lack of autonomy are still today the lot of large numbers of financially dependent women and children whose husbands and fathers are by no means low paid. BI subverts men's power to conceal, withhold and control their family's financial resources.

Beyond this elementary blow against patriarchy the implications of BI for domestic work and the sexual division of labour are difficult to assess. Recent research (see Lewis and O'Brien (eds), 1987) suggests that changes in the respective contributions of men and women to childcare and housework have been glacially slow. Real, as opposed to promised or imaginary, sightings of a new, caring and domesticated species of human male remain rare. BI will certainly alter the climate of family relations, and this in the end will dissolve the frozen frontiers of domestic responsibility. But the timescale of the melting process may turn out to be measured in generations rather than a single lifetime.

Several interim developments are possible. The option of genuine financial independence outside marriage may raise the rate of separation and divorce, and lower the rate of marriage and remarriage. Combined with the spread of artificial insemination by donor, these trends could further expand the number of one-parent families headed by women. Arrangements within conventional families would depend on whether the underlying sexual division of labour remained intact. Women who continue to shoulder disproportionate responsibility for housework and childcare may be tempted to withdraw from part-time labour market activity. BI rebalances the attraction of full-time domestic labour compared with the wages, companionship and stimulation offered by a paid job, even if tax incentives are rigged so as to discourage exit from employment. Women who select the former option at least escape the burden of the double shift without losing all financial, and therefore personal, autonomy. The status of domestic labour is also likely to improve when those who do it are no longer unpaid and unnoticed family servants. BI cannot be equated with the old feminist demand for 'wages for housework': it is every citizen's unconditional right, not a monetary compensation for contributions to social labour. Nevertheless, by dislocating the absurd equation of work with employment, it achieves much the same result.

Finally there is the possibility of renegotiating the sexual division of labour. We have seen how by enhancing personal income security BI removes certain obstacles to shorter employment hours, particularly on a weekly basis. An expansion of men's job-free time permits, though does not ensure, a fall in male absenteeism from domestic labour. How far men's and women's familial roles move towards genuine symmetry would depend on women's success in asserting their claims to life's opportunities, and on men's willingness to transfer time released from factory and office to their homes and children rather than the pursuit of ego-gratification. At all events BI marks a new stage in the unfinished revolution against the gender system.

Men's anxiety over loss of status, power and material reward can hardly be expected to vanish overnight. But if BI threatens masculine privileges and values, it also opens up compensating possibilities of personal growth and fulfilment both inside and outside the formal job market. The fact that the division of labour is a functional necessity in any advanced society by no means entails a fixed, inflexible and hierarchical allocation of persons to its various specialised branches and positions. Just as BI prompts men and women to negotiate a freer interchange of roles between home and labour market, so it also helps to prise apart the technical and cultural aspects of the division of labour generally.

Industrialists and politicians are fond of urging workers to show greater willingness to switch between work stations in the course of their working lives. But this kind of admonition usually reflects a one-sided concern to equip industry with a pliant and adaptable labour force. It is meant to rouse society to meet the challenge of technical and structural change and to guard against the placid, but lethal ways of the museum. There is, however, another, neglected side to labour mobility.

Consider, first, the entire array of occupations and activities involved in the process of social reproduction. According to the classification scheme presented in Chapter 5, some of these will be waged, others unwaged; some contribute primarily to the production of people, others are mainly object-producing; and some give rise to commodities for sale, others to goods or services intended for direct use. Consider next the disposition of the working population across this array. Taking each generational cohort societies can be arranged in a spectrum according to the openness of this disposition. By this is meant how far, given society's rules and conventions, its individual members are able and willing to transfer across the various positions in the array over the course of their working lives, and thus acquire a variety of different *kinds* of work experience.

At the closed end of the spectrum are stationary caste and feudal societies in which occupational mobility and experiential diversity are zero: all persons are assigned at birth to predetermined slots in the work array and stay there until overtaken by death or incapacity, whereupon one of their kin takes over. At the other extreme is a society in which each able-bodied citizen is free from social restraints on work mobility and enjoys the opportunity and desire to engage in a multiplicity of different types and levels of activity in the course of his or her lifetime.

Actual societies stand somewhere between these extremes. But it seems safe to say that contemporary capitalist societies are closer to the lower than the upper limit. Erikson *et al.* (1983) conclude that considered *net* of the effects of structural change, social mobility chances in Western nations have displayed considerable stability over post-war decades. Goldthorpe *et al.* (1980) argue that although the Western working classes are now somewhat reduced in numbers, their internal homogeneity has actually increased. Downward mobility into working-class positions has declined; the influx of labour from greatly contracted agricultural sectors has slowed down; as a result these classes are now predominantly self-recruiting. The decisive importance of education as a channel for upward mobility means that those who do break away do so when they are young. The bulk of working-class kids who pass on into working-class jobs can expect a lifelong affiliation to their hereditary class and a correspondingly restricted work-life experience.

BI does not in itself and immediately push society towards the open end of the mobility spectrum. But it does create a base for exerting pressure in this direction. With BI as a safe anchorage for their material needs, individuals acquire more real options in the choice of life itineraries. Part-time work, job-splitting, flexitime, sabbaticals and lifelong access to education and training become so many channels leading on to new horizons. Broader layers of the population can begin to savour the varied and rounded lifestyle which hitherto has been the prerogative of the privileged few.

Obviously there are limits on work mobility: natural, economic and social. It is physically impossible for anyone to sample more than a handful of the vast number of positions in the occupational/activity array. Further constraints are imposed by efficiency considerations. The technical demands of jobs should not exceed the capacities of their occupants. (The opposite kind of inefficiency arising from the *under-utilisation* and *suppression* of individuals' capacities should also be considered a problem.) In addition labour allocation owes some regard to the principle of comparative advantage: not just absolute abilities, but also relative suitabilities are relevant in matching people to jobs. Finally the structure of social power is likely to restrict the scope for threading new pathways through the work matrix: wider mobility options may at first be more or less confined to the *horizontal* plane.

As in the case of the sexual division of labour, how far the *vertical* dimension of the general division of labour will succumb to improved mobility chances is uncertain. It is important to distinguish between better opportunities for ascent within structures which preserve clear lines of superordination and privilege, and the compression of the structures themselves. Nevertheless over the long run a BI system creates space for an egalitarian dynamic to deconstruct the hierarchical order of society's labour. This dynamic is further discussed in Section 5 and in the next chapter. The culmination of this process would be arrangements which enabled and encouraged each person to participate sequentially in each major *category* of social labour. For example, activities might be classified according to their material characteristics, social purpose and relations of production. This might yield, say, a fivefold division into menial, caring, administrative, skilled and creative types of work. Apart from time spent undergoing education and training, everyone would expect to spend a portion of their lives in work subsumed under each of these headings.

Long before this point BI immediately improves the eligibility of one particular work option outside the sphere of conventional employment. As things stand today, the opportunity to become self-employed, or to set up a small business – whether on an owner-proprietor, partnership or cooperative basis – is limited by the requirements of commercial viability. All such projects must provide their workers with a subsistence income as well as covering their other costs. In a BI system the commercial imperatives become less exacting. Whatever happens subsistence is guaranteed. Projects need cover only the costs of energy, materials and overheads to remain financially viable. Indeed, workers in the alternative economy might be content with little or no personal monetary return provided the intrinsic satisfaction of their work was sufficiently great. Intrinsic rewards might derive from the nature of the task – as in the case of artistic production; or from the purpose of the activity – such as service to the community; or from the relations of production involved – as with self-managing producers' cooperatives.

The promotion of the alternative economy is one of the ways in which BI signals the need for a new approach to the measurement of social reproduction. Another is the collection of unemployment and underemployment data. Statistics based on the number of people claiming social security benefits would be obsolete. The extent of idleness might still be gauged by a headcount of the numbers registering as jobless at official job centres. But since contingent unemployment benefit has been superseded by unconditional BI payments, the financial incentive to register disappears. In addition many of those using the centres to seek employment might well be engaged in unpaid or alternative economy work. In these conditions it would make good sense to introduce regular and wide-ranging population activity surveys. One of their objectives would be to ascertain the size of the labour surplus in the monetised economy. Unemployment in the old sense might be unmeasurable; but the labour surplus would not have been abolished by a mere definitional sleight of hand. Improved statistics on desired and actual aggregate hours of employment would enable debate to focus in an informed way on the appropriate mix of policy remedies as between demand expansion, labour supply contraction and the redistribution of job opportunities.

Activity surveys would also encourage the adoption of new indicators of well-being and the quality of life. In contrast to the old measures of employment and unemployment these would be more comprehensive and less tied to the labour market. For example, one important task would be the compilation of time-activity profiles by sex, age, marital status, household type, and so on. The object would be to discover the numbers of people participating in various categories of social activity and the amount of time devoted to each. A major advantage of tracking social reproduction in this way is that important areas of social life are not hidden from observation by the observer's own perceptual framework. Domestic labour and the alternative economy suddenly leap into view.

Statistical innovation along these lines is the BI analogue of the system of national income accounting devised during the Second World War as an adjunct to demand management. But the concepts and techniques of welfare capitalism were designed for specific historical purposes. Basic income capitalism demands new methods of social auditing to complement, amend or transcend the established computations of GDP. It is, for instance, quite inappropriate to attempt to widen the ambit of social measurement by imputing a *monetary* value to the output of the non-monetised sector. Similarly national income conventions are seriously flawed in their treatment of what have been called *defensive* expenditures.[4] These are costs incurred in eliminating or neutralising deteriorations in living, working and environmental conditions. Examples are pollution control, the treatment of illness directly caused by prevailing patterns of consumption, and extra insurance and security precautions against theft and burglary. It is decidedly eccentric to count such expenses as net *additions* to, rather than *subtractions* from, the flow of goods and services delivered for final use.

Two final reasons for developing alternative records of social activity are suggested by the argument of this section: first, to consolidate a long overdue reconceptualisation of work; and, second, to inform a transition beyond basic income capitalism to a more fully egalitarian order.

5 Abating Toil

In Chapter 7 attention was drawn to the internal, subjective aspect of 'toil'. The implication is that toil abatement involves more than the crude reduction of job-time. It also calls for the suppression of types of work which are intrinsically unrewarding, and the promotion of those in which labour ceases to be experienced as a sacrifice requiring monetary or other external compensations, and becomes instead an agreeable and purposeful activity conferring its own psychic rewards. In a pure free market economy the logic of BI spontaneously favours both forms of toil-reduction. In reality this logic is likely to require an organised and concerted push.

Imagine a society whose labour markets are completely de-regulated: all incumbent or prospective job holders are freely mobile; there is unrestricted access to all job slots; wages are fully responsive in both directions to surpluses and shortages of labour. Wage flexibility implies that labour markets always tend to clear: the number of hours of labour employed both in the aggregate and in each micro labour market corresponds to a point on the relevant labour supply schedule. It follows that Keynes's 'second classical postulate' (see Keynes (1936), ch. 2) is satisfied: the marginal utility of the real wage is equal to the marginal disutility of labour, 'disutility' being understood to include every kind of circumstance that might lead workers to withhold their labour. Furthermore, *relative* wages reflect the *relative* disutilities of different jobs.

Imagine now that this society decides to introduce BI. To study what happens next it is essential to appreciate that waged work has become genuinely optional. Employers can rely on neither starvation nor duress to recruit and retain a labour force. Equally, the supports which used to set a minimum floor to wage levels have been removed: an unconditionally guaranteed subsistence income is available outside the labour market; and conditional, out of work, social security benefits have been withdrawn. So the situation is as follows: workers are neither slaves nor wage slaves; employers need no longer pay a 'living wage'; wages are free to adjust in response to workers' preferences for different kinds of work; and workers are able to make their preferences effective.

Now, given the array of jobs on offer, each with its associated toil value, workers will tend to shun intrinsically unrewarding tasks, and seek out those with lower toil ratings. In the short run employers have to raise wages in the former case and will lower them in the latter. In the long run the logic of cost minimisation leads employers to substitute either capital or low toil labour for relatively more expensive, high toil labour. Boring, dangerous, dirty, menial and generally oppressive tasks are automated, technology permitting; otherwise, their quality is improved through job enrichment, more congenial working conditions, less autocratic forms of management, and so on. These toil-reducing consequences of relative wage movements and factor substitution are further reinforced by wider opportunities for low income, but also low toil, work in the alternative economy.

Unfortunately this pleasant vista is likely to be clouded by the presence of labour market segmentation. Where the labour market is divided into a regulated core and commodified periphery, it would be unwise to put too much faith in the liberating potency of market forces. For it has to be remembered that the starting level of BI provides only the barest subsistence living: the purely material incentives to labour market activity remain strong. In addition the removal of the poverty, unemployment and idleness traps releases on to the market a fresh stream of workers whose endowments of skill, work experience and character are generally poor. If the labour market is segmented, and if entry into desirable, but inaccessible core jobs is denied, this increased supply of low quality labour flows into the periphery. There is, therefore, a risk that sectoral labour gluts will actually *worsen* pay and conditions in high toil jobs.

The neo-liberal solution to this problem is to break down restrictions on job access by extending the sway of market competition. But even if it were feasible to subject all employment positions to a perpetual competitive race open to all comers, this would still leave intact the conditions which today cause the pay structure to reinforce, rather than compensate for, inequalities in the toil ratings of different jobs. Competitive equality of opportunity and meritocratic career progression are quite consistent with vertical stratification at both ends of the race. Competitors arrive at the starting line already handicapped or advantaged by unequal initial endowments of marketable attibutes. The order in which they pass the finishing post determines their rank in the employing organisation's hierarchy of authority and responsibility.

In practice deregulation is likely to be only *partial*, extending the width of the periphery by flaking off the outer fringes from the core. For core employment is not a monolithic citadel of privilege. Even in regulated labour markets toil ratings and wages tend to be inversely correlated. Hospital ancillaries, for example, have a high ratio of drudgery to pay. BI will hardly succeed in reversing this ratio if the queue of applicants for menial hospital jobs grows longer because the jobless have no realistic hope of gaining any other type of paid work; still less if ancillary services have been sub-contracted out to competitive tender. If deregulation is likely to twist wage relativities in the wrong direction, it would be better to maintain statutory controls or collective bargaining for labour markets vulnerable to chronic excess supply. Minimum wages and non-wage conditions restrain employers from taking advantage of the fact that society has relieved them of responsibility for paying a living wage, encouraging them instead to search out other, productivity-raising and toil-reducing ways of holding down unit labour costs. However, this still leaves the problem of peripheral overcrowding and an unabsorbed labour surplus.

At this point the enterprise must steer clear of a further cul-de-sac. Suppose BI scales are uprated above bare subsistence in an attempt to drain off the labour surplus. Employment privilege now becomes entrenched. Having been eased out of the labour market, an idle underclass is pacified by the ancient Roman expedient of bread and circuses. Meanwhile tax-paying job-holders are liable to resent the burden on their pockets. Once again, as on previous occasions in this chapter, it appears that the institution of BI lays down a marker for the direction of social development, but cannot alone ensure that society follows it. Additional momentum is needed to expedite the progressive dynamic of toil abatement.

Some clues as to how the extra motivational energy might be generated can be gleaned by considering the effects of shorter working hours within the enterprise. In microcosm this case anticipates the broader prospects explored in the next chapter. It was pointed out in Chapter 8 that if standards of work intensity are held constant, a generalised reduction in hours of employment entails some combination of upwards promotion, new recruitment and job upgrading at each level of the hierarchy of authority and responsibility. The first two of these options increase the ratio between senior and junior staff; the third redistributes downwards some of the more highly prized and responsible tasks formerly incorporated in senior job specifications. In all three cases the shape of the organisational pyramid is modified to look more like a somewhat flattened, rectangular block: the vertical distance between horizontal sections is reduced; and the width of the upper sections is extended relative to those lower down.

The distributional consequences of internal restructuring exactly parallel those discussed earlier in connection with shorter working hours and increased employment. The positional value of jobs at any given organisational level is diluted. To the extent that senior job-holders cleave to a hierarchical mentality, they suffer a welfare loss. If, on the other hand, they become convinced that the new enterprise relations of production represent a superior mode of collective collaboration, they experience a transformatory welfare gain. But even if their preference for the old regime remains unreconstructed, their disappointment has to be weighed against the headway made by others.

All three responses to shorter working hours produce gains for someone. But from the standpoint of toil reduction particular importance attaches to the third, job enrichment option. Suppose that toil scores depend only on the range of material activities assigned to the workers in each job specification, and on the proportion of their working day devoted to each activity. Since toilsomeness is a subjective matter, the relevant scores are, of course, those which are (or would be) awarded on average by the workers who actually perform each job. Ratings vary between 0 and 1 depending on how far each job group obtains intrinsic rewards from its designated time-activity profile, and would want to maintain the same profile even if they received gratis (some of) the income for which they currently have to work. Jobs whose incumbents find them unappealing in every respect have a toil value of 1. Those in which work is 'no longer a means, but life's prime want'[5] score 0.

The rank order of toil scores is likely to correlate fairly closely with the enterprise hierarchy. If so, a downwards redistribution of the more intrinsically satisfying work packages not only reshapes the organisation into a more egalitarian mould, but also tends to reduce the collective labourer's aggregate toil factor. Job enrichment helps to reduce high toil ratings attached to the more humble posts. At the same time some marginal impoverishment of the more exalted posts still affords their occupants enough high quality work to leave their lower toil ratings unaffected. Toilsomeness probably also depends on the social as well as the material relations of production. If the recomposition of the labour process is accompanied by, say, more relaxed methods of supervision, or a more democratic managerial control system, the effect on collective toil is even more pronounced. The whole operation relieves toil twice over: once on account of shorter job times, and again by lowering the toil factor.

Rearranging the detail division of labour within the enterprise may incur adjustment costs and some short-run loss of allocative efficiency. There may, however, be offsetting, dynamic gains in X-efficiency if toil abatement raises standards of work intensity. In the longer run, once job satisfaction has become a salient feature of industrial culture, the quality of working life is likely to receive higher priority in decisions about job design and the choice of techniques. Job enrichment also points to the converse possibility of sharing out responsibility for any residual dead-end tasks, thereby contributing to the kind of versatile and egalitarian working lifecycle envisaged in Section 4.

In order to realise this benign vision, however, there would have to be a veritable cultural revolution within each enterprise and within the wider society. The next chapter outlines the way forward.

Notes to Chapter 10

1. See, for example, Miller (1983); Ashby (1984); Boulanger *et al.* (eds) (1985); van der Veen and van Parijs (1987). The arguments presented in this chapter draw heavily on these references.
2. This terminology is due to van der Veen and van Parijs (1987) who helpfully decompose what they call 'a capitalist road to communism' into two stretches comprising two distinct transitions. The first covers the move from welfare state capitalism to basic income capitalism. The second starts where the first leaves off and leads to communism, which they define as a society in which the social product is distributed entirely in the form of basic income allocations, and no one is coerced into performing social labour ('from each according to his abilities to each according to his needs').
3. Claims might be temporarily transferred after death as bereavement grants available to surviving partners or orphans.
4. See C. Leipert, 'From Gross to Adjusted National Product', in Ekins (ed.) (1986), pp. 132–9.
5. This is Marx's famous characterisation of labour in a future communist society. See Marx (1951), p. 23.

11
Basic Income: Incentives, Ethics and Political Strategy

1 Introduction

This final chapter deals with the ethical and political aspects of basic income. Section 2 seeks to defend BI against the charge that the high tax rate needed to sustain it would destroy economic incentives. Section 3 rebuts a number of moral objections to a transfer system in which guaranteed incomes are both unconditional and universal. Section 4 acts as a bridge between these abstract disputations and the political context which a transformatory strategy is obliged to address. Having noted that BI belongs to the more general class of 'citizenship rights', the argument draws out the tension between these rights and the logic of the market. A movement committed to the BI project could re-empower the claims of citizenship, infusing them with the moral appeal, motivational energy and political direction which are needed not just to shake off the debilitating consequences of the neo-liberal counter-revolution, but to establish an entrenched, gradualist dynamic of egalitarian transformation.

The issue examined in Section 5 is whether such a strategy is politically feasible. It is suggested that even on short-term and narrowly self-interested criteria a majority of the population stands to gain from the introduction of BI. But this majority is unstable, weak and unlikely to acquire an adequate political form without the active support of the organised labour movement. Sections 6 and 7 tackle the labour movement's reservations about BI and conclude that they are unfounded. By embracing the BI strategy as its own the labour movement can revitalise its political fortunes and reclaim its historic title as an agent of human emancipation.

2   Economic Incentives

From a strictly economic standpoint the main objection to BI is that it could prove to be a recipe for general impoverishment. If no one is obliged to earn a living, why should anyone wish to? What if the higher tax rate needed to sustain universal BI allocations so diminished labour market incentives as to reduce national income? Any fall in income would contract the tax base. The same volume of BI transfers could then be maintained only by raising the tax rate. But this would further erode incentives and cause the whole productive system to collapse in a vicious, downward spiral.

In responding to this anxiety three preliminary points are worth reiterating. First, one of the central objectives of BI is to promote reduced working time and redistribute job opportunities within the formal, public sphere of employment. Necessarily this entails a marginal *withdrawal* of labour supplied by 'over-employed' workers, particularly prime age males in core jobs. At the same time for workers previously caught in the unemployment, poverty and idleness traps BI actually strengthens labour market incentives compared with the system it replaces. Second, to the extent that formerly illicit waged or self-employed work in the 'black economy' is regularised, *measured* GDP rises and the tax base is broadened. Third, BI promotes work in the self-employed, cooperative and small business sectors. If new projects are fully commercialised, any re-allocation of labour away from the conventional labour market entails no corresponding reduction in national income. Indeed, if diverted labour were previously idle, national income rises. If labour flows into non-monetised, alternative economy activities, any fall in measured GDP should, in principle, be adjusted for the increased output of non-traded use values.

Let us, however, set aside these complications and concentrate on the macroeconomic issue whether, if everyone's subsistence were guaranteed, the aggregate supply of hours to the conventional labour market would fail to provide an adequate tax base for BI. Recall first that BI preserves the traditional principle of lesser eligibility. Those who wish to enhance their personal incomes above the minimum guaranteed level still have an incentive to do so, particularly since this level would at first hardly be princely. As Chapter 10 showed, BI induces labour supply adjustment *at the margin* – precisely what is wanted – not a wholesale exodus from the labour market.

A rather more fundamental point to be borne in mind in judging the incentive issue is that it is not the supply of labour that determines the overall level of output and employment, but the demand for labour emanating from the decisions of employers. The labour supply schedule is a *frontier*. It sets an upper limit to the extent to which output and employment can be increased at any given real wage. Actual employment may lie anywhere between zero and this upper limit depending on how much output employers decide to produce, and therefore, with given equipment and techniques, how much labour they require.

In Figure 11.1 below the range of possible *sustainable* levels of employment is represented by that section of the labour demand schedule, D_L, above the point E corresponding to the market-clearing wage $(\frac{w}{p})^*$. Points on D_L below E are not sustainable. At a point such as B firms encounter physical shortages of staff which threaten to reduce their output below planned levels. Their normal response will be to raise wages either to attract new employees to unfilled vacancies or to elicit extra hours/higher intensity standards from their incumbent workforce. What happens thereafter depends on the macroeconomic repercussions of these micro-level adjustments. Micro wage setting serves only to determine the *money* wage. But it is the *real* wage to which labour demand and supply respond; and the movement of the real wage depends on the cumulative outcome of all wage and price decisions across the economy as a whole. If a generalised rise in money wages succeeds in driving the real wage up towards the market clearing level, the labour shortage at B is eased and employment rises along the labour supply curve, S_L, towards E. If, on the other hand, rising money wages are accompanied by an equiproportionate rise in product prices, the

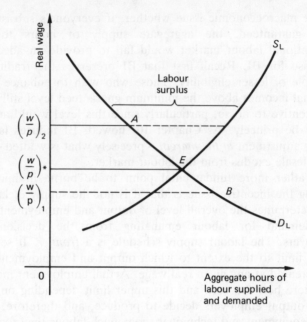

Figure 11.1

real wage remains unchanged, the labour shortage persists, and an inflationary wage-price spiral ensues. Sooner or later macro intervention will be required to correct the underlying disequilibrium and induce employers to cut back their demand for labour along D_L.

By contrast a point such as *A is* sustainable. Here firms' output plans are not constrained: they can obtain all the labour they need. There is, however, a labour surplus measured by the distance between S_L and D_L along the horizontal corresponding to the real wage $(\frac{w}{p})_2$. Mainstream economists continue to dispute whether, if wages were fully flexible, downwards as well as upwards, the range of possible employment levels would in effect reduce to the single point *E*. What is not in doubt is that for the foreseeable future Britain and most other advanced capitalist countries will continue to experience a large and chronic labour surplus. Against this background fears that BI will precipitate a drastic labour shortage seem decidedly eccentric.

There are three broad strategies for reducing the labour surplus.

Neo-liberals advocate the commodification of the labour market in the belief that greater wage flexibility will induce the economy to move along D_L from A to E. Keynesians agree on the desirability of the destination, but hold several reasons for doubting whether it can be reached via the neo-liberal route. First, even in the absence of trade unions money wages tend to be sticky except in rare instances where jobs are open to permanent competition and hiring is casual. Second, a generalised fall in money wages cannot be guaranteed to reduce the *real* wage. Third, even if real wages fall, the consequences for aggregate output and employment are uncertain and difficult to determine a priori. Economy-wide wage cuts not only lower firms' costs, but also produce complex effects on the real demand for goods and services. Demand may rise, fall or remain unchanged depending entirely on contingent and volatile conjunctural circumstances. Hence the move from A to E is best accomplished by direct action to stimulate aggregate demand, buttressed by supply-side planning to improve the economy's responsiveness to demand expansion, and by controls to curb its unwanted side effects, notably inflation.

The combination of BI and reduced working time stands in marked contrast to these growthist, employment-expanding strategies. Changes in job time patterns allow more job openings to be created: hours of paid work at point A are shared out more equitably and the number of persons wholly unemployed falls. At the same time the labour supply frontier is pulled inwards as hours currently supplied to the conventional labour market are diverted into alternative forms of useful non-employment. The contrast need not be absolute: elements of the Keynesian and neo-liberal approaches could still find a place within a redistributive employment policy. There is, for example, no warrant for the fatalism which has overtaken macroeconomic policy since the neo-liberal counter-revolution destroyed the faith of informed opinion in demand management. Modest, but sustained demand stimulation remains an important tool in averting or escaping from recession. Similarly, shorn of the doctrinaire demand for deregulation, the idea of pricing labour into jobs becomes relevant when the policy problem at hand is to change the *composition* rather than the *level* of employment. Thus in an economy following a deliberately chosen path of restrained growth selective marginal employment subsidies could be used to reduce labour costs in

246 The Future of the Labour Market

priority sectors and steer employment towards energy-saving, non-polluting or labour-intensive activities.

As part of suitably modulated employment programme it ought not to be impossible to design BI scales and tax rates so as to reduce the prevailing labour surplus without overshooting the target and creating an overall labour shortage. Admittedly, firm knowledge of labour supply responses to BI is sparse and is unlikely to be consolidated until the system is actually tried. This is not, however, a decisive objection to the *principle* of BI, any more than comparable uncertainty about the effects of widening the franchise on the conduct and outcomes of the political process, constituted a principled objection to universal suffrage. At most uncertainty is a reason for proceeding with caution. A step by step, gradual approach is indicated: first in fixing BI scales and tax rates; and second in widening the range of eligibility for BI during the transition to a universal system covering the whole national population. It would also need to be acknowledged beforehand that incremental advances in the level and coverage of BI might need to be reversed if unforeseen and undesired consequences arise.

This last point provides one of the reasons for insisting that BI and personal income taxation should form a fully integrated, self-contained system. Entitlements and tax rates are thereby subject to the discipline of the tax base, and hence become properly articulated with the performance of the monetised economy. The implications of marginal adjustments can then be more easily assessed and monitored, and a clear focus exists for public debate and negotiation over the conduct of policy. Incentive problems and the avoidance of labour shortage will inevitably figure among the items discussed. The broader coverage of the agenda is considered in Section 7 below.

3 Ethical Objections to Basic Income

The BI principle provokes two kinds of moral disapproval. One rests on meritocratic grounds, the other invokes a needs-based standard of distributive justice.

(i) The meritocratic objection

Some people allege that it is morally wrong and socially unjust for the state to transfer income to those who have done nothing to deserve it. The assumption here is that able-bodied citizens establish desert either by their past or current contribution to social labour or by satisfying some other test of their willingness to work. There are really two strands to this objection. One is disapproval of social parasitism: no one should be able or encouraged to rely on unreciprocated handouts levied from the rest of society. The other involves a judgement of equity: it is (a) unfair and (b) socially divisive that those who have made no sacrifice by contributing to society's work should be treated in the same way as those who have. It is unfair by virtue of the principle that equal sacrifices should attract equal rewards. It is socially divisive because deserving citizens who have (or believe themselves to have) fulfilled their obligations to society are liable to become resentful towards 'scroungers'.

These two strands are commonly woven together. They are, however, logically distinct: parasitism could still be a problem even when, as is in fact the case with BI, no question arises of inequitable treatment. BI treats everyone alike with due allowance for age and disability. Holding property ownership and unearned income constant, the income of anyone who works in the monetised economy exceeds that of anyone who chooses either to work outside the monetised economy, or to do no work at all. The personal distribution of income in a BI society may fail to be just in some broader sense. Just as happens now, inequalities of income will continue to arise from inequalities in endowments of income-yielding assets and in market opportunities. Constraints on individuals' choices about how much of what kinds of work they do and on what pecuniary and non-pecuniary terms will still be subject to various consciously contrived or unintended structural inequalities in power. As explained in Section 4 below, basic income capitalism directs public attention to sources of social injustice and supplies a ready made channel of redress. It does not automatically produce any momentous levelling of incomes. It certainly does not violate the widely held norm enjoining some degree of proportionality between sacrifice and reward.

This leaves the parasitism argument: Is it not corrupting and degrading to permit any able-bodied adult to live on other people's backs? Before answering we first need to clarify whose backs we are talking about. That contemporary society can afford to present an unrequited gift to all its members without destroying its economic base is a consequence of its advanced level of productivity. This enviable option has been inherited from the work and inventiveness of all our forebears going back to Adam and Eve. The usufruct of our material and cultural heritage does not have to be distributed as a social dividend available equally to all. But if society chooses to use its patrimony in this way, then the option of workless subsistence is extended to everyone without distinction. To this extent both the idle who elect to exercise this option and the industrious who do not, stand on the same footing – or backs.

This does not, of course, mean that industriousness ceases to be a virtue. Work is still needed to maintain and develop society's reproductive forces. What counts as work and how far its performance exacts a toilsome sacrifice are, as we have seen, questions which cannot sensibly be answered solely by reference to activities in the labour market. Anyone who contributes to any aspect of social reproduction must be regarded as working. Certainly it is desirable that everyone who is able to do so should make some contribution to society's work. It is also desirable that, as far as possible, work roles should be freely chosen and neither punitively nor structurally enforced.

Basic income is perfectly compatible with the precept that work is preferable to idleness. There is no disagreement on the importance of continuing to uphold a moral and cultural climate prescribing work both as a social duty and as an integral part of any rounded human experience. The only outstanding issue is how society is to ensure that its members assimilate and abide by this norm. Sheer economic necessity is now less critical to the choice of methods for enlisting labour performance than at any time since the neolithic agricultural revolution. Society is able to dispense with the crude threats of coercion and starvation. As long as material incentives sustain an adequate supply of labour to the monetised economy, both in the aggregate and at the micro level, there is no binding reason to make BI entitlement conditional on work contributions. Incipient labour shortages can be averted by wage increases and readjustments in BI scales and tax rates.

The choice of compliance methods rests, therefore, largely on political and social criteria. A system of compulsory labour backed by legal sanctions against the workshy would be difficult to police and enforce. Not the least of the reasons for this is the broad sweep of the activities which can all legitimately be subsumed under the heading of work. There is also the enhanced opportunity and desire for a mobile working lifecycle which BI would encourage. On both counts it would be virtually impossible to devise administration routines for distinguishing between bona fide workers and lazy drones. Labour compulsion would in any case strike a jarring, anachronistic note at a stage in human development when waged labour had become genuinely optional and the realm of free time was expanding as the average employee's time commitment to waged labour shrank.

Suppose that a minority of citizens opts for impoverished idleness. As long as the size of this minority does not threaten to deplete the supply of labour to the monetised economy, the only reason for punishing their behaviour would be to appease the working majority. But the same factors which make skiving difficult to detect also reduce its social visibility. To the extent that skivers continued to be noticed and to cause offence, they would attract pity, contempt or ostracism. It is not obvious why these social penalties need to be compounded by legal retribution.

(ii) Why pay basic income to those who do not need it?

Like any universal benefit BI conflicts with the principle that income transfers should be restricted to those who need them and weighted in favour of those whose needs are greatest. By this standard it is unjust to spread transfers evenly, but thinly, across the whole population. A selective transfer system could do more for the poor at a lesser total cost by withdrawing superfluous benefits and retargeting them towards those whose incomes are inadequate to meet their needs.

This classic rationale for selectivity glosses over the practical problems of means testing discussed in Chapter 9. But even if these problems did not exist, any selective benefit system is bound to be socially divisive. It cannot avoid driving an institutional wedge between net beneficiaries and net taxpayers. Certainly benefit recipients are less humiliated and less dependent on the goodwill of donors when the state mediates between them. But as long as the principle of selectivity remains, state-sponsored transfers are only a half-way house between private charity and guaranteed rights. The dependency relationship is socialised, but not abolished. BI, by contrast, minimises the disconnection between taxpayers and beneficiaries and creates a more robust basis for social solidarity. The prevention of poverty becomes an entrenched public responsibility in which everyone acquires a stake.

Moreover the status of income distribution as a *res publica* is far more transparent in a BI society than under any other income transfer regime. Everyone receives a regular reminder of the financial resources available to the least privileged sections of society, and of their own position relative to this base-line. As argued in Section 4 below, these institutional arrangements create fertile ground for the progressive growth of citizenship rights and the gradual abatement of unjustifiable economic inequalities. The argument for selectivity takes altogether two static a view of social justice and ignores the dynamics of a BI society.

There is a more immediate riposte to popular incomprehension and unease about paying the rich as much as the poor. Those who neither need nor wish to claim their entitlements are under no obligation to take them up. Without in any way forfeiting their rights, people with ample private means could be issued with a standing invitation to top up their compulsory tax payments by voluntarily foregoing their BI allocations. Voluntary donations would be retained within the system and applied either to raising BI scales or reducing the tax rate. In a fully self-contained transfer system donors could be confident that the state would refrain from exploiting their generosity by raiding the BI fund to finance other public spending programmes. Alternatively donors might be given the option of directing unwanted benefits into a separate overseas aid fund to supplement whatever official aid finance the government proposed to provide. Finally, anyone who was reluctant simply to leave what was due to them in the public coffers, would still have the option of continuing to draw their benefit in order to hand it over to the charity or voluntary organisation of their choice. Indeed, the whole voluntary sector might be expected to broaden its fund-raising activities beyond flag days, sponsorship and tax convenants to include mass appeals for secondary transfers of BI.

Admittedly, there is no strong incentive for the rich to behave in any of these ways. Individual donations are microscopic relative to the aggregate magnitudes involved. Charitable acts are always vulnerable to the taunt that barring some miraculous multiplication of loaves and fishes, crumbs from the tables of the rich can never fill many hungry bellies. On the other hand, charitable impulses might flourish if offered a partnership with the state in a secular effort to refute the belief that the poor are always with us.

There is, however, one respect in which the needs-based argument deserves to be taken seriously. This concerns the starting level of BI scales. BI is expensive and its introduction is likely to encounter considerable resistance. It is not difficult to envisage a political compromise in which in return for acceptance of the principle of BI, scales are initially set at such levels that they would be inadequate for anyone with no other source of income. But if the price of BI is that poor people become financially worse off than they are under the *existing* system, it is unacceptable. This is a minimum requirement which the design of any new system must satisfy. At the same time it would not be reasonable to demand that the poor should become immediately better off under BI than they would be under any *conceivable* reform of the tax and benefit system. This demand cannot be met. It will always be possible to devise some hypothetical scheme based on selective and conditional criteria which would outperform BI in this respect. But purely static calculations of immediate distributive outcomes are only one, and by no means the most important, basis for comparing alternative transfer systems. In the long run what matters is transformatory potential.

4 The Logic of Citizenship

In the previous section it was argued that compared with other transfer arrangements BI minimises the social distance between beneficiaries and taxpayers. This point exemplifies a broader characteristic of a BI society which can be summed up in the phrase 'the logic of citizenship'.

In T. H. Marshall's classic statement (Marshall, 1950) citizenship is realised to the extent that all members of a national society enjoy in common a body of civil, political and social rights.

The achievement of citizenship is thus an inherently egalitarian undertaking. Marshall further contends that the gradual extension of citizenship rights from the political to the social sphere brought about by the creation of the welfare state, is also a means of 'class abatement'. By this he means that the welfare of individuals and groups comes, up to a point, to be independent of market contingency: economic inequalities rooted in market relations are in some measure offset and their wider social implications attenuated.

Goldthorpe, commenting on Marshall's analysis some thirty years later, adds the following postscript: '. . . with the realisation of citizenship, the contrast between the principled equality of rights that it bestows and the unprincipled inequalities thrown up by the market will be highlighted, and . . . the latter will thus increasingly be called into question' (see Goldthorpe, 1978, p. 202). And not only does the advance of citizenship delegitimise market inequalities; it also makes for progressively greater equality in the conditions of conflict. Political and civil rights, including the secondary system of 'industrial citizenship' based on independent trade unions and the apparatus of collective bargaining, establish an institutional platform from which social rights can be fought for. Each fresh conquest opens up new opportunities and aspirations. Trade unions and other collective associations in civil society are encouraged to press for extensions in the range and standards of citizenship rights. As Goldthorpe puts it: '. . . the working out of the logic of citizenship, in its ongoing war with class, is specifically aimed against the idea, coeval with capitalism, of labour as a commodity' (Goldthorpe, 1978, p. 203).

The context of Goldthorpe's remarks was the post-war evolution of the Keynesian-social democratic state. By the 1970s this state had become dynamically unstable. The contradictions between citizenship and market were acute. They could be resolved only by recombining these principles in a new state formation in which one or the other predominated. Trade unions and other interest groups stepped up their efforts to improve on market outcomes and resist market logic. The consequences were intensified inflationary conflict over distribution, and an emergent, though more fitful bid to democratise the control of production.[1] Arguably these conflicts reached their highest pitch in Britain. Here a labour movement which was economically strong, but politically weak, proved incapable either of appreciating the nature of the dynamic in which it was caught up, or of forging a strategy for advancing the claims of citizenship in a reconstructed state. As a result the disequilibrium of the existing state remained unresolved. Eventually the initiative and responsibility for rectifying it passed into the hands of political forces deeply hostile to the citizenship principle, and radically determined to reassert the primacy of the market. The long march of citizenship was halted and turned into a partial retreat.

Viewed against this background the BI principle holds out the prospect of resuming the struggle not just to recover ground lost during the years of the neo-liberal ascendancy, but to re-establish forward momentum along a new line of advance. For a society which can be persuaded to embark on it, basic income opens up a path of development which runs in a direct line from advanced capitalism to what used to be called communism. At this end of the path property ownership, market privilege, bargaining power and sheer luck tip the distributive scales heavily against the feeble counterweight of a decrepit system of social security. At the further end work and distribution are based on the celebrated (but rarely investigated) principle: 'From each according to his abilities to each according to his needs'.

The starting level of basic income is the current state-approved standard of subsistence as laid down in supplementary benefit scales. But there is no reason why BI should forever remain at this parsimonious level. Once the BI principle has been culturally assimilated and embedded into the functioning of the economy, the mutual relationship between BI scales, income from other sources and the tax rate can be rearranged. The timing, speed and magnitude of each successive upward regearing would depend on society's capacity to absorb far-reaching transformations. On general grounds it seems probable that once the force of social inertia has been overcome in the first and most critical transition from welfare capitalism to basic income capitalism, subsequent shifts of gear would present fewer problems of novelty, stress and resistance. Essentially the decision to advance from one income transfer ratio to the next would be a political one to be settled through the normal political processes of argument, pressure and compromise.

The timescale of this trajectory is unpredictable, its end-state perhaps always receding into the future and never completely attained. The important point is that BI inserts into the structure of social relations a permanent mechanism for emancipating work and income distribution from market contingency and social power. Moreover the installation of BI within one nation state would highlight the absence of any comparable institutionalised arrangements for transferring resources between states. The progressive mitigation of inequalities within advanced capitalism might be expected to raise public awareness and lower public tolerance of the much wider gulfs between North and South that continue to disfigure our global social order.

5   The Political Feasibility of a Basic Income Strategy

It is not enough to show that there is a strategy for resuming the conquest of citizenship rights which is ethically desirable, economically viable and historically opportune. This strategy must also be politically feasible. These requirements are not, of course, entirely independent of each other. For 'the art of the possible' has both a 'realist' and a 'transformatory' side. It consists not simply in correctly identifying probable resistances and constraints on political action; but also in judging whether, by what means, how far and how fast such foreseeable limitations can be relaxed or circumvented. Arguments about the desirability and viability of alternative futures are one means by which the currently prevailing boundaries of political realism can be changed. Hence even if it could be shown that the basic income strategy had little prospect of taking root in a political movement capable of translating its vision into achievement, it would not follow that there was no point in discussing the strategy's other virtues.

Nevertheless, the political feasibility of a proposal is not reducible to its abstract ethical and economic qualities either. The best is sometimes the enemy of the good, and there are at least three strictly political issues which deserve to be considered in their own right: first, whether there is potential majority support for BI; second, whether, if so, this majority can generate a political movement capable of waging an effective campaign for BI; and third, whether, if so, this movement will be able to overcome the resistance of its opponents.

There are obvious difficulties in generalising about the probable distribution of support for BI. As we have seen, its effects are complex, especially when longer-term dynamic changes are taken into account. Any given individual may be favourably affected in one respect and unfavourably in another. People's assessments may differ depending on whether their point of reference is their own personal situation or that of their household (or indeed some wider community). And, finally, interest definitions are never passively predetermined by objective social position, but acquired or learned through social interaction. In particular preferences as between different patterns of living and working may come to be revised in the course of the transition to a BI society. To cut through these complexities consider only the short-term effects of BI and take individuals roughly as they are now. Assume further that people's attitudes to BI are determined entirely by whether they personally expect to gain or lose from its introduction either because it alters their net disposable income or because it changes their effective range of choice.

On these assumptions it can be deduced from the analysis of Chapters 9 and 10 that the gainers would include many low paid and/or part-time workers, many of the self-employed, and virtually everyone engaged in alternative economy activities or in the early stages of setting up their own businesses. People currently unemployed enjoy improved job prospects; even if they remain jobless and receive a net income no higher than before, their freedom of action is enlarged thanks to the unconditional nature of BI. The same is true of the handicapped and disabled. Those who are unemployable for whatever reason no longer have to feign willingness to work. Students make no financial gain from the conversion of maintenance grants into BI allocations, but at least they are no longer subject to the parental means test. Most married women can be expected to welcome their greatly enhanced financial independence, whether they work in the labour market or at home. Low income single parents benefit financially, and all single parents acquire a wider set of eligible options in the disposition of their time. Elderly single pensioners with no significant unearned income are unaffected financially. But couples now receive twice the single old age benefit, and everyone over what was formerly the official retirement age now obtains the opportunity to continue gainful work without incurring any financial penalty.

On the same criteria the list of losers would consist primarily of individuals with above average gross incomes – earned or unearned – whose BI allocations failed to compensate for their increased tax liabilities. Some of the categories of gainers overlap. But even excluding double counting, it seems probable on general grounds that the gainers will outnumber the losers. Gainers are heavily concentrated in the non-employed section of the population – half or more of all adults in the advanced capitalist countries today. But the beneficiaries also include certain disadvantaged groups of employees. Although these are a minority of all employees they are nevertheless likely to outnumber the opposite minority of relatively privileged non-employees who are financially worse off under BI. Moreover some of those who lose as *individuals* may still derive compensation from belonging to *households* which either gain in some overall sense, or at least contain other members who are individually better off than before. (Of course, a similar interpersonal welfare effect may also work in reverse to take the edge off gains enjoyed by individual beneficiaries.)[2]

However, from the standpoint of political effectiveness this simple numerical majority of potential BI supporters suffers from three qualitative weaknesses. First, many of its sections are unstable in composition. They consist of people who either do not expect or do not wish to remain in their current socio-economic state. Their temporary or undesired position provides them with no strong source of identification or interest affiliation. Second, the list of gainers reads like a litany of the alienated and dispossessed. It would be extremely difficult to weld such a disparate and poorly organised series into a coherent political force. Third, the losers, though in the minority, are nevertheless a substantial minority. And they encompass not only the wealthiest social strata with the greatest direct or indirect influence over public policy, but also large numbers of workers in the core sector of employment, including the majority of trade union members.

To make matters worse organised labour has suffered grievous defeats over the past decade, whether electoral disasters, as in Britain, or forced reversals of policy, as in France. Everywhere trade unionism is in decline and socialism debilitated. Historically the labour movement has supplied a democratic resistance to capitalist power, and a powerful motor, or at least umbrella, for the advance of citizenship rights. With labour's defeat citizenship loses its political cutting edge and society's ideological balances begin to realign. As traditional values and allegiances decay workers become more receptive or less resistant to definitions of interest emphasising market freedom, personal property ownership, enterprise, competition and selectivity. Class de-alignment clears the way for the construction of a new dominant social bloc. Though the bloc is by no means complete or solid, the design and foundations are already prepared for a real or imaginary community of interest uniting the highest powerholders in industry and state with the workplace rank and file. There is an evident risk that the basic income strategy will simply consolidate this emergent coalition in opposition to its demands. For whatever else may divide its various factions they all stand to lose from a policy of radical redistribution.

But a strategy which ranges the poor and disinherited against an unholy alliance of the state, big business and organised labour is doomed to failure. Clearly some way has to be found of avoiding this adverse balance of forces. The critical factor is the position of the organised labour movement. If trade unions and socialist parties oppose BI, its fate is sealed. If they remain on the sidelines, it lacks credible force. Even if they become its champions, there is no guarantee of success. They still have to carry members and voters with them as well as fending off resistance from other quarters. But at least with the labour movement firmly committed to it, the strategy has a fighting chance.

6   Basic Income and the Labour Movement

To argue that the position of organised labour is critical to the political prospects of a BI strategy is not to reinstate some fundamentalist notion of 'class politics'. It is the destructiveness and irrelevance of what passes for 'class politics' which has contributed in no small measure to the labour movement's defeat and the triumph of neo-liberalism. Nor is it to imply that the strategy calls for the altruistic use of trade union muscle to force concessions out of employers or the state. If anything, muscular methods of industrial struggle are likely to hinder rather than help the cause of egalitarian transformation.

Apart from the negative argument that the BI project is certainly doomed without the labour movement's active support, the positive reason for stressing its role is intrinsic to the project itself. For at almost every point BI impinges on workers' interests, challenges established definitions of interests and proposes an alternative design for the organisation and distribution of work and resources. This inevitably brings into sharp focus a multitude of overlapping lines of social division – between employed and unemployed, secure and insecure, high paid and low paid, mental labour and manual labour, men and women. In order to transcend or at least ameliorate conflicts of interest along these fault lines, a redistributive strategy requires something akin to a continuous session of internal negotiation within the ranks of the collective social labourer both across the economy as a whole and in each of its departments. It would be Utopian to expect either the process or outcome to be free from tension. The point is to create the institutional and cultural conditions in which the various agents of social reproduction perpetually strive towards interest integration and solidaristic social policies. Without this effort they can never become subjects of their collective destiny, but are destined to remain subject to partial interests rooted in the prevailing configuration of social power.

The work of strategic reconstruction is scarcely conceivable without some organised focus, stability and continuity. The 'collective labourer' is a conceptual abstraction from a more or less inchoate mass of individuals and groups. An enduring framework is needed if those who undertake society's reproductive work are to discover anything resembling a 'popular will'. It is true that the labour movement is in a sadly reduced and subjugated state. Its representational coverage remains limited. The hallowed god of free collective bargaining bears a strong resemblance to the totems of neo-liberalism. The themes of labour's economic programme – industrial regeneration, full employment, central planning, corporatist policy concertation and state welfare – are not so much misconceived as misdirected: they all face squarely backwards towards a past which has irretrievably departed, and desperately need to be refocused on the future. The backwardness of organised labour is indeed a major reason for seeking a new strategic direction for the advance of citizenship. But in a structural sense the labour movement is also part of the solution to this problem. It occupies the ground on which the strategy will be won or lost.

And no other coherent political force looks even remotely capable of supplying the requisite organisational architecture and communicational fluency.

The BI project needs ideas, stimuli, pressure and commitment from all kinds of social movements – claimants' unions, the poverty lobby, women's organisations, ethnic minority interests and ecological pressure groups. Similarly, if the project is to have any chance of success it must build a broad social alliance comparable to those which accomplished earlier advances in citizenship. But if something like the labour movement had not already established a structure to receive and transmit the strategy's political inputs and outputs, then it would have to be invented.

BI needs the labour movement. But does the labour movement either need or want BI? Certainly BI conflicts with the classical objectives of organised labour. It abandons the principle of social insurance; it appears to surrender the goal of 'full employment'; and it might be thought to narrow the scope of trade union responsibility. In a BI society workers who lack either marketable skills or monopolistic control over labour supply, cease to depend on trade unions to protect their living standards. More generally, the role of trade unions in determining the distribution of income appears to be weakened. Income distribution comes to depend more on the political process and less on the mobilisation of economic power in the process of wage bargaining.

The first two of these reservations have been sufficiently discussed before. The social insurance principle has outlived its useful purpose and should be consigned to the museum. Worries about giving up on 'full employment' are ill defined. The traditional interpretation of this objective was a state in which there are sufficient paid jobs for all who might wish to take them on prevailing wage and non-wage terms. But among the background conditions ignored by this formula are: (1) patterns of weekly, annual and lifetime hours of work; (2) the distribution of access to paid employment by sex, age, ethnic identity, skill and education; and (3) the composition of total social labour both by persons and by category of reproductive activity, including work in the alternative economy and work outside the monetised economy altogether. Merely to enumerate the social parameters which 'full employment' in the traditional sense takes for granted and would leave intact, even if it were feasible, is to condemn it as both conservative and unrealistic.

On the other hand, the labour movement could set its sights on a new employment policy which aimed to: (1) reduce average hours of employment; (2) redistribute job opportunities in favour of marginalised and oppressed social groups; (3) promote both technical and organisational methods of abating the toilsomeness of waged labour; (4) encourage the growth of non-materially motivated, unwaged work; (5) deconstruct the sexual division of labour and recompose the social division of labour generally. Within this perspective 'full employment' has to be redefined as a condition in which the aggregate supply of hours to the waged sector of the monetised economy is equal to the total hours demanded by employers. If this condition is not satisfied and there is a labour surplus, the policy problem ceases to be crudely identified as one of finding feasible ways to set idle hands to idle wheels. Instead it calls for debate and decision on the appropriate mix of demand- and supply-side measures to reduce the surplus without converting it into a shortage.

The fear that BI renders trade unions redundant, or at least detracts from their social power and significance, itself reflects a narrow and economistic view of trade union purposes. It is not trade unionism in general which is threatened by BI, but a particular, historically evolved trade union strategy. This strategy has now exhausted its progressive potential, leaving the labour movement politically stranded and economically impotent.

7   Sectionalism, Trade Unions and Incomes Policy

The key to appreciating the role of trade unions in a BI society lies in the concept of sectionalism. In order to analyse this concept it is useful first to classify the various general fronts of trade union activity. The nature and consequences of sectionalism can then be illustrated by reviewing the particular ways in which the British trade union movement has marshalled its forces across these different fronts.

From their earliest origins trade unions have sought to participate in the regulation of employment: both its terms and conditions and at least some areas of production control. Apart from now largely defunct mutual insurance functions, trade unions have also acted as a political pressure group. And, intermittently, they have crossed the threshold between civil society and the state to collaborate with government and employers' representatives in the formation and administration of economic policy.[3]

In Britain the unions' primary activities have centred on job regulation and (partial) production control. Collective bargaining has been the main institutional channel for these activities and British unions are deeply entrenched in its complex pathways. If anything, this traditional priority has been strengthened since the neo-liberal counter-revolution closed down access to government and severely circumscribed the unions' pressure group role.

By comparison with, say, French trade unions the British unions' relatively solid base within the collective bargaining network is a great source of organisational strength. At the same time it is a source of ideological and political weakness. For the claims which unions press under normal collective bargaining tend to be seen as, and usually really are, *sectional* claims. Except in rare circumstances, such as war,[4] and except on certain special issues, such as production safety standards, it is normally quite specious to pretend that the interests of a particular section of workers coincide with the *general* interests of society as a whole. Indeed, as often as not, the two are in direct conflict.[5] In any specific context there may be uncertainty and dispute about what exactly the 'general social interest' is. And not infrequently this formula is hijacked as a cover for some other, merely sectional interest, as in the dictum that what is good for General Motors is good for America. Nevertheless the phrase is not a purely emotive noise, devoid of semantic substance. The difficulty of ascertaining the general social interest complicates, but does not remove, the contradiction between this interest, however defined, and the particular interest of any individual or group.

There is nothing reprehensible or illegitimate about such a conflict: it continually recurs in all kinds of social situations. Sectional interests are no less real than general social interests, and have every right to expression and action. The problem of sectionalism is not the mere existence or vigorous pursuit of sectional demands in themselves. Nor are sectional struggles necessarily pugnacious and recalcitrant. After all, trade unions specialise in the art of power broking and compromise. The problem is rather that, by definition, sectionalism lacks any broader societal perspective.

A *purely* sectional approach to contested issues leaves their outcome to emerge from the interplay of power struggles (the first dimension of power). But these struggles unfold within a social framework in which certain interests are structurally privileged (dimensions two and three). The outcome is, therefore, likely to be least satisfactory to those with least resources and least power. And the underlying conflict is liable to recur, forcing sectional interests into repeated, and essentially defensive mobilisations. In short, sectionalism offers no way of reconstructing either the agenda of conflict or the relationships of power. If the *only* notes which trade unions ever sound and the public ever hears are the discords of sectional interest, there is no harmonic theme to modulate either sectional claims themselves or the public's perception of them. And there is certainly no possibility of articulating an integrated perspective, strategy and programme which can be held out as serving the best interests of society as a whole.

The BI project supplies the orchestration which is missing from a mere summation of sectional demands. As its standard bearer the labour movement could validate its claim to be the authentic voice of labour, speaking not just for well organised wage earners, but for all who contribute in any way whatsoever to society's reproductive work; and, indeed, since BI involves literally everyone, for those who choose or are unable to make any contribution at all. This comprehensive sweep is due not simply to the fact that BI is, by definition, a universally inclusive device; but also to its ability to bring together two levels of discourse which rarely connect, and are often at odds. At one level the project addresses individual human beings in all their singularity. At the other it deals with the totality of their relationships which we call society as a whole. The individual person has been conspicuously absent from the socialist and labour movement tradition, almost anathematised as a category of thought. This has been a grave deficiency, relentlessly exploited by the movement's enemies. BI closes this lacuna. It enables its advocates to engage with neo-liberal concepts of individual freedom and rights, without abandoning a proper concern for the collective, social dimension of human life.

It is not suggested that trade unions either should or could cease to represent their members' sectional interests. This would be an oppressive, totalitarian conception. The contradiction between sectional and societal interests cannot be made to go away. It can, however, be internalised within the trade union movement so that its energy is converted from a negative fetter into a positive source of creative tension. There is, in other words, a distinction between giving voice to sectional concerns and unrestrained sectionalism.

The unions have a world to gain from basic income and nothing to lose but the golden chains of privileged subordination. The broadening of their representative credentials and programmatic ambit would improve their tarnished image and check the centrifugal pull of sectionalism. On both counts they would be better placed to break out of the cramped, defensive ground to which they have been forced to retreat. They could recover momentum as a political pressure group and again bid to resume their rightful place as an estate of the realm. There is plenty of work for the unions to do at the level of the state. The transition to basic income capitalism and beyond calls for a permanent process of triangular collaboration, hard bargaining and power politics between unions, government and employers.

Nor does BI remove the need for collective bargaining at the levels of industry, enterprise and workplace. Some institutionalised method of wage determination is still required. Employers who now recognise trade unions as legitimate negotiating agents have no reason to withdraw recognition. The same motives impelling employers to concede that wage issues are proper matters for joint regulation rather than managerial prerogative, continue to operate – administrative convenience, the preservation of orderly industrial relations and the maintenance of employee consent. At the same time BI encourages workers to reorder their bargaining priorities. With enhanced income security, reduced working hours and more flexible working lives, some of the energy which is currently absorbed in job protection, status fetishism, time pilfering and slow down is released for more constructive outlets, notably the abatement of toil. As we have seen, toil-reducing demands have immense ramifications for work organisation and the control of production. Heightened aspirations for participation in the management of workplace and enterprise will still run up against opposition from professional managers. But workers can now avail themselves of a powerful counterforce against such resistance. For employers are under pressure to make jobs sufficiently attractive compared with other uses of time to enable them to recruit and retain adequate supplies of suitably qualified, trained and motivated staff.

The progressive democratisation of employment relations should relieve some of the compensatory psychological and social motivations behind wage inflation. But at the same time an employment policy which eliminates the labour surplus and eases fears of unemployment, also removes the classic economic discipline on wage bargaining. With permanent full employment a decentralised and uncoordinated system of wage bargaining is inherently inflation-prone. In the past the failure to regulate wage-price anarchy by means of a negotiated and lasting incomes policy was the Achilles heel of the Keynesian-social democratic state. In a BI society too the requirements of macroeconomic balance must be brought to bear on wage and price decisions at the micro level. It remains important to preserve a tolerable degree of price stability, less for its own sake than as an index of the underlying state of social conflict over the distribution of real output between rival uses and users.

But the context of an incomes policy in a BI society is quite different from the past. Since wage bargaining has to be coordinated with the setting of BI scales and tax rates, wage norms cease to be a temporary expedient and become a permanent fixture. The remit of the policy makers necessarily extends to a general assessment of the performance of the national economy. And as the object of the policy is the behaviour of wage negotiators, it would hardly be just or prudent to exclude the unions from the policy-making process. Both democratic principle and practical statecraft demand that major stakeholders should be involved in the formation of policies affecting their vital interests. So whatever the form of incomes policy adopted, traditional or tax-based,[6] its parameters have to be settled through triangular negotiation between government and the peak organisations of capital and labour. The scene is thus set for a grand integration of wages policy with the BI system, each in turn linked with lower level collective bargaining over working hours, toil and industrial democracy.

To illustrate the dynamics involved suppose that a tax-based incomes policy is in operation. There is no central review body to vet claims and settlements, and no direct control over settlements in breach of policy norms. Negotiators at the micro level are free to reach their own decisions without direct, third party intervention. However, employers who allow their employees' average gross hourly earnings to grow at a rate in excess of the basic norm incur a tax penalty levied according to a predetermined rising scale on either their payroll or their profits. Employers thus receive an incentive to resist settlements above the norm, and most unions can be expected to take this into account in framing their wage demands and bargaining strategies. Provided the norm itself is 'realistic', the degree of norm violation should be minimised, and the conditions for preserving public trust in the policy satisfied.

Of course, *ex ante* no one can be sure what a 'realistic' norm will be. This emerges only *ex post* as deals are struck and hindsight reveals whether the norm has been strained by an outbreak of tax-penalised settlements. At the point in time when the norm is being fixed the outcome of wage bargaining is necessarily uncertain. This is why it is wise, as well as democratic, to harness the intelligence and authority of the principal industrial organisations to the norm-setting process.

In the course of tripartite negotiation the national union leadership, having previously evolved a bargaining platform which commands the general assent of its constituents, lays out its preferred terms for endorsing a particular wage norm. If agreement is reached with the other two parties, a figure is duly authorised. To the extent that the terms being pressed by the employers or the state fall short of the unions' asking price, then any proposed figure for the norm becomes that much less 'realistic'. At this point one of three things must happen: either the figure is revised upwards, or the non-wage terms on offer are improved, or, in the final analysis, the parties simply register a failure to agree. In this third case the state, as norm-fixer of last resort, must specify a figure unilaterally. Then, assuming the union leadership have accurately gauged the mood of their members, the norm is liable to come under pressure during subsequent wage bargaining. This experience then feeds into the next round of tripartite negotiation.

There is, of course, no guarantee that this institutional framework will keep sectionalism permanently at bay. The bottom line of a democratic society has to be the right of dissent, however misguided or anti-social the dissenters might appear. This is why the right to idleness was earlier defended alongside the presumption that all who can do so should take part in society's work. Nevertheless by encouraging the unions to redirect their bargaining goals at the micro level, and to adopt a concerted approach to incomes planning at the macro level, and all of this within a pluralistic political and economic system, the rules of the game are stacked against the recrudescence of sectionalist tendencies.

It should now be clear that there are no grounds for believing that basic income would put trade unionism out of business. On the contrary, basic income would emancipate the suppressed potential of workers and their organisations, broaden and deepen the range of their concerns, and reconnect their efforts with the long haul towards a society which deliberately and habitually adjusts the patterns of its reproductive activities to meet the needs of all its members. Without the labour movement basic income lacks political coherence and weight. Without basic income the labour movement is incarcerated in a merciless ghetto of economism and sectionalism. We seem to have a project in search of a movement and a movement in search of a project. This sounds like a suitable case for partnership.

Notes to Chapter 11

1. For an analysis of the relationship between the control of inflation and the democratisation of economic decision-making at state, sectoral and enterprise levels during the period of the Social Contract in Britain from 1974 to 1979 see Purdy, D. L., 'The Social Contract and Socialist Policy', in Prior (ed.) (1981).
2. As non-voting financial dependants children are excluded from this rough headcount. Some relatively privileged children with large holdings of income-yielding assets will be worse off financially. But a much larger number will gain materially either because their parents gain, or because BI breaks the grip of patriarchal control over family resources, or because the financial implications of separation and divorce become less vexatious as causes of parental discord and litigation. The entrenchment of children's entitlement to state transfers might also strengthen children's legal rights generally, particularly in relation to custodial provisions, and contribute towards a social climate in which children were less likely to be treated by adults as unpersons lacking even the most elementary human rights.
3. The history of what he calls 'corporate bias' in the British political system is retailed by Middlemas (1979). For more general discussions

of corporatist tendencies in the advanced capitalist countries see Schmitter and Lehmbruch (eds) (1979) and Goldthorpe (ed.) (1984).

4. In both the world wars of the twentieth century the traditional distinction between civilian and combatant became blurred. The overriding need to gear the national economy to the war effort and to avoid the risk of internal disaffection produced an unwonted coincidence between the sectional interests of workers in improved wages and conditions and the interests of the nation in gaining military victory or avoiding military defeat.

5. This explains why organised labour frequently justifies its claims in terms which invoke the general social interest. One classic example of this phenomenon is the economy of high wages argument. According to this militant wage demands galvanise employers into searching out methods of raising productivity which they would otherwise overlook. If this is true, workers gain self-financing pay rises and society benefits from technical progress. Another example is the underconsumption argument that by boosting workers' spending power generalised wage increases rescue society as a whole from being dragged down by capitalism's allegedly chronic tendency to demand deficiency.

6. Tax-based incomes policies are more in keeping with the general spirit of a system which seeks to reconcile market freedoms with the protection of personal security and the maintenance of social cohesion. Traditional policies are replete with opportunities for damaging collisions between policy makers and sectional groups. Such confrontations generate cumulative aggravation, and constantly threaten to discredit both the policy, the government presiding over it and the general principle of macroeconomic wage regulation. However, which type of policy is chosen is a secondary matter. The discussion in the text is illustrative and can easily be recast to accommodate other forms.

References

Addison, J. T. and Siebert, W. S. (1979) *The Market for Labor: an Analytical Treatment* (Santa Monica, California: Goodyear).

Anderson, P. (1980) *Arguments Within English Marxism* (London: New Left Books/Verso).

Ashby, P. (1984) *Social Security After Beveridge: What Next?* (London: National Council for Voluntary Organisations).

Ashenfelter, O. and Johnson, G. E. (1972) 'Unionism, Relative Wages and Labor Quality in US Manufacturing Industry', *International Economic Review*, vol. 13, pp. 488–508.

Atkinson, A. B. (1984) *The Economics of Inequality*, 2nd edn, (Oxford: Oxford UP).

Bahro, R. (1978) *The Alternative in Eastern Europe* (London: New Left Books).

Bain, G. S. (ed.) (1983) *Industrial Relations in Britain* (Oxford: Basil Blackwell).

Baldamus, W. (1961) *Efficiency and Effort: an Analysis of Industrial Administration* (London: Tavistock).

Basic Income Research Group Bulletin (1985–6) Nos 3–6 (London: National Council for Voluntary Organisations).

Becker, G. (1971) *The Economics of Discrimination*, 2nd edn (Chicago: Chicago UP).

Becker, G. (1975) *Human Capital*, 2nd edn (New York: National Bureau of Economic Research).

Beveridge, W. H. (1944) *Full Employment in a Free Society* (London: Allen & Unwin).

Blumberg, P. (1968) *Industrial Democracy: the Sociology of Participation* (London: Constable).

Boulanger, P-M., Defeyt, P. and Van Parijs, P. (1985) 'L'Allocation Universelle: Une Idée Pour Vivre Autrement?', *La Revue Nouvelle*, vol. LXXXI, No 4 (Bruxelles).

Bowles, S. and Gintis, H. (1975) 'The Problem with Human Capital Theory: a Marxian Critique', *American Economic Review, Papers and Proceedings*, vol. 65, pp. 74–82.

Brannen, J. and Wilson, G. (eds) (1987) *Give and Take in Families: Studies in Resource Distribution* (London: Allen & Unwin).

Braverman, H. (1974) *Labor and Monopoly Capital* (New York: Monthly Review Press).

Brecht, B. (1985) *Collected Plays, Volume 6, Part One* (London: Methuen).

Brody, D. (1980) *Workers in Industrial America* (Oxford: Oxford UP).

Bullock, A. (1967) *The Life and Times of Ernest Bevin, II, Minister of Labour 1940–45* (London: Heinemann).

Burton, J. and Addison, J. T. (1977) 'The Institutionalist Analysis of Wage Inflation: a Critical Appraisal', *Research in Labour Economics*, vol. 1, pp. 333–76 (Connecticut: JAI Press).

Burton, J. and Addison, J. T. (1978) 'Wage Adjustment Processes: a Synthetic Treatment', *British Journal of Industrial Relations*, vol. xvi, pp. 208–23.

Cammett, J. M. (1967) *Antonio Gramsci and the Origins of Italian Communism* (Stanford, California: Stanford UP).

Campbell, B. (1984) *The Road to Wigan Pier Revisited* (London: Virago).

Chick, V. (1983) *Macroeconomics After Keynes* (Oxford: Philip Allan).

Child, J. (1964) 'Quaker Employers and Industrial Relations', *Sociological Review*, vol. 12, pp. 293–315.

Coates, K. (ed.) (1978) *The Right to Useful Work* (Nottingham: Spokesman/Institution for Workers Control).

Coddington, A. (1968) *Theories of the Bargaining Process* (London: Allen & Unwin).

Cohen, G. A. (1978) *Karl Marx's Theory of History: a Defence* (Oxford: Oxford UP).

Collectif Charles Fourier (1984) 'L'Allocation Universelle', in *Le Travail dans L'Avenir* (Bruxelles: Fondation Roi Baudouin).

Confederation of British Industry (1981) *Working Time: Guidelines for Managers* (London: CBI).

Coote, A. and Campbell, B. (1982) *Sweet Freedom: the Struggle for Women's Liberation* (London: Pan).

Crouch, C. (1982) *Trade Unions: the Logic of Collective Action* (Glasgow: Fontana).

Currie, R. (1979) *Industrial Politics* (Oxford: Clarendon Press).

Dahl, R. A. (1971) *Polyarchy: Participation and Opposition* (New Haven: Yale UP).

Davis, M. (1980) 'Why the US Working Class is Different', *New Left Review*, 123.

Department of Employment and Productivity (1971) *British Labour Statistics Historical Abstract 1886–1968* (London: HMSO).

Dilnot, A. W., Kay, J. A. and Morris, C. N. (1984) *The Reform of Social Security* (Oxford: Oxford UP/Institute for Fiscal Studies).

Ekins, P. (ed.) (1986) *The Living Economy: a New Economics in the Making* (London: Routledge & Kegan Paul).

Engels, F. (1972) *The Origin of the Family, Private Property and the State* (London: Lawrence & Wishart).

Equal Opportunities Commission (1981) *Job Sharing: Improving the Quality and Availability of Part-Time Work* (Manchester: EOC).

Erikson, R., Goldthorpe, J. H. and Portocarero, L. (1983) 'Intergenerational Class Mobility and the Convergence Thesis', *British Journal of Sociology*, vol. 34, pp. 303–43.

European Trade Union Institute (1980) *The Reduction of Working Hours in Western Europe: an Analysis of the Social and Economic Consequences* (Brussels: ETUI).

Fernbach, D. (1981) *The Spiral Path: a Gay Contribution to Human Survival* (London: Heretic Press).

Flanders, A. (1970) *Management and Unions: the Theory and Reform of Industrial Relations* (London: Faber).

Ford, H. (1973) *My Life and Work* (New York: Arno Press).

Fraser, R. (ed.) (1968) *Work: Twenty Personal Accounts* (Harmondsworth: Penguin/New Left Review).

French, M. (1978) *The Women's Room* (London: Andre Deutsch).

Goldthorpe, J. H. (1978) 'The Current Inflation: Towards a Sociological Account', in Goldthorpe, J. H. and Hirsch, F. (eds) *The Political Economy of Inflation* (London: Martin Robertson).

Goldthorpe, J. H. (with Llewellyn, C. and Payne, C.) (1980) *Social Mobility and Class Structure in Modern Britain* (Oxford: Clarendon Press).

Goldthorpe, J. H. (ed.) (1984) *Order and Conflict in Contemporary Capitalism* (Oxford: Clarendon Press).

Goodrich, C. L. (1975) *The Frontier of Control* (London: Pluto Press).

Greenleaf, W. H. (1975) 'The Character of Modern British Politics', *Parliamentary Affairs*, vol. 28, pp. 368–85.

Hakim, J. (1979) *Occupational Segregation*, Research Paper No 9 (London: Department of Employment).

Hašek, J. (1942) *The Good Soldier Schweik* (Harmondsworth: Penguin).

Hayek, F. A. (1967) *Studies in Philosophy, Politics and Economics* (London: Routledge & Kegan Paul).

Hicks, J. (1963) *The Theory of Wages*, 2nd edn (London: Macmillan).

Hindess, B. (1982) 'Power, Interests and the Outcomes of Struggles', *Sociology*, vol. 16, pp. 498–511.

Hinton, J. (1973) *The First Shop Stewards' Movement* (London: Allen & Unwin).

Hobsbawm, E. J. (1964) 'Trends in the British Labour Movement since 1850', in *Labouring Men* (London: Weidenfeld & Nicolson).

Hobsbawm, E. J. (1969) *Industry and Empire* (Harmondsworth: Penguin).

Hobsbawm, E. J. (1978) 'The Forward March of Labour Halted?', *Marxism Today*, September.

Hodgson, G. A. (1982) 'Theoretical and Policy Implications of Variable Productivity', *Cambridge Journal of Economics*, vol. 6, pp. 213–26.

Hodgson, G. A. (1984) *The Democratic Economy* (Harmondsworth: Penguin).

Hughes, J. (1980) 'The Reduction in the Working Week: a Critical Look at Target 35', *British Journal of Industrial Relations*, vol. XVIII, pp. 287–96.

Hyman, R. (1971) *Marxism and the Sociology of Trade Unionism* (London: Pluto Press).

Johnson, G. E. (1975) 'Economic Analysis of Trade Unionism', *American Economic Review, Papers and Proceedings*, vol. 65, pp. 23–8.

Kerr, C. (1954) 'The Balkanisation of Labor Markets', in Bakke, E. W. *et al.*, *Labour Mobility and Economic Opportunity* (Cambridge, Mass.: MIT Press).

Keynes, J. M. (1930) *A Treatise on Money*, vol. ii (London: Macmillan).

Keynes, J. M. (1936) *The General Theory of Employment, Interest and Money* (London: Macmillan).

Layard, R., Metcalf, D. and Nickell, S. (1978) 'The Effect of Collective Bargaining on Relative and Absolute Wages', *British Journal of Industrial Relations*, vol. xvi, pp. 287–302.

Le Guin, U. (1981) *The Left Hand of Darkness* (London: Futura).

Lewis, C. and O'Brien, M. (eds) (1987) *Re-assessing Fatherhood: New Observations on Fathers and the Modern Family* (London: Sage).

Lewis, H. G. (1963) *Unionism and Relative Wages in the United States* (Chicago: Chicago UP).

Lindblom, C. E. (1977) *Politics and Markets* (New York: Basic Books).

Lipsey, R. (1983) *An Introduction to Positive Economics*, 6th edn (London: Weidenfeld & Nicolson).

Lively, J. (1975) *Democracy* (Oxford: Basil Blackwell).

Lukes, S. (1974) *Power: a Radical View* (London: Macmillan).

Lynd, R. and Lynd, H. (1929) *Middletown: a Study in Contemporary American Culture* (New York: Harcourt Brace).

MacIntyre, A. (1967) *A Short History of Ethics* (London: Routledge & Kegan Paul).

Maddison, A. (1977) 'Phases of Capitalist Development', *Banca Nazionale del Lavoro Quarterly Review*, vol. xxxii, pp. 103–39.

Marsden, D. (1986) *The End of Economic Man? Custom and Competition in Labour Markets* (Brighton: Wheatsheaf).

Marshall, A. (1920) *Principles of Economics*, 8th edn (London: Macmillan).

Marshall, T. H. (1950) *Citizenship and Social Class* (Cambridge: Cambridge UP).

Marx, K. (1951) 'Critique of the Gotha Programme', in *Marx–Engels Selected Works*, vol. ii (Moscow: Foreign Language Publishing House).

Marx, K. (1976) *Capital: Volume One* (Harmondsworth: Penguin).

Marx, K. and Engels, F. (1962) 'Manifesto of the Communist Party 1848', in *Marx–Engels Selected Works*, vol. i (Moscow: Foreign Language Publishing House).

Matthews, R. C. O. (1968) 'Why Has Britain Had Full Employment Since the War?', *Economic Journal*, vol. lxviii, pp. 555–69.

Maurice, S. C. (1975) 'On the Importance of Being Unimportant: an Analysis of the Paradox in Marshall's Third Rule of Derived Demand', *Economica*, vol. 42, pp. 385–93.

Meek, R. L. (1973) *Studies in the Labour Theory of Value*, 2nd edn (London: Lawrence & Wishart).

Metcalf, D. (1977) 'Unions, Incomes Policy and Relative Wages in Britain', *British Journal of Industrial Relations*, vol. xv, pp. 157–75.

Metcalf, D. (1982) 'Special Employment Measures: an Analysis of Wage Subsidies, Growth Schemes and Worksharing, *Midland Bank Review*, Autumn/Winter, pp. 9–19.

Middlemas, K. (1979) *Politics in Industrial Society: the Experience of the British System since 1911* (London: Andre Deutsch).

Mill, J. S. (1983) *The Subjection of Women* (London: Virago).

Miller, A. (1983) 'In Praise of Social Dividends', Working Paper No. 1 (Edinburgh: Heriot Watt University Department of Economics).

Moore Jr, Barrington (1978) *Injustice: the Social Bases of Obedience and Revolt* (London: Macmillan).

Morley-Fletcher, E. (1980–1) "Per una Storia dell Idea di 'Minimo Sociale Garantito'", *Quaderni della Rivista Trimestrale*, pp. 64–6.

Mulvey, C. (1976) 'Collective Agreements and Relative Earnings in UK Manufacturing in 1973', *Economica*, vol. 43, pp. 419–27.

Mulvey, C. and Abowd, J. M. (1980) 'Estimating the Union/Non-Union Wage Differential: a Statistical Issue', *Economica*, vol. 47, pp. 73–9.

Murgatroyd, L. (1983) 'The Production of People and Domestic Labour Revisited', in Sawyer, M. and Schott, K. (eds) *Socialist Economic Review 1983* (London: Merlin).

Nairn, T. (1965) 'The Nature of the Labour Party', in Anderson, P. and Blackburn, R. (eds) *Towards Socialism* (London: Fontana/New Left Review).

National Board for Prices and Incomes (1971) Report No 169, *General Problems of Low Pay*, Cmnd 4648 (London: HMSO).

Offe, C. and Wiesenthal, H. (1980) 'Two Logics of Collective Action: Theoretical Notes on Social Class and Organisational Form', in *Political Power and Social Theory*, vol. i, pp. 67–115 (Connecticut: JAI Press).

Orwell, G. (1962) *The Road to Wigan Pier* (Harmondsworth: Penguin).

Paine, T. (1792) *Rights of Man* (Dublin: P. Byrne).

Paine, T. (1796) *Agrarian Justice* (London: J. Adlard and J. Parsons).

Parker, H. (1985) 'Costing Basic Incomes', *Basic Income Research Group Bulletin*, no. 3, pp. 4–15.

Parsons, T. (1969) *Politics and Social Structure* (New York: The Free Press).

Peattie, L. and Rein, M. (1983) *Women's Claims: a Study in Political Economy* (Oxford: Oxford UP).

Pencavel, J. H. (1974) 'Relative Wages and Trade Unions in the United Kingdom', *Economica*, vol. 41, pp. 194–210.

Phelps, E. S. *et al.* (1970) *Microeconomic Foundations of Employment and Inflation Theory* (New York: Norton).

Phelps Brown, E. H. and Browne, M. H. (1968) *A Century of Pay* (London: Macmillan).

Phelps Brown, E. H. (1975) 'A non-Monetarist View of the Pay Explosion', *Three Banks Review*, vol. 105, pp. 3–24.

Poole, M. (1984) *Theories of Trade Unionism*, Revised edn (London: Routledge & Kegan Paul).

Poole, M. (1986) *Industrial Relations: Origins and Patterns of National Diversity* (London: Routledge & Kegal Paul).

Prior, M. (ed.) (1981) *The Popular and the Political: Essays on Socialism in the 1980s* (London: Routledge & Kegan Paul).

Purdy, D. L. (1976) 'British Capitalism Since the War – Part One: "Origins of the Crisis" and Part Two: "Deline and Prospects"', *Marxism Today*, September–October.

Ricardo, D. (1951) *Works and Correspondence*, edited by P. Sraffa, Volume One (Cambridge, Cambridge UP).

Robertson, J. (1985) *Future Work* (Aldershot: Gower).

Robinson, D. and Mayhew, K. (eds) (1983) *Pay Policies for the Future* (Oxford: Oxford UP).

Rose, M. (1978) *Industrial Behaviour: Theoretical Development Since Taylor* (Harmondsworth: Penguin).

Rosen, S. (1969) 'Trade Union Power, Threat Effects and the Extent of Organisation', *Review of Economic Studies*, vol. 39, pp. 185–96.

Rowthorn, R. (1974) 'Neo-Classicism, Neo-Ricardianism and Marxism', *New Left Review*, 86, reprinted in Rowthorn, R. (1980) *Capitalism, Conflict and Inflation* (London: Lawrence & Wishart).

Rubery, J. (1978) 'Structured Labour Markets, Worker Organisation and Low Pay', *Cambridge Journal of Economics*, vol. 2, pp. 17–36.

Runciman, W. G. (1972) *Relative Deprivation and Social Justice* (Harmondsworth: Penguin).

Schmitter, P. and Lehmbruch, G. (eds) (1979) *Trends Towards Corporatist Intermediation* (Beverly Hills: Sage).

Seabrook, J. (1978) *What Went Wrong?* (London: Gollancz).

Sharpe, S. (1976) *Just Like a Girl: How Girls Learn to be Women* (Harmondsworth: Penguin).

Showler, B. and Sinfield, A. (eds) (1981) *The Workless State* (Oxford: Martin Robertson).

Singer, P. (1976) *Animal Liberation* (London: Jonathan Cape).

Smith, T. (1979) *The Politics of the Corporate Economy* (London: Martin Robertson).

Spence, M. A. (1973) 'Job Market Signalling', *Quarterly Journal of Economics*, vol. 87, pp. 355–74.

Sraffa, P. (1960) *Production of Commodities by Means of Commodities* (Cambridge: Cambridge UP).

Stamworth, M. (1981) *Gender and Schooling: a Study of Sexual Divisions in the Classroom*, Explorations in Feminism No 7 (London: Women's Research and Resources Centre).

Standing, G. (1986) 'Meshing Labour Flexibility with Security: an Answer to British Unemployment?', *International Labour Review*, vol. 125, pp. 87–106.

Steedman, I. (1977) *Marx After Sraffa* (London: New Left Books).

Terry, M. (1977) 'The Inevitable Growth of Informality', *British Journal of Industrial Relations*, vol. xv, pp. 75–90.

Thompson, E. P. (1963) *The Making of the English Working Class* (London: Gollancz).

Townsend, P. (1979) *Poverty in the United Kingdom* (Harmondsworth: Penguin).

Trades Union Congress (1980–83) *Progress Reports: TUC Campaign for Economic and Social Advance/European Trade Union Confederation Campaign for Reduced Working Time* (London: TUC).

Tressell, R. (1955) *The Ragged Trousered Philanthropist* (London: Lawrence & Wishart).

Trist, E. L. and Bamforth, K. W. (1951) 'Some Social and Psychological Consequences of the Longwall Method of Coal-Getting', *Human Relations*, vol. 4, pp. 3–38.

van der Veen, R. and van Parijs, P. (1987) 'A Capitalist Road to Communism' *Theory and Society*, vol. 15, pp. 635–55.

Wainright, H. and Elliott, D. (1982) *The Lucas Plan: a New Trade Unionism in the Making* (London: Allison & Busby).

Watt, R. M. (1973) *The Kings Depart: The German Revolution and the Treaty of Versailles 1918–19* (Harmondsworth: Penguin).

Weber, M. (1968) *Economy and Society* (New York: Bedminster Press).

White, M. (1980) *Shorter Working Time* (Policy Studies Institute No. 589).

Wilensky, H. (1961) 'The Uneven Distribution of Leisure: the Impact of Economic Growth on "Free Time"', *Social Problems*, vol. 9, pp. 32–56.

Williams, B. (1983) 'Technical Change and Life Hours of Work', Manchester Statistical Society, Proceedings and Papers of the Sesquicentennial Conference.

Wittgenstein, L. (1969) *On Certainty* (Oxford: Basil Blackwell).

Wood, A. (1978) *A Theory of Pay* (Cambridge: Cambridge UP).

Index

275